THE
W**OO**LMAN WAY

A HISTORY OF **JOHN WOOLMAN SCHOOL**

LISA FRANKEL & CATHERINE LENOX

WRITE
CONTACT

Seattle, Washington, USA

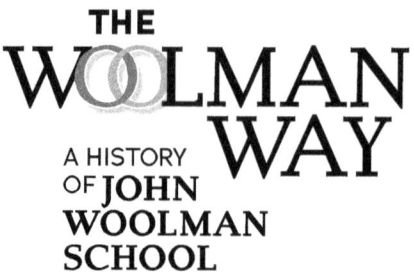

THE WOOLMAN WAY

A HISTORY OF JOHN WOOLMAN SCHOOL

Published by Write Contact
www.WriteContact.com

Book cover illustration by Sophie Wood Brinker
Book cover layout by Sonja Gerard

Book design by Sonja Gerard

Chapter divider illustrations by Sophie Wood Brinker

Printed in the United States of America.
Paperbound edition of this book originally printed by:
Ingram Spark/Ingram Content Group, One Ingram Blvd., La Vergne, TN 37086
www.ingramspark.com

ISBN 979-8-218-27672-0 (pb)

10 9 8 7 6 5 4 3

Dedicated to the inspired Woolman School founders who worked tirelessly to make their vision a reality.

Special recognition is given to founders Russ and Mary Jorgensen, whose lifelong belief in Woolman and dedication to its longevity was exemplary.

CONTENTS

Preface vii

Introduction xv

①

SECTION ONE:

THE HISTORY

Chapter 1   Rooted in Quaker Tradition 1

Chapter 2   Toward a Friends Secondary Boarding School
             in Northern California 5

Chapter 3   Making the Dream a Reality 27

Chapter 4   Teachers but No Toilets 45

Chapter 5   Building Community 53

Chapter 6   Work is Love Made Visible 77

Chapter 7   Students in Action 91

Chapter 8   Trials and Tribulations 113

Chapter 9   We're Living Life in Light at the End of the Road 139

Chapter 10   The Phoenix Metaphor is Apt 151

Notes 167

◯◯

PHOTO GALLERY

The Experience 169

Community 183

Special Projects 195

SECTION TWO:

THE MEMOIRS:
WOMBATS IN THE REAL WORLD

Chapter 11   Influence and Legacy 209

Chapter 12   Experiential Learning 229

Chapter 13   Living Together 235

Chapter 14   Quaker Contemplation 243

Chapter 15   The Eco-Campus 247

Chapter 16   Work Jobs 257

Chapter 17   A Space for Healing 261

Chapter 18   Sense of Place 267

Chapter 19   The Natural World 271

Chapter 20   Teachers 281

Chapter 21   Conscientious Objection 295

Chapter 22   Crafting Clay 305

Chapter 23   Staging Creativity 309

Chapter 24   Visual Interpretation 315

Chapter 25   Meaning, Myth, and Magic 319

Chapter 26   Pluck Your Magic Twanger 327

Chapter 27   Special Projects 335

Chapter 28   Goat Herding in Arizona 347

Chapter 29   The Shadow Side 355

Chapter 30   The Woolman Semester 365

Chapter 31   Reunions 369

Postface 373

Acknowledgements 375

About the Creatives 376

| THE WOOLMAN WAY |

PREFACE

By Lisa Frankel & Catherine Lenox

Talk to former students of the John Woolman School, and chances are you will hear the phrase "the Woolman Way." A way of being and a way to follow. Everyone will have a story to tell. The land speaks too. It is the ancestral home of the Nisenan Tribe of the Nevada City Rancheria, the original residents of this place.

There are the stories of the early Quakers whose belief in the importance of education is reflected in the many Quaker educational institutions in the United States and the world, including the John Woolman School. Of course, you will also hear stories of students' lives, the teachers, the people who have lived and worked on the campus from 1963 until today. There are the Quakers who come to the meeting house, the youngsters who come to camp who sleep under the stars and sing around the campfire. There are the Quaker families who volunteer on weekend work crews on the campus, as they have done since the school was conceived. So many stories that deserve to be preserved so that we can remember. Our lives are shaped by particular places, and our physical place in the world is a major determinant of how we live our lives. This is the story of a place, and way of being in that place, that shaped the lives of many people during the past 60 years.

Once we started writing, we talked to many, many people, and even more people are important to the story. If you aren't in the book and you think you should be, we sincerely apologize.

We bring two different perspectives to this story. Lisa is a strategic planning consultant for nonprofits and a public historian who writes about community history. She worked with the Board in 2018 to develop the "Woolman Rising" strategic plan. Catherine is a writer and alumna of John Woolman School whose association goes back to the early 1970s. Our sources for the story overlap, and our narratives are complementary. Without both perspectives, The History, (Lisa) and The Memoirs: Wombats in the Real World (Catherine), the story would be incomplete. Here are our perspectives on the storytelling.

ABOUT THE HISTORY:

I ran into Amy Cooke in the fall of 2017, soon after I'd noticed a small article in the local paper announcing that she had been appointed Interim Executive Director of the John Woolman School. We had a passing acquaintance, but I knew nothing about her Quaker affiliations. My curiosity was piqued, and I soon learned that this was not her first stint leading the school—about which I knew very little. I had had only two associations with Woolman before getting to know Amy; one was with the place itself and the other with people.

The Woolman campus is situated about seven miles outside of the towns of Grass Valley and Nevada City, California, and I had been there only once in the 20 years I lived in Grass Valley. On a cold day in early December 2001, I visited the campus for the firing of the "Noborigama climbing kiln." Potters and artists from around the country gathered for the event, as they had annually for three decades. Friends and colleagues of the potters took turns stoking a massive blaze that burned inside a rare, multi-chambered kiln. Built on the slope of a hill in 1971 with the help of the students, the kiln was part of the Earth Air Fire Water program at Woolman, and the annual firing tradition had continued from that time. I was among the community visitors assembled that day to see it.

On that first visit, as I drove down the hill toward the campus, the green meadow, old farm buildings, and huge oak trees revealed themselves behind the screen of massive gray pines that surrounded the property. The campus sits in the quintessential Sierra Foothills landscape of gray pines, massive blue oaks, manzanita, and chamise, and in the winter, the rains bring out the emerald radiance of the central meadow. Deer browse along the edges, accustomed to the harmless human hubbub. It is the landscape of my own Foothill home, and it always enchants me, open and inviting but also curiously complex, full of flowers and birds and creatures hiding in the forest. So I was intrigued. What goes on here I wondered; how did I not know about this place only a few miles from my house?

A few years after that visit, I had my first experience with the students and staff of the Woolman Semester. As one of the organizers of a monthly contra dance in nearby Nevada City, I received a call one autumn day from a teacher from the Woolman Semester program who wanted to bring about 20 young people to the upcoming dance on Saturday night. Always delighted to have some youthful energy and enthusiasm at our small community dance, I assured her that they would be most welcome. When the students arrived at the door that Saturday—a loud, lively, diverse, enthusiastic bunch of teens—they enchanted the regular crowd of dancers. They threw themselves wholeheartedly into the community dance with people who ranged in age from 8 to 80. When they asked about returning, they were given a unanimous thumbs-up. During that semester and in the following several years, the Woolman Semester students came to the dances when their schedules permitted. Gradually I learned a little about the program at Woolman. I could see that the students were a close-knit bunch, and that they brought their warm sense of community with them to infect our group. Both the experience of place and people struck a chord with me; there was something intangible but special there.

In 2017, I learned that the Woolman School was an institution in transition. After 40 years as a boarding school, followed by 10 years as a semester program for high-school students, the institution was struggling and needed help finding a new direction. As with any institution, over the course of sixty years there had been good times and hard times. The history of Woolman embodies hundreds of individual stories and community history, encompassing the influences that the school had locally through the projects of those who graduated from or taught at Woolman and then remained in the local area. Woolman's history reflects the history of Quaker education, and a time of cultural change and turmoil in the United States as it manifested in an insular academic community. It seemed to me that many people knew parts of the story, but no one had assembled the whole historical narrative in detail from the beginning to the present day. I wanted to tell the story for posterity.

One day in August 2019, Catherine and I joined Don Elton Smith, one of the founders of Woolman, for a long conversation. At the time, Don was 95 years old and had driven to California from his home in Colorado, stopping to visit friends at Woolman on the way to the coast. He brought his razor-sharp memory, and we recorded as he answered many questions and reminisced about his decades at Woolman. That interview was the launchpad for my research. Fortunately, Quakers keep great records, and I discovered a treasure trove of material in the school archives. Boxes and boxes of correspondence, meeting notes, newsletters, brochures, photos, and newspaper clippings sat waiting for me. It was thrilling to find folders with hundreds of letters that Don exchanged with members of the College Park Friends Educational Association (CPFEA) as the school was being created. Don was on site in Nevada County right from the beginning, and nearly all his communication with the Bay Area Quakers was through written correspondence, sometimes several letters a week. He and the committee members talked about all the details—the purchase of the land, the bank loans, the goals of the school, the daily challenges of creating an educational institution out of a rural ranch.

In addition to reading the materials from the archives that form the core of the historical narrative, I also had the delightful experience of talking to many people who have lived and worked at Woolman through the years. I am deeply grateful to each of you who spent time answering my questions and reminiscing with me. A few months ago, I had the pleasure of spending time again with Don Smith at his home in Colorado. At nearly 100 years of age, he is the only one of the original founders of Woolman, present at the first planning meetings in Berkeley and Palo Alto in the late 1950s, who I was privileged to meet. And he entrusted me with some of his personal papers, which I am adding to the archives and have used in the book.

We thought it would take a year to write the book, and it's been more than four years since our first meeting with Don Smith at Woolman. I thank my most patient friends for listening to me talk endlessly about Woolman and Quaker history all this time, and to all who encouraged me in the challenging endeavor of writing a book. Thanks to Catherine, my persistent and motivated co-author. To Paul Jolly, who has handled the fundraising and administrative efforts. To the people who supported this project. And above all, to my sister Deena Frankel, who shares my love of books and ideas, and is my indefatigable developmental editor and cheerleader. She kept me going when I thought I just couldn't find the words or organize my thoughts. And last, but far from least, thanks to my dear husband, Eric Engles, who has been the most loving, patient, and supportive partner in life, and indirectly in this project. We've talked about books nearly every day for the past 25 years. He has been teaching me to write by osmosis as he shared with me the developmental editing work he has done for his clients, and I hope some of that magically acquired knowledge shines through.

~ Lisa Frankel, Grass Valley, California

ABOUT THE MEMOIRS:
WOMBATS IN THE REAL WORLD

Some time ago, I approached Amy Cooke about writing a book about John Woolman School, something I had wanted to do for many years. Amy told me about Lisa's interest in preserving the history of Woolman and suggested that we should get together. On a summer afternoon basking on the banks of the Yuba River with Amy, and later, gathered around a picnic table on the dining-hall deck, we began to brainstorm how we might move a writing project forward. This book is the result of that collaboration.

It was my keen memories of being a student at John Woolman School and the love of my experience there that inspired me to approach Amy. For many years, I have had it in my heart to write a book about Woolman. Doing so has been a nostalgic journey for me. In many ways, I have felt what it was like to be sixteen years old again, with all its thrills and fragility. Like many Woolman students, the story of how I came to Woolman was one of disenfranchisement. When I was fifteen years old and in public school, I was given a writing assignment to write a poem or story. At the time, I was acting in a children's theater and thought that writing a play would be an interesting way to respond to the story assignment. After all, what is a play, if not a story? I worked for days writing a play taken from my dream about a man who faces a judge in a courtroom and is juried by a cast of characters representing birth, life, and death. I had worked hard on my 30-page, handwritten play and was quite pleased with it when I turned it in. But my enthusiasm was short-lived. I was mortified when the teacher gave me a giant red F.

Once home, I announced to my mother that I was never going back to public high school. An English instructor herself, she marched right down to the school with a head of steam to demand that the English teacher change my grade to A. The teacher refused, saying that I had plagiarized the Greek playwright Aeschylus because "no teenager thinks like that," to which mother replied, "she does."

Aeschylus was born in Eleusis in Western Attica in 525 BC and wrote his first plays in 498 B.C.E. Though his work did include moral themes, what perplexed me then and still amazes me now is that a high-school English teacher could believe that a 15-year-old teenager would know who Aeschylus was, much less have the temerity to plagiarize him!

When we got home, my mother looked at me soberly and said firmly, "You will be ruined in public school." Coincidentally, she was friends with Ellie Foster, one of the founders of John Woolman School, and had high regard for the Quakers and the Foster family. I also knew Quakers through the local children's theater and had been attending Quaker meetings on my own. I liked their emphasis on peace and community.

Bumping down the dusty road to Woolman, I caught a flash of goats grazing on a manzanita-swept ridge. Sweet, hot pine scent lingered in the air as a young woman in a long muslin dress skipped across a sloping meadow, barefoot. I was immediately drawn in. After talking with staff, my parents and I both knew that Woolman would be a perfect place for me to grow my native abilities and personality. I moved in the next week.

Interviewing students and staff for this book, I began to see thematic similarities in the life choices they made after attending or teaching at John Woolman School. Rather than tell their stories chronologically, I decided to group these similarities to illustrate that throughout Woolman's history, from its beginning to more recent years, the impact the school and its unique approach to education and community had on people was similar. What emerged were groups of students and staff through all the years who were drawn to the arts, healing therapies, environmental protection, peace action, and social justice—choices that most people said originated in their experience at Woolman. Many were also imbued with Quaker values and a sense of responsibility for bettering their communities and the life of people around them, which they traced back to their experience at the school.

I know that the foundation I got at Woolman is what led me into every aspect of writing in my life and career. Like many other Woolman students, as German author Herman Hesse once wrote in *Beneath the Wheel*, I sincerely believe that I would have been "crushed beneath the wheel" and perhaps never made it through high school or college without the benefit of John Woolman School. It changed my life. This is how I felt as a student and still feel today. Without question, the story of Woolman is well worth sharing.

My part of this book would not have been possible without the generous contribution of time from former students, instructors, and staff at John Woolman School and the Woolman Semester. My heartfelt thanks go to each person who took time out of their busy lives to meet with me personally or talk online. Your participation was invaluable. It was also a joyful experience getting to know you. I felt fully welcomed as a Wombat—and as the Quakers have been known to say, "You are now in my basket." In the community spirit of Woolman, I hope that we all stay connected. Big thanks also go to Lisa Frankel, whose dogged determination to sort through countless documents and files has given this book its rich historical perspective.

~ Catherine Lenox, Duvall, Washington

We, Catherine Lenox and Lisa Frankel, extend a very, very special thank you to Sophie Brinker, who created the lovely illustrations found throughout the book, to Anita Anderson for her precise and thoughtful copyediting, and to Sonja Gerard for applying her artistry to the design of the book. We set out to tell the story of the John Woolman School. It turned out that we were not the only ones who thought it was a good idea to write a book to preserve this history. Paul Jolly, also an alumnus, created a Kickstarter online fundraising campaign to raise money to pay for the writing, editing, design, printing, and distribution of the book. Many generous donors stepped up to contribute funds, and they will receive the first copies. All proceeds from book sales will go to Sierra Friends Center.

JOHN WOOLMAN SCHOOL
QUAKER COEDUCATIONAL
BOARDING SCHOOL
Grades 10, 11, 12
JONES BAR ROAD

INTRODUCTION

Residents of Jones Bar Road noticed an unusual amount of traffic motoring past on the quiet country road leading to the old Hedrick's property outside Nevada City, California, on Sunday, September 15, 1963. Family cars, mostly arriving from the San Francisco Bay area and carrying a high-school student and a pile of gear, crested the hill and rolled down to the expansive campus of the new John Woolman School. Thirty-three students gathered for the beginning of Orientation Week at the first Quaker boarding high school west of the Mississippi. Despite frantic efforts to prepare, the campus wasn't quite ready for them, and for the next two weeks students moved back and forth between the Woolman property and their temporary quarters at a nearby summer camp while the dormitory was readied for occupancy.

The story of the John Woolman School begins long before this moment. It includes the people who conceived of establishing a Quaker school, the process of building and the challenges of operating the school, the eventual evolution of the institution into a new form, and the memories of the people who participated. The first half of this book sets forth a chronological historical narrative, and the second half brings together the voices of students, staff, volunteers and Friends (Quakers), telling stories about their involvement with Woolman and how it affected their lives.

The story of Woolman has many facets. The physical place has always figured prominently in the memories of those who spent time there. Meadows and forests surround the school's buildings. Situated as it is in the Sierra Nevada foothills, it is a mostly peaceful and welcoming landscape that has been home to humans and wild creatures for eons. It sits above the South Fork of the Yuba River, and its meadows and springs provided sustenance to the Nisenan people long before colonizers arrived in the 1850s to wreak havoc on the landscape and the Native people in their search for gold. Mining was the primary lure, but agriculture also drew white settlers. By 1885, the Marshall family owned the property, which included "a house, two barns, a fenced enclosure, 20 head of horned cattle, one sorrel horse, 30 chickens, 17 hogs, one plow and two sets of harness." In the mid-1940s, the Stillens family bought the property and built some of the buildings still in use today. The Hedricks purchased it from Jack Stillens in 1959 and then sold and optioned half the land to the College Park Friends Educational Association (CPFEA) in 1962, and the remaining portion in 1968. Today, the school owns approximately 230 acres. Much of the Woolman story involves the efforts to maintain the property and infrastructure.

The John Woolman School evolved from the strong desire of Quaker families to have an educational institution, a boarding high school, on the West Coast, where they could send their children to "live" and learn Quaker values. The school was built, guided, and sustained throughout the years by the strongly held Quaker values of simplicity, peace, integrity, community, equality, and stewardship. Simplicity meant using financial resources carefully and valuing spirit over material objects. Seeking peace meant focusing on conflict resolution and decision-making based on consensus or "a sense of the meeting," as well as a belief in empowering students to share in the development of school culture. Integrity, particularly with respect to curriculum, encouraged inner motivation rather than the pressure of grades, as well as a more thematic and integrated approach to academic topics. Connection within the community was an all-important focus, with a deep appreciation of the idea that everyone holds a piece of the truth within. Gathering at school for Meeting for Worship and allowing anyone to speak their mind conferred respect on every group member, welcoming into the community people of all faiths, ethnicities, genders, beliefs, and cultures. And finally, Woolman promoted environmental and economic sustainability through the lens of social justice.

Students who attended Woolman over the years reported profoundly meaningful experiences of all kinds. Hundreds of students and campers participated in a wide variety of activities during the past 60 years. A sampling of their stories includes some of the most wonderful, most challenging, and sometimes most ordinary moments you could imagine. But a throughline in the stories is a dedication to doing good in the world, working for peace, standing against injustice, bearing witness, and being dedicated to learning and service of all kinds. These values pervaded the campus, and the students inevitably absorbed them. And it wasn't only the students; so many people who worked at Woolman over the years also encountered the magic of place and people, and were inspired to succeed in impactful and especially creative careers.

Adherence to Quaker values proved to be a double-edged sword for Woolman: a source of strength and of weakness. The idea of creating a Quaker boarding school for high-school students was wonderfully ambitious, and an amazing group of dedicated and talented people participated in making it happen. Quaker values strongly encourage volunteerism, and many people gave remarkable amounts of time and energy to creating the school and keeping it going. Woolman always relied on energy and enthusiasm to get the job done, yet there were times when having expert advice and assistance might have avoided some pitfalls. The dedication of the planners to student empowerment, as well as the social change afoot nationally in the 1960s, translated at first into an environment that did not include a lot of rules. However, Nevada County was more conservative than the San Francisco Bay Area, where many of the students had grown up, and the local community sometimes looked askance at the students who didn't have a dress code or restrictions on the length of their hair, at a time when these constraints were still the norm for youth in the area. Empowering students to share in the development of school culture was both a wonderful and fulfilling opportunity for students, and also contributed to a challenging situation when students felt empowered to choose a path that made their elders uncomfortable.

The acceptance and almost prioritization of simplicity sometimes resulted in having to make do with less than ideal material resources, or without adequate funding. One consequence of this approach was that the school opened without sufficient financial reserves, a situation that had long-lasting consequences. Other challenges that Woolman faced over the years were truly out of the leadership's control. Economic changes in the world included increased expenses due to inflation, and sometimes lessened public support for certain kinds of educational programs while increasing the emphasis on others. As time passed, the cost of running a school skyrocketed beyond the wildest dreams of the founders.

Though the theme of financial difficulties runs through the whole historical narrative, interestingly, it is only occasionally mentioned in the personal reminiscences of students and staff. Over 60 years, thousands of people—students, staff, volunteers, and Friends—were affiliated with Woolman in one way or another. Those who have told their personal stories here repeat over and over the intense feeling of community, often joyful connection to others, pleasure in an intense sense of "place" and love of the land, and inspiration to act, create, and work in the world inspired by their experience at Woolman. Whatever challenges the faculty or board faced seemed not to change the general love of place expressed by so many. However, nothing as long-lasting and complex as a 60-year history can be all rosy for the participants. There are stories of good times and bad times for everyone involved.

The details of Woolman's history came from many sources. Quakers are notorious for their diligent documentation. Unselfconscious about the enormity of the undertaking, the founders had an idea that they believed in, and they threw themselves into the process of bringing that idea to fruition. The archives of the school include minutes of meetings from the late 1950s, when Quakers first gathered to discuss the idea of starting a school. Later, there are hundreds of pages of letters, mostly between Don Smith (who was tasked with first finding suitable property for the school and then managing the build out of the campus) and various members of the College Park Friends Education Association (CPFEA) , the Quaker nonprofit entity established to create and govern the school. They discussed everything by letter for almost two years, at a time when the toll calls between the San Francisco Bay Area (where most of the board members lived) and Nevada County (where the school property was) would have been prohibitively expensive. Once the school opened, the nature of the historical documentation changed. The minutes of meetings of the CPFEA and its subcommittees fill folders. The CPFEA made regular reports at the College Park Quarterly Meeting (CPQM), a quarterly meeting of the Religious Society of Friends (Quakers) in northern California and northern Nevada. The minutes of those meetings (with some exceptions) are available online. Woolman students and staff published newsletters throughout the years reporting on the activities on campus, and boxes of photos and memorabilia, three-ring binders full of staff meeting notes, and files of a wide variety of correspondence provided sources from which to piece together the history of Woolman.

Quaker documentation has its own unique vocabulary used in meetings and reflected in the minutes of those meetings. Throughout the archives, repeated and defined here when appropriate, are phrases that might be unfamiliar to non-Quaker readers.

Part I, the chronological history, begins by looking deep into the past and briefly examining Quaker history and attitudes toward education. This history strongly influenced the Quaker founders of the school, who intentionally chose to imbue the school culture with Quaker values. The history of Woolman spans more than six decades, beginning in the late 1950s, when the founders began meeting to talk and plan. The creation decade is the 1960s, and both the campus and "the Woolman Way" came to be in a time of great social upheaval in the United States. The 1970s, '80s, and '90s each had their distinctive cultural and social backgrounds that affected the direction of both the academic and social aspects of Woolman. In the early 2000s, John Woolman School ceased to be a boarding high school. In 2003, a new educational program, the Woolman Semester, was started and continued until 2016. When that program closed, the CPFEA spent a couple of years struggling to develop new sustainable programming on the campus. On August 17, 2020, a long-feared natural disaster occurred. The Jones fire, a lightning-sparked wildfire, swept through the campus, destroying much of the natural surroundings and burning to the ground many buildings large and small. Ever undaunted, rebuilding began with new plans and opportunities for reconstruction and revival, and the CPFEA continued to plan a new future direction.

Part II, "Wombats in the Real World," provides a different perspective on the story through interviews with dozens of former students and staff members, capturing and preserving memories of the time they spent at Woolman. Sometimes memories don't exactly match the facts of the written record, names are forgotten, dates are uncertain, and events confused. Despite the occasional confusion, the memories are imbued with vividness and energy. They reflect the lived experiences incorporated into the personal histories of each individual. The memoir portion is organized by the themes that recurred in the telling of these tales. Some involve everyday experiences of students as they did their assigned "work jobs" or engaged their creative energies crafting clay. Others reflect the incorporation of Quaker values, recalling Meeting for Worship, Quaker contemplation, and conscientious objection. There are stories of joy and sorrow, and sometimes pain and emotional distress that reflect the complexity, challenges, and intensity of life lived in community where education is a critical focus.

This book brings together documentation that has never been assembled in one place before. It preserves a record of a unique Quaker educational enterprise.

Woolman outdoor wooden sign, some of the inspiration for the cover of this book

SECTION ONE:

THE HISTORY

| QUAKERISM |

ROOTED IN QUAKER TRADITION

Today there are fewer than a hundred Quaker or Friends Schools in the United States, the lasting embodiment of deep Quaker educational roots that stretch back to the mid-seventeenth century. From the beginning, universal learning was a religious obligation of Quakers. The lineage of John Woolman School goes back to the late 1600s, when Quakers opened schools to educate boys and girls "not to live in the world that was, but in the world Friends hoped to help create." They believed that a distinct way of life demanded a distinct type of education.

The Quaker movement began in 1647, when George Fox started preaching in England and quickly created a following in the form of the Society of Friends, or practitioners of Quakerism. The Quakers believe that God exists in everyone, and that consequently there is no need for churches, rituals, holy days, or sacraments to practice religion. With no formal creed or dogma, they are instead committed to a set of core values of simplicity, peace, integrity, community, equality, and service. They are interested in the transformation of not only of individuals but society as a whole; from this outlook has come the traditions of working for civil liberties, civil rights, peace, and justice.

In the 17th century, the Quaker beliefs and form of religious practice directly flouted the prevailing political priority of strict uniformity of religious worship. Those who did not support the Church of England were seen by monarchs and their advisers as a threat to the state and the social order. The 1662 Act of Uniformity required strict adherence to the rites and ceremonies of the Church. The rules were onerous and specific for

clergy and followers, and failure to adhere to them resulted in penalties, including being banned from government office or any role in the church. The Quakers were one of about twenty groups of religious dissenters who fled England for the American colonies during the seventeenth century in search of religious freedom.

There is more than one theory about how Quaker educational goals developed. About twenty years after he began to preach, George Fox advised Friends to set up schools. He regretted his own lack of education and saw value in establishing schools. In addition to children experiencing restricted educational opportunities, he and other nonconformists in England were denied higher education in colleges and universities because they were not members of the Church of England. In the early days of Quakerism, some well-educated members of society who joined the Friends also recognized that if they were to instill their values in young people through education, they would need to establish their own schools.

The fundamental concepts of spirituality, simplicity, equality, and nonviolence serve as the founding principles of Quaker education. The concept of universal learning looked very different in the 1600s, so associated educational methods have metamorphosed over time as the role of religion in society has evolved. Quaker educational philosophy reflected the northern European Christian values (such as those reflecting gender roles, attitudes toward poverty, and assessments of moral failings) when the religion was founded. The approaches to education varied in the many Quaker branches and sects that began in Europe and spread into the Americas, however wherever they lived, they started schools.

Early Quakers believed that many of society's problems, particularly poverty and criminality, were due to a lack of education. They also believed in spiritual equality. In order to cure the ills of society and to give everyone the opportunity to fulfill their spiritual nature, they supported universal education regardless of financial status, gender, or race. In spite of these lofty goals, the concept of equal pay for equal work was centuries away, and women were not paid the same as men for their teaching skills. Nor was the curriculum the same for the boys and girls. Women were seen as nurturers, and teaching reflected these ideas. Additionally, in spite of the belief in nonviolence, the teachers in English Quaker schools meted out corporal punishment until 1839. As society has continued to change, Quakers have adapted, including evolving attitudes towards race and gender in the community and in schools.

Friends schools had some distinct characteristics. Meeting for Worship (akin to going to chapel in Christian schools) was fundamental to the curriculum. There was no music, art, or drama for the first 250 years of Quaker schools, since such activities were frowned on by Friends; instead, they emphasized practical subjects like science and nature. Because Quakers believed that no physical labor was degrading, manual labor as well as academic subjects were the norm. This idea reemerged in the twentieth century and was incorporated into the curriculum of modern Quaker education; this, along with an emphasis on social service, is distinctive of Quaker schools.

Acknowledging that Quaker education has many peculiarities, for more than 50 years there has been discussion in Quaker circles of "What should a Friends school be." In 1982, Douglas Heath wrote the pamphlet "The Peculiar Mission of a Quaker School" for Pendle Hill (225). He reflected that, among the many Quaker schools he visited, there was a feeling that the schools had a sense of purpose that went beyond academic excellence—yet they also were "vulnerable to the corrosive effects of a pervasively seductive and secular society." He observed that this threat was intensified because so few students, teachers, and administrators in the Quaker schools came from a Quaker background. Early Quakers wanted what they referred to as "guarded education" for their children, providing an educational environment that protected students from the influences of the world that were thought harmful to their development. Teaching the Quaker way of life was another key goal. One problem was that there were so few Quakers; if they restricted Quaker education to Quakers exclusively, the schools ran the risk of not being able to survive. It is difficult for schools to identify, let alone live up to, the ideals and traditions of a Quaker education. There is the added need to adapt those ideals to the changing mores of contemporary society. To survive and thrive as Quaker institutions, the schools must identify the "peculiar" element: the empowering of students, faculty, and administrators to live more fully in Truth. Consequently, the question emerged early on, how could Quaker schools successfully reflect both the distinctive cultural and spiritual heritage of Quakerism if they admitted students who were not Quakers? These were issues that John Woolman School grappled with.

The principles of early Quaker educational philosophy provided a solid foundation for the goals of Woolman. At the same time, the intention of embracing traditional values in the midst of rapidly changing social norms of the second half of the 20th and early 21st century presented an immense challenge. As we explore the history of the school from its inception through its evolution to the present day's reimagined programming, the still solid core values of simplicity, peace, integrity, community, equality, and service remain evident. In these pages, we seek to follow that through-line. Students and staff who sometimes remember challenges and hard times inevitably cite these foundational values. Sixty years later, they are inspiring new ways of executing them while preserving longstanding tradition.

Stone House

2

....

TOWARD A FRIENDS SECONDARY
BOARDING SCHOOL
IN NORTHERN CALIFORNIA

As the 1950s drew to a close, a group of Quaker families in the greater San Francisco Bay Area began thinking about the educational opportunities for their children. This diverse group had a variety of interests, concerns, and dreams specific to the educational needs of their families. In particular, families with young children were thinking forward to their secondary-school options. They could consider sending them to Quaker schools in Pennsylvania, such as Scattergood School or other boarding schools, but among their concerns, sending a youngster to boarding school in the East was an expensive proposition. Why wasn't there a Quaker school in California? Some families felt that a West Coast Quaker school could be better, be local, more rigorous, and offer more depth than the local public schools.

Further fueling the conversation was a general concern, not just among the Quakers, that the American education system needed reforming, concerns that were partly inspired by the success of the Soviet Union's launch of the Sputnik satellite in 1957. These worries prompted fears that U.S. students could not compete with the Soviet Union in the areas of science and technology. In response, Congress passed the National Defense Education Act of 1958 to fund the improvement of U.S. schools and promotion of post-secondary education. Ideas about how this was to be accomplished varied, and these concerns inspired lively debate among the Quakers.

The national movement for educational reform brought to some a sense of urgency to offer a more rigorous traditional curriculum for their children. Others had an interest in alternative educational philosophies. Some of those interested in more unconventional approaches knew about and were interested in the Summerhill School founded in England by A. S. Neill in the early 1920s. Summerhill's educational system promoted giving freedom to children and staff through democratic governance. Replicating that kind of approach to education in the mountains and woods of California appealed to some of the group. However, not surprisingly, there was a wide range of ideas and possibilities for educational approaches.

Serious political issues were also driving the desire for a West Coast alternative to the public schools. The McCarthy trials were in full swing, and the idea of requiring public school teachers to sign a loyalty oath was anathema to Quaker beliefs. These concerns were not theoretical; sixty-nine professors were fired nationwide for political reasons during the McCarthy era, nearly half of them from the University of California, so this issue was very close to home and added to the motivation to develop a new school.

The early planning for a Quaker school began in April 1957. Several dozen people, mostly families from the College Park Quarterly Meeting of the Northern California Pacific Yearly Meeting, met formally for the first time to discuss the establishment of a Friends secondary school on the West Coast. They met at Hidden Villa Ranch in the mountains west of Palo Alto, home of the Josephine and Frank Duveneck family. Josephine Duveneck was originally a member of the Berkeley Friends Meeting, and later organized the San Francisco Monthly Meeting. The Duvenecks had established a center for social, educational, environmental, and humanitarian activities at Hidden Villa Ranch. In summer, it was a youth camp, to which Josephine and her husband Frank brought minority and disadvantaged children, and minority counselors—given the mostly white demographics of the San Francisco Peninsula, this was particularly unusual and innovative. By the late 1950s, Hidden Villa Camp was incorporated as a nonprofit, so it was a very appropriate venue at which to discuss the creation of a new educational facility.

A group of Quakers gathered for the Friends Secondary School Conference at Hidden Villa Ranch on April 16 and 17, 1957, and began discussing the basic organizational structure for a proposed school. There were so many issues to consider. They felt it was necessary that the school should have a director. But there was no precedent, and they debated who should choose the director, concluding that it made sense to appoint a board of trustees or some similar body. But again, who was to choose them? They deliberated at length and finally reached some conclusions about a number of important issues that were to shape the ultimate creation of the school. They felt that every effort should be made, in spite of probable geographic difficulties,

> "to develop a school community among the parents students and staff; that this should be a Friends school, openly and frankly, but not limited to Friends alone; that the school should be, as much as possible, a part of the present organization of Friends, such as this Quarterly Meeting, rather than a completely separate organization; that while the board of trustees should not be limited to friends alone it should be so organized that it would always be under the control of Friends and express their attitudes."

At the end of the weekend of discussion, the group established a committee, the College Park Friends Educational Association (hereafter referred to as the "CPFEA," the "association," the "committee" the "board") with representatives from several meetings of the Quarter, Palo Alto, Delta, Monterey, College Park, Sacramento, and San Francisco groups. In the first year after the establishment of the CPFEA, the group met once a month. Generally, about ten or a dozen people attended, though occasionally more people joined. They regularly alternated meetings between Berkeley and Palo Alto (about 40 miles away). After the first year, they recognized the need to incorporate as a formal legal organization, and the official papers establishing the nonprofit educational corporation were filed on July 3, 1958.

Among those present at the first meeting, along with the Duvenecks, was an eclectic and dedicated group of Friends including Don and Harriette Smith, who lived in Watsonville and owned a chicken farm at the time; Mary and Russ Jorgensen, who (according to the history of the Berkeley Friends Meeting) had been members since 1946 and were counted among the "giants" of Berkeley Meeting's history; Meg and Marshall Palley, who lived in Berkeley with their six children, where Marshall was a faculty member at UC Berkeley in the Department of Forestry; and Bob Beloof and his wife (Bob was a graduate of a Friend's school in Wichita, Kansas, and consequently very interested in Quaker education). Don Smith recalls someone remarking that "We Quakers were all a bunch of queer, different people." Some in the group were involved for the long haul, and others eventually lost interest or their circumstances changed before the school opened its doors.

Complicating the conversation was the fact that Quaker education was undergoing its own soul-searching process. Society had become increasingly secularized and materialistic in the mid-twentieth century, and values were becoming more homogeneous across the culture, driven in part by the ubiquity of radio and television. Were these changes compatible with Quaker education, particularly for a new school, which would need a significant input of resources to get established? Clearly there was rebellion afoot among the generation of students who would be served by the school, and it wouldn't be long before the school authorities would be dealing with some difficult social issues. Questions that arose included how to retain an identity as a Friends school in the face of contemporary societal pressures. Further, it was likely that many students and staff would not be Quakers, nor necessarily even acquainted with Quaker values. In the face of these challenges, what would it take to maintain Quaker identity?

Among one contingent of West Coast Quakers, there was also philosophical opposition to the idea of starting a Quaker boarding school. This group felt that keeping the energy of Quaker families in local communities would "infect" those places with Quaker values and raise the standards of education for everyone. In addition, the money spent on the new school, which would be considerable, could be used more effectively to support other projects. Some felt that a boarding school would be separatist and elitist. Debates among Friends about whether to have a private school moved from the early planners' conversations to discussions in the wider Quaker community as the plans became known. To a certain extent, the attitude was that one ought to be seen in the public schools helping to bring up the quality of the public schools, reaching all these kids instead of a select group from families who can afford to pay tuition. Not the least of the challenges of starting a new school was the question of financial resources and support. The conflicted feeling about private versus public education did not help this issue. Historically, Quaker meetings in the eastern United States have had well-supported, well-funded Quaker education as a tradition. In many areas where Quakers had started schools, the early generations of English settlers bequeathed money and property when they died to support the Quaker schools. It was also a tradition to serve both students who could pay and those who couldn't. By the mid 1800s, during the Western Expansion, settlers expected towns to offer public education, which reduced the pressure on Quakers to provide schooling. Though Quakers did start some schools in the West during the second half of the 20th century, most of them were grade schools, without the financial endowments that boosted the early Eastern institutions. Though there are eastern Quaker schools without extensive financial support, most that are well known (such as Scattergood, Westtown, and Georgetown) have secure financial foundations. No robust financial foundation existed for the ambitious project of starting a boarding school in California.

Josephine Duveneck, who did not mince words, said at the opening of the "On A Friends School for the West Coast" conference, April 26-27, 1957:

> "We should not fool ourselves no matter how glamorous the dream. We ourselves might afford to take a chance, but can we do so for our children? If we had an angel bearing under the shadow of his wings heavy and substantial money bags, I am sure a wonderful school could emerge from the thinking and enthusiasm of this group and others involved."

At the suggestion of those who had extensive experience in Quaker education, the newly established Interim Planning Committee for a Friend's Secondary School decided (among its first actions) to start a monthlong summer school for the young people of the Pacific Yearly Meeting. Members of the original committee included Clarence and Polly Ash, Bob and Ruth Beloof, Thornton and Sarah Conrow, Orval and Mary Etter, Russ and Mary Jorgensen, Armand and Virginia Jackson, Mary King, Josiah and Adele Lancaster, Isaiah and Vanita Meyer, Claire Milliken, Ada Roberts, Don and Harriette Smith, Alan and Joan Strain, Mildred Thierman, and Ken Stevens. The summer school provided an opportunity for the CPFEA to develop as an organization, gain experience working with young people, and broaden its contacts in the community. Also at this point, the CPFEA began appealing to the Monthly Meetings of the Quarter to establish a regular amount in their annual budgets to help support the process of establishing a school.

The first summer program was held in southern California in 1958 (Claremont) and in northern California during the following summers. Unlike the typical summer schools of the time, designed primarily as remedial courses for students struggling with school, this was an enrichment program. Each summer, the program focused on a challenging topic designed to involve the students intensively in a specialized subject— including the science of brain surgery, Gandhian nonviolence, painting, and world faiths. They were led by experts in the field, with field trips and student participation, and these served as a practice model for those involved in planning the school. The program continued for six summers through 1963.

The CPFEA met often, preparing for and running the summer school. After the successful 1958 summer, discussion turned more fully to the proposed regular-term school, though not until the staunchly Quaker group had concluded a long discussion about paying taxes. Some members of the group were strongly opposed to sending the Federal tax withholding payment (for summer wages) to the government. One suggestion was the following statement:

"We are opposed to acting as an agent of the government in collecting from unwilling individuals taxes which will be used for war purposes."

After discussing various problems arising from the payment or nonpayment of withholding taxes, the group agreed that a letter of protest would be sent along with the payment. The discussion demonstrated the strong political motivations of some of the participants, viewpoints that often influenced their thinking about the future school plans.

The issue of deciding on a clearly stated purpose and goals for the school dogged the committee for the next few years. In various forms, this remained a recurrent theme for the next sixty years. A few members, including the Strains, rejected the idea of a statement of purpose, expressing their belief that the quality of teachers was more important. They also felt that the group was not asking the right, but difficult, questions about the purpose of the school. Another committee member argued that the Meeting School, which was often held up as an example, moved away from its original statement of purpose but then had returned to it, reinforcing the belief of some that it was a moving target. Some on the committee felt that a statement of purpose would be critical to use when recruiting a director and students; others felt that they should hire a director and that it would be up to that leader to set the "the emphasis of the school." Another committee member suggested asking the question, "What sort of education do I want for my children?" and keeping a file of 15-20 written answers to the question for future faculty to use for guidance. There was a vague statement of goals in a new brochure advertising the school, but some committee members were dissatisfied with that version as well.

While the CPFEA grappled with these questions, some of the original group fell away as their circumstances changed; in some cases, individuals (including the Strains and the Conrows) became disenchanted with the process and resigned. But at the Second Annual Conference of the

CPFEA, held at Tilden Park in Berkeley on May 16, 1959, a new slate of officers was elected for the coming year: Marshall and Meg Palley, chairpeople; Mary Etter, secretary; and Jim Estes, treasurer. The rest of the association members were Don and Harriette Smith; Mildred Thiermann; Edith Vernon, Larry and Polly Ash; Eugenia Sorenson; and Art and Helen Currier.

And where should the new school be? This was a very big challenge for the committee. Some were drawn to the mountains of northern California, and others favored a San Francisco Bay Area location. The consensus was that kids should have an experience away from home, and it shouldn't be where their mothers could drop in any afternoon. On the other hand, it shouldn't be a whole day's drive away—that would be too far. Some of the Friends in Berkeley had become acquainted with Alfred Heller, a well-to-do newspaperman who owned quite a bit of property in western Nevada County, California, about 150 miles east of San Francisco in the Sierra Nevada foothills. He ran a weekly newspaper called the Nevada County Nugget. When he learned of the Quaker interest in Northern California, he enthusiastically promoted the area to the committee, saying "we'd love to have you up here [Western Nevada County]—it's a great idea to have a Quaker school here." His encouragement, and the possibility that he might be a source of donor support, contributed to the decision to look for property in the foothills. With these factors in mind, the committee decided that Nevada County was about the right distance from the Bay Area. "You can get a bus home if you don't drive up, and it's out in the country."

Before the formal search for a site began, the committee proceeded with conversations and preliminary planning for establishing a school. The school needed a name. After deliberating for some months, the committee decided on the John Woolman School. A revered Quaker who practiced contemplative spirituality and energetic social activism, John Woolman, who was born in 1720 in New Jersey, worked as a clerk and a scribe, and learned tailoring. As a young man, he began to question and speak out against slavery, and soon the abolition of slavery became one of his main interests. Later, as an active and influential member of the Philadelphia Yearly Meeting, he was closely associated with their anti-slavery publications. Among his other concerns were the plight of the poor and the rights of Native Americans. He traveled to England in 1772 to preach, and while he was there died of smallpox. The *Journal of John Woolman* (1774) has been continuously in print since its initial publication. Numerous schools and institutions have adopted his name in honor of his teachings, including the Woolman Institute at Wilmington College, the John Woolman College of Active Peace, the John Woolman room at the Friends House in London, and the Woolman Peacemaking Forum at George Fox University. Both his spirit and his activism made his name a fitting one for the nascent school to adopt.

The CPFEA also worked on identifying the challenges that they would encounter in the complex process of locating property and developing it. By the end of 1961, it formally committed to finding property and doing whatever work was necessary to open a school in the fall of 1963. Marshall, Claire, and Bob went to Grass Valley, the largest town in western Nevada County, to have a look at some of the available properties. Members enjoyed looking around at some interesting rural properties, but the trip brought up issues such as "...how do you go from wildland with no improvements in the spring of 1962 to a school with open doors (or flaps— think tents!) in the fall of 1963." These were important questions, and the busy CPFEA committee considered them as it organized house meetings to present its ideas and progress and pursued fundraising for the school to interested Friends and others.

During this period, Don Smith, one of the original committee members, expressed enthusiasm for being involved in the site search and development of the school facilities. He wrote a thoughtful letter to Marshall Palley, also a longtime committee member, proposing some ideas to move the practical aspects of the project forward. For example, if a site was purchased, as many Friends as possible should visit to generate more enthusiasm for the project. He mentioned other ideas for promoting the school, including holding summer school and family camp on the property and bringing groups of Friends for meetings and volunteer work parties to make improvements. He thought that other Pacific Yearly

Meeting or American Friend Service Committee groups might also be interested in using the site. Don also suggested that a resident on the property could handle arrangements for getting groups there, act as a host, and lead tours for visitors. He recognized that if people became personally involved, they were much more likely to become financial contributors, and their enthusiasm would help bring in additional donors. He acknowledged that a lot of work would need to be done even to prepare for visitors of this type. He was looking forward, imagining the days when faculty and students could move in once they met some minimum standard of accommodation. His preliminary thoughts also reflected the serious financial questions that needed to be addressed, such as whether the association would be able to afford to have such a resident manager. These questions in the letter to Marshall and the committee planted the seed for the work that was to come and for Don's future involvement.

Early in 1962, both Don and Marshall began to feel pressure to move the process along more quickly to meet the timeline for opening that they envisioned. They needed to locate and purchase a property as soon as possible. It was far too inefficient for committee members to drive 150 miles up to Nevada County from the coast on weekends to look for property. The committee asked Don, who was highly respected and had expressed his strong commitment to working on developing the school, if he and his wife Harriette and their girls would consider relocating to Nevada County to take over the search for a suitable property. Although it would be a big change for his family, Don was favorably disposed to make the move to Nevada County from Watsonville, where he had been farming. He was waiting for the CPFEA to make a firm decision before he rented out his house, but he was in the process of shutting down his poultry farm operation in anticipation. At this point, Don and Marshall were in constant communication by letter; Don asked Marshall about financial plans for the new school and wondered about the CPFEA's ability to borrow money to buy the property. In spite of the known challenges, he was optimistic about the future and wrote words that reflected his Quaker upbringing, "...if we have faith enough not to block it, the way will open." When the job of searching for property in Nevada County was officially offered, Don agreed, and he and his family prepared to make a big move. He knew that living there would be a great advantage to the search, as they could get to know the area well.

To formalize the job and give Don some security as he uprooted his family, the CPFEA drew up a proposed employment contract for him in February 1962. The job was titled Resident Manager for the John Woolman School, and the position it described was no small task. Much of the responsibility for establishing the Woolman School was on Don's shoulders. The job description read as follows:

"To direct and coordinate an effort to provide a home for the Woolman School by September 1963, in some of the following and other ways:
- Conceive and recommend a general plan
- Explore and recommend acquisition of a site
- Oversee preparation of a site development plan
- Supervise construction of buildings and improvements
- Broaden and increase support of the school
- Co-ordinate contributed services
- Do visiting and fundraising
- Make effective use of Association membership and other supporters

Aid in physical arrangements for summer school and other groups using the school site, suggesting and overseeing suitable work projects where feasible."

Of course, Don was not expected to do this alone; a sub-committee of the CPFEA backed him up. However, he was the person on the ground in Nevada County, and the only one who was *employed* to accomplish the task—all other committee members were volunteers. Once his position as Resident Manager was made official, Don communicated about once a week with the CPFEA committee, and more often when urgent matters arose. Most of the letters were addressed to Marshall Palley, later also to Delbert (Del) Reynolds when the latter was hired as the Head of School for the 1963-1964 academic year. Marshall, who lived in Berkeley, was an important liaison with the Bay Area Friends. Much of this early history is based on those letters.

Site acquisition was the first priority for Don in his new job. He began working with local realtors searching for a suitable location and available property of at least 10-20 acres. Later, he laughingly recalled that he often felt like he had a job "site-seeing" as, for months, he spent much of his time traveling around the region with realtors looking at properties on offer. The fundraising and promotional materials for the school at the time included this colorful description of the region:

> "The Motherlode country of the Sierra. Starting from the Bay Area you go northwest on the Super Highway, US 40, through Sacramento. You continue beyond Sacramento on US 40 to Auburn, where you turn northerly on the State Highway 49, an excellent road, to a point due west of Lake Tahoe. Here the towns of Nevada City and Grass Valley, situated within 4 miles of each other, form the largest urban center of the foothills around, 8000 people. These are towns rich in history with buildings going back to Gold Rush days such as the famous National Hotel, the assay office where the first nugget of the Comstock Lode was assayed, and handsome Victorian homes. Dotting the countryside are old towns with names like Rough and Ready, Scotch Hill, Bourbon Hill, You Bet, Delirium Tremens, and even, by a circumstance lost to history, Quaker Hill.
>
> At an elevation of approximately 2500 feet, the area is within less than an hour's drive of prime winter sports areas, with sledding, skiing and skating. It is not so high as to be involved in serious winterizing problems, yet it is high enough to avoid the worst of the valley summer heat. It is an area of immemorial pastoral dramas, creeks, trees, rushing mountains rivers, clear air, and days that conclude satisfactorily."

Before any property had even been secured, at the end of March,

Marshall connected with a young architect, Dick Bergstrom. who would be taking the State Boards in June. He had been hired to design some of the new buildings, though Don had yet to meet him and decide whether he felt that he could work with him on a site plan.

In April, Don found a rental house in Grass Valley for his family, a two-bedroom bungalow on Bragg Avenue. As they settled in, Don visited potential school site properties with area realtors. He dutifully sent detailed descriptions of all the properties he visited; there were seventeen on the list by the end of the process. Several were possible contenders, some with buildings and improvements and others without.

During this period, there was an interesting twist that involved the Bureau of Land Management (BLM). Buying property was a significant cost of starting the school. Don and Marshall were constantly on the lookout for opportunities to minimize that expense. They learned that property might be available under the Reservation and Public Purposes Act. This act, which was passed in 1926, authorized the Secretary of the Interior to lease or convey public lands for recreational and public purposes under specified conditions, including lease or sale to nonprofit organizations and foundations, with special pricing for schools. Don heard that there might be some available land held by the BLM in Nevada County, but the location was unclear. They needed to determine the exact location of the land, confirm that it was not suitable for BLM purposes, and preferably was without an occupant, as well as obtain a legal description of it. Complicating the process was a lot of confusion in the BLM offices in Sacramento about the location of available property. They also learned that the Grass Valley School District was also potentially interested in acquiring land, so there might be some competition. Don did a lot of sleuthing around the county and eventually realized that pursuing that option could take a long time and be very frustrating, so they abandoned the effort.

While he was searching, Don and Harriette got to know a group of local Quakers who were interested in the idea of the school. Isabel Hedrick and her husband Mel were part of this group. One day, Mel asked Don what size property he was looking for, and when Don told him about 10-20 acres, Mel said nothing more. Don was well into the process when, in mid-May, the realtor he was working with invited him to see a property that admittedly was much bigger than what Don had in mind; he suggested that Don should come and see it anyway. Don agreed to see it, though when he learned that it was 160 acres he remembers declaring that the Committee would never go for that. It turned out to be owned by the Hedricks. It was number 14 out of a total of 17 properties that he visited in his search. Don wrote later that:

> "The road to the property was rough and narrow, but the sweeping view as you crest the hill of the wide expanse of green pasture, the white ranch house, the cattle sheds, great oaks shading the brook at the bottom, all surrounded by tall grey pines, captured his imagination. Once you start down the hill a reservoir for irrigation, a ranch house, a garage and a few other outbuildings, all less than ten years old come into view. The ranch house faces south and the large level pasture behind it looked like a perfect area for school sports. The central pasture is surrounded by small creeks. The price was reasonable for the amount of land."

Don wrote up a description of the Hedrick property for the CPFEA. It exceeded the committee's original expectations both in size and the amount of existing infrastructure, and consequently the price was more than they originally intended to pay. However, it was a beautiful piece of land, the price was modest for its value, and it turned out to be especially significant that the Hedricks were enthusiastic about having a Quaker school on the land. The Hedrick's place was looking better and better in comparison to others that were available. The only property at a similar price was much further out of town.

Now that they were getting closer to identifying land to purchase, and would soon need to be actively fundraising, Don and Marshall realized the need for a prospectus of some kind outlining the ideas for the school. They knew that this critical document needed to come from more than just the two of them and might take a while to develop. With the help of other committee members, they assembled information for public promotion of the school project. Realizing the need to publicize the school to more people, the CPFEA held a banquet in Berkeley in the middle of May. They invited Dr. Beulah Parker, a psychiatrist who talked about the role of communication in child development. The event attracted seventy people, many of whom were Quakers and potential supporters of the new school. Following Dr. Parker's talk, Marshall Palley spoke about the aims of the CPFEA, and Don Smith presented a set of slides illustrating the properties being considered for the school. There were to be many more of these public presentations in the coming months.

In his letters to Marshall, Don sometimes speculated about the future of the school and his role in it. He was tasked for the moment with organizing and developing the physical plant, but he was also involved in the conversations about finding a director so they could begin looking for staff and developing curriculum. He was already predicting that they might be opening the school with unfinished building projects. If the students were to be involved in any of those projects, they would need guidance. Additionally, they were planning to establish a farm program that would need to be designed and then overseen. These were all important questions for the future regardless of which property they purchased.

In addition to public relations, there was the issue of financing. It was clear, even before they had decided on a property to purchase, that completing loan applications was going to be a lot of work. They needed to assemble three years of CPFEA financial statements, a list of existing improvements on the property they intended to purchase, and a projection of earnings and expenses of the school operation. Another essential element would be a schedule of future building. Much of this involved guesswork, but the exercise would have tremendous value whether or not a particular bank would offer a loan. It would give the CPFEA a comprehensive picture of its finances for the project. At the same time, Don continued to improve and expand the promotional materials they were using both to recruit students and/or get pledges for donations, knowing that this source of funds was also crucial to their success.

By the beginning of June 1962, Don decided that he had seen enough properties, especially because there were two that he felt might work for the Quaker school, the Franzen property and the Hedrick's. The Franzen property was more expensive, but there was the possibility of selling off a piece of land to help finance the rest. The details were complicated, and Don thought the seller's representative was being somewhat "cagey" about the actual asking price. In addition, even if they were to sell off a piece, the total cost looked like it would be about $15,000 more. Don felt that it was important to compare the two properties as the CPFEA made a final decision on which one to purchase, and also to have a backup if the first choice fell through for some reason. He had several reasons for being more optimistic about the Hedrick's property, so as the discussions continued with the sellers, he worked with the Hedricks and the CPFEA to host a joint picnic with the Sacramento and Reno Friends on the site on June 10, 1962. The committee liked the idea that this would give the already interested parties, and the potential student families and donors, an opportunity to "inspect" it. Don was pleased at the interest in the property, but he was also a little concerned that he and the CPFEA might find the situation embarrassing if they decided not to purchase the land from the Hedricks.

Even before the day of the picnic and after much deliberation and negotiation, the CPFEA decided to move ahead with a formal offer to the Hedricks. The purchase price was to be $55,000, with an additional $9,200 to be paid to the title company at the close of escrow. Don and Marshall wrote back and forth about the details as they worked on the required financial information. At least one of the lenders questioned how the organization would be able to begin loan payments immediately, with no prospect of income until the school opened in September 1963. Lenders also asked whether members of the Quaker Meeting would guarantee the loans—to which Don had to reply no. The Meeting had clearly state that they were not willing to guarantee a loan. Don told Marshall that he felt let down after the discussions with the bankers. This wasn't going to be as straightforward as he had hoped; obtaining the loan they needed would entail much negotiating and possibly more time than they had originally expected.

In spite of concerns about obtaining a loan, on June 18, 1962, Don Smith wrote enthusiastically to Marshall that he had completed the negotiations that morning to purchase the property from the Hedricks. The contract was being drawn up that week. Of the 170 acres, 110 acres would be purchased immediately with a $19,200 down payment (an $800 deposit had already been given) at the close of escrow, and the remaining $30,000 was subject to getting a bank loan. They also took an option to purchase an additional 68 acres, promising an $800 deposit at the close of escrow and $200 to be paid when the purchase was completed, by August 21, 1962. A very important factor in making the sale work for the CPFEA was that the Hedricks were giving a generous donation of $5,000 to CPFEA at the close of escrow and another $5,000 by February 1, 1963. Isabel Hedrick's interest in the place as a home for a Quaker institution helped make the price more within reach; however, the committee couldn't sink all its money into the land, as it would still need a considerable amount for development.

Decisions needed to be made about which parcels of land to include in the initial purchase. In the past, some surveying had already been done on the northern sections of the Hedrick's property, with the four corners established. However, apparently the original survey field notes resided with the BLM office in Sacramento and were not easily retrieved. A full survey was needed for the real-estate transaction. Dave Russell, who attended the Berkeley Meeting and worked as a land surveyor with a firm in Vallejo, offered to help with the survey. Dave had only a New Mexico license at that point; he would be taking his California exams in August. He planned to ask his boss if he could borrow equipment to do the survey, and he also he needed his boss to sign the survey when it was completed, which he believed he would willingly do, since he knew and respected Dave's work. This was one of many significant tasks that were accomplished with volunteer labor. In the future, many people stepped up to take on tasks because they saw the need, whether or not they had the *official* qualifications or even the expertise.

In addition to the big projects like the land survey, there were other minor obstacles. And, like the lack of a land survey, they were often related to the rural nature of Nevada County. The property wasn't clearly associated with either of the two nearby towns. It was more or less equidistant from the town centers of Grass Valley and Nevada City. Don wrote to Marshall that "...it has a Nevada City mailing address, but road access is better and slightly shorter from Grass Valley. Also the phone prefix (273) is a Grass Valley one rather than Nevada City's prefix (265). It's something to mull over." None of these issues were obstacles to the purchase, but they complicated the process for Don, who had to deal with every detail.

Don talked to various lenders, including the Auburn branch of the Bank of California. They would potentially lend only up to a maximum of 50% of the appraised value, and even then, they would need a lot of financial information, including lists of all the pledges to date, details of how much money had already come in, a set of financial reports for the last three years, and budgetary projections for the establishment of the school—no small feat. The finance committee went into high gear to provide the financial reports to the lenders.

On a less stressful note and lighter side of the financial considerations, Mr. Hedricks planned to leave the chickens, geese, and turkeys that were currently on the ranch. He also offered some of his other livestock for sale, though Don felt that because it was not clear when someone would be living on the site full time, he should not take on any animal-care responsibilities. He planned to be away drumming up support for the school and making various arrangements for the improvements to the property during parts of the summer and early fall. He told Marshall that the price was fair, and they should consider keeping a young steer and heifer who could range free, as long as there was adequate water for them. Once the school was established, they would provide a good meat supply and would "mow" the pasture in the meantime. Possibly prompted by these considerations, around this time, Marshall first floated the possibility that Don and Harriette Smith might move from the rented house in Nevada City onto the property to live in the ranch house.

Meanwhile, the work of gaining new donors and supporters for the school continued with increasing fervor. It helped that the committee could now use photos and descriptions of the property to entice audiences. Whenever Don visited the Bay Area, members of the committee who were busy drumming up potential donors arranged for him to meet with various Friends who were interested in the school. Other association members also met with individuals and groups of potential donors and interested parties. Don went to Tacoma, Washington at the end of June, where he attended the Tacoma Meeting and promoted the school. There, once again, Friends questioned the role of independent schools versus public schools, and this reinforced Don's awareness that this was a continuing issue in the Quaker community. He used the opportunity to share the intentions of the CPFEA to emphasize Quaker values such as community, equality, and stewardship in order to try to increase goodwill for the project. The Association also floated the idea of homesites on the property for families who would pay rent to the school as a way to raise more capital for the operation. This idea had appeal to some Quakers. Interest and goodwill was essential to fundraising efforts, which at this point were also being scrutinized by the potential lenders. The CPFEA needed to show that it had the financial backing to be a viable risk for the banks.

When Don Smith returned to the house that the school rented for him and his family on Bragg Avenue in Grass Valley, mail from Berkeley finally caught up with him there. In one of those letters, Marshall assumed that the sale of the "ranch," as he called it, would be completed in August, and said that the CPFEA wanted Don to be in residence on the property. They planned to arrange for Don and Harriette to use the main ranch house and some outbuildings. In addition to struggling with financial details, the committee was toying with various ideas for setting up the land for summer visitors, volunteers who would be coming to do work and others who might come to see the property. One option was to make a comfortable and functional camping space complete with an outdoor kitchen.

During July, Don had information for Marshall and the committee about progress on the loan applications, but no offers yet. He found that factors and restrictions varied among the banks. One bank would make loans only for multiuse commercial properties (and the school was considered "single use"); others had limits on the amounts they would lend on certain types of projects. In general, the lenders were taking their time considering the loans, while Marshall and Bob definitely felt a sense of urgency to get the matter resolved. This was a pivotal time—they needed the loan to secure the property, but they also felt great pressure to maintain and expand the potential donor community. Marshall wrote in late July:

> "I have been trying for a few weeks to say this. I have been concerned that we have not been reaching the people who are active in social concerns. Many of them seem to feel the school is not acutely relevant to the burning issues. That it is visionary and is taking money and effort from the classes they feel are paramount, so I have tried to show how the school is basic to any solid expression of such activities. I do not expect that this group by and large, has large sums of money to give, but I do want their moral support and enthusiasm. I leave it to you to deliver to this sort of friend, either written or spoken. I hope to deliver it to the San Luis Obispo friends next Sunday."
>
> [Marshall letter to Don 072362]

Trying to leave no stone unturned, the committee investigated the possibility of applying for grant funding; though that never happened, it did receive a donation of 35 cartons of books for the library from a Bay Area bookstore, as well as other incidental items. Feeling anxious about the financing, the CPFEA explored a number of alternative options. The committee considered the pros and cons of commercial loans (versus private funding). As it awaited an answer from the banks, it toyed with the idea of staging the borrowing, taking only what it needed for the immediate work, and borrowing more later for another phase of getting ready to open. While the lenders deliberated, Marshall worked with Charles Hornig to set up the accounting for the coming year; Charles offered to be the auditor and to join the CPFEA as a representative from San Jose. This was an important development for future financial stability.

The committee moved forward with other tasks, setting up a post office box for school correspondence and pursuing donors (and possibly loans from private individuals). The survey of the property was almost completed, and this would help inform the process of designing the school facilities. They also requested information from five Friends boarding schools in the east and Midwest about their physical plants and layouts. It was clearly time to begin thinking about the detailed plan for the school buildings on the property. The committee was also getting ready for the formal announcement of the purchase of the school site, with press releases to local and regional newspapers.

Finally, on August 24, 1962, Don informed the CPFEA officers that he had three loan offers in hand. He stressed how important it was to make a decision and move forward quickly, to complete the title insurance on the property, and to have enough money to complete the build-out of the campus, so as to be ready for students the following fall. This was a momentous occasion. Escrow closed on the property on September 11, 1962.

The stones at Jones Bar, Yuba River

| FORWARD |

3

MAKING THE DREAM A REALITY

The school had a home! More than five years had passed since the first serious discussions took place among Quaker families in northern California who dreamed of creating a school for their children. In addition, hours of physical effort and a great deal of money had been spent making this dream a reality. There was no time to waste now. Once the monumental formality of purchasing the property was complete, there were endless immediate details to address: from simple tasks, like making sure the school phone number was listed in the phone directory, to more challenging problems, like repairing two bad leaks in the irrigation lines and roofing the camp facility. These tasks were precursors to the enormous project of preparing the physical site to be a boarding high-school campus within twelve months. This had to be accomplished at the same time as fundraising for the construction and the future operation of the school, and recruiting staff and students.

There were so many needs to consider. Members of the CPFEA participated in the planning decisions; however, Don Smith was at the center of most of the projects on the campus. Various companies promoted products to the school, like gymnasium or auditorium bleachers, the kinds of things that planners were not ready to think about until the basic building projects were under way. On the other hand, someone donated a new typewriter, an item that Don badly needed, as his was wearing out! And volunteers continued to show up to help in essential ways. Harold Berliner, a Nevada County lawyer, district attorney, and printer, offered free legal services to the school. CPFEA members and Don began to address future staffing needs, but more immediately, the appointment of architect Richard (Dick) Bergstrom of Berkeley was announced. Marshall had recruited him even before the land was purchased. The completed aerial survey of the property and a map showing the location of all the existing buildings, fences, roads, and large trees in the building areas was in the hands of the planners. The next step in preparation for construction was to create a shop and tool room; a group of volunteers cleared out the ranch's stock-feeding room for this purpose. At the end of October, a weekend work party arrived to help with maintenance. They cleared the haybarn of feed racks and barn paraphernalia so that it could be remodeled as a recreation hall.

To communicate with donors and to entice other Friends to become involved and contribute, the CPFEA began sending regular newsletters out to a large mailing list. Newsletter Number 1, dated August-September, 1962, announced the purchase of the land for the school and the general financial status. Finances were always at the forefront of everyone's mind. At the end of September, 1962, the John Woolman School had assets of $56,281; however, the construction project budget would take at least $40,000 of additional funding. The financial report in the fall newsletter, which was intended to drum up financial support as well as report on building progress, announced that fifteen Quaker Meetings had pledged financial backing to the school development fund, and most of that money had come in. Friends were reminded that they could contribute by donating their Blue Chip stamps (BCS). (The stamps were a promotional device used by grocery stores and pharmacies to create customer loyalty. The stores dispensed the stamps in proportion to the amount spent by a customer. Customers pasted them into booklets that could then be traded for merchandise like lawn furniture, cutlery, and kitchenware. They also could be exchanged for cash in certain circumstances, and because Woolman had religious nonprofit status, they were eligible for the BCS matching program; for every two books donated, the company would give one book, and all could be redeemed at the rate of $1.20 a book.) These small contributions could not hope to bridge the $40,000 gap, but every bit of additional support helped. Between December, 1961 and

November, 1962, financial support came from three main sources: the Quaker meetings in northern California; individuals from whom funds were solicited, mostly from mailings, but some from personal phone calls; and several very large gifts.

Many people put effort into fundraising, and those involved were keenly aware of the questions that would arise as they solicited support. One common topic was whether it was right to support a private school. Potential donors asked over and over: was a private school elitist; couldn't public education meet the needs of all children and families? In answer to these questions, Woolman supporters promoted the idea that a private, nonpublic education sector served an important role in our lives. They argued that education for service, an important concept in Friends education, is lacking in our society. They strongly emphasized that there would be scholarships and financial support for needy students so that they could be recruited from a wide variety of backgrounds. When potential donors asked questions about the value of Quaker education specifically, Howard Brinton's book *Quaker Education* was cited as a good source for articulating the ways in which it had contributed to general education in the past. Would-be contributors were reminded that Friends who were working to build the school had also worked hard for public education and been active in the parent-teacher associations where their children went to elementary school. The same Quaker families who might send their older children to Woolman were still actively involved in education in their communities.

Prospective supporters and students also needed to know the purpose of the new school and the details of the proposed educational structure and policies. Though these issues had been discussed from the beginning by the CPFEA, they were not formalized until Marshall Palley wrote an initial document, "John Woolman School Statement of Purpose and Policies—Fall 1962." It was the first comprehensive statement of the planned organization of the school, and it is reproduced here because it lay the foundation for what was to come.

"John Woolman School Statement of
Purpose and Policies—Fall 1962

John Woolman School is to be an educational community designed to help its members discover purposes that will challenge their gifts and powers. Experience through intellectual and aesthetic as well as work, social and worship relationships will be the chief agents toward these ends. To discover his bent, to challenge his potential, in furtherance of spiritually directed goals, these are what we hope for the John Woolman student. Our labor in founding this school has been undertaken with the clear knowledge that the hope of the world lies in the moving forward of such young people.

Policies

The School: John Woolman School is planned as a co-educational boarding high school with approximately 40 students in the 10th, 11th, and 12th grades growing to a projected enrollment of 120. Some qualified day students may be included. A sound college preparatory program will be offered., along with opportunity in the arts and in real work experience.

The Students: Boys and girls who are familiar with the ways of the Society of Friends will form an important element in the student body. A group of students representative of the racial, ethnic, and economic groupings in the region will be sought, including a normal range of academic abilities. The ability of the school to meet the needs of potential students, and the contribution of each student is likely to make to the school community, will be carefully weighed in considering applications.

Teachers: We seek a staff having unity of outlook with high capability in both teaching and in evoking and sustaining creative relationships. Teachers will be selected for their competence, enthusiasm, and their understanding and love for young people. The principal particularly must be strong in the experience and insights of Friends. We hope for a unity of outlook which does not exclude individual ideas and approaches.

Work Program: The students will take part in work program consisting of two main elements: 1) a modest farm operation designed to produce milk, eggs, beef and perhaps other products for the school; 2) maintenance on grounds and structures and semi-skilled work in the kitchen and office. The purpose of this work program will again be two-fold; to help keep tuition low so as to enable more families to consider John Woolman School as a real possibility, and to show the students the value and dignity of the individual to the community.

Tuition: We aim to keep tuition and board as low as equitable salaries for the teachers, wholesome diet, and reasonable outlays for equipment and supplies will allow. Requests for tuition reduction grants will be considered in proportion to need and in relation to the limited funds available.

The Association: The members of the Educational Association will appoint a principal to carry out the policies listed here and will assist him in appropriate ways. The principal will be the administrative head of the school. In consultation with the Association he will choose the teachers and staff and with them develop the educational program and the guiding framework for other activities.

The Neighborhood: The school is meant to take root in the landscape and among the people who live nearby as well as the wider community of Friends. The chances for outdoor study and recreation in the nearby Sierra will not be neglected. Visitors and friends from the nearby towns will be received warmly. Conference and camp retreat activities of the Friends community will be accommodated to the extent consistent with smooth operations of the school program.

Religion: The unprogrammed silent meeting for worship, found meaningful by young people of all faith in Friends schools and summer activities, will be a central part of the school experience. The Quaker approach of openness to truth will be impressed on students through a life which everyday expresses that spirit."

With no experience yet of building and operating a school behind it, it was an aspirational document; however, it captured the spirit of the founders as they built the school. It also set the stage for some of the challenges the school would face in the future. It was vague about the educational goals, promised generous financial support for students in need, and incorporated the work of unskilled or semiskilled labor in the maintenance of the facility. In various forms, these ideas would become future challenging issues.

By November, 1962, it was clear that "an organization with sufficient vigor, personnel, and fixed responsibility" (letter from Marshall Palley) was needed to establish consistent coordination of fundraising efforts. This meant getting enough people involved to accomplish the tasks. Don Smith planned to work closely with a person or committee, but he also had plenty of other responsibilities on his plate, so it was good that the CPFEA formed a Finance Committee focused on improving fundraising techniques. It created a packet of materials including brochures, a formal Development Plan with site photographs, the "Purpose and Policies of John Woolman School" statement, and (to help answer the concerns of the skeptics) a pamphlet entitled "Response to the Critics of John Woolman School." All this activity necessitated a lot of additional help—all of it from volunteers. Don planned the publicity campaign that included press releases and newsletters. Meg Palley and Mappie Seabury kept the mailing list of over 800 names, which grew as names were gathered at meetings held to promote the school, and were suggested by alumnae of other Quaker schools.

Friends meetings provided some support for the school. The Berkeley, Palo Alto, and San Francisco Friends meetings were the most generous; however, money also came from about a dozen other meetings that were solicited by mail, and surprisingly, a few of the contributions were from meetings in other parts of the country. More than 100 individuals made one-time or ongoing donations. The fundraising effort welcomed many forms of financial support, including outright gifts and pledges, interest-free loans, guarantees of a portion of the bank loan, advance tuition for students who wanted to attend, gifts of furniture and books or other in-kind gifts and other contributed services that the school might need, but also—and especially—help raising funds from others. In the flurry of responses to a big mailing, there were offers of assistance of various kinds from Quakers, designers, architects, teachers, and musicians. Also, at a meeting on December 17, 1962, the Berkeley Meeting decided to incorporate its giving to the CPFEA into regular budgeting for the next year; they allocated an additional contribution for 1963. The previous year, the budgeted amount had been only $200, and it was in a special fund designated for contributions. The amount for the new year included 24 pledges or contributions to the school development fund, financial support for Don Smith's job, some undesignated funds, and $900 of funding that depended on performance or other issues.

At this point. the CPFEA needed to review the Development Plan to make sure that the funds it was seeking were consistent with the ever-changing projected costs. Frustratingly, the target for the fundraising effort had to be adjusted as cost estimates fluctuated for the design, material, and construction work. The architectural plan was not finalized, and that also complicated the financial picture. In addition, the Personnel Committee was in the process of searching for a Head of School. Once that person was known, it was expected that he/she would help with the fundraising efforts. In the meantime, key committee members continued making presentations in the Quaker community, helping to keep up the momentum.

Concurrent with the fundraising push, for a few months the CPFEA Personnel Committee had been engaged in lengthy conversation with Delbert (Del) Reynolds, a candidate for the principal's job. Del had a master's degree in philosophy, and worked at the Friendsville Academy, a Quaker boarding school in Knoxville, Tennessee, where he met and married Julia White. During college, he had become interested in the Holy Land, and that led the young couple to teach at the Friends Schools in Ramallah, Jordan (now part of the occupied territories of Palestine) in 1951, but within a year, the Director of the school abruptly left, and Del found himself conscripted as Director of the Boy's School. Their first two children were born in Jerusalem. When their five-year service mission was complete, the family returned to the U.S., where Del worked as a school administrator in Illinois and the family grew to five children. His experience and qualifications, as well as his keen interest in the position, impressed the hiring committee. They recommended him to the full board, and at the January 1963 meeting the CPFEA approved hiring him as of June 15, 1963. In addition to his salary, he would receive housing, meals for his family in the school dining room, and gas for his car from the school pump, all provided by the Association. Moving expenses for the Reynolds family from Illinois to Grass Valley would also be paid by the association, and he would have an annual vacation of two months beginning in the summer of 1964. After that decision, the CPFEA also "minuted"—that is, in the tradition of Quaker meeting, formally recorded —the following:

> "It is the policy of this association to help to meet the health cultural and educational needs of John Woolman School staff members and their families. With particular reference to high school and college age members of staff families, the following policy will be followed: Children of a full-time staff member resident staff members may attend John Woolman school, free of tuition. They will be given preference in summer work opportunities on the school property. The Association recognizes an obligation to share in the college expenses of faculty children."

At the beginning of 1963, yet another big fundraising appeal mailing was about to go out. Bob Beloof, who was on the committee, and Don Smith traveled to Southern California to meet with a group of potential donors, taking with them the "Statement of Purpose and Policies." In this round of fundraising efforts, they emphasized that this project was actually happening with concrete plans—land and funds for a real school that would be important to young people, the state, the world, and the future of the Society of Friends on the West Coast.

When he wasn't out fundraising, Don was busy on the property. The weather was very cold, and the road needed repairs, though it remained passable for the various visitors who showed up daily. To facilitate their arrival, signs were made and placed at the important intersections between town and the school, including atop the mailbox at the beginning of Woolman Lane. And then, around the middle of January, a spate of mild and clear weather allowed a big push to complete some important outdoor projects. These included fencing off the upper corner of the pasture in preparation for building the stock barn. Mel Hedrick was supposed to help level the site with his bulldozer, but the bulldozer got stuck in the creek, and the crew spent half a day trying to liberate it in vain. Finally, with the help of Mel's backhoe, they prepared the site and set the building corners and bench boards, and began digging the footings. Fortunately, the building didn't require a permit, and Don found a way to save several hundred dollars by repurposing some corrugated iron roofing. They had already purchased the cedar and white fir for the framing and siding of the stock barn, and soon the foundation was poured. The barn construction was well under way and Don arranged for an engineer from Pacific Gas and Electric to plan an electrical supply to the property.

As work progressed on the physical plant, there was also much to do to determine the actual curriculum for the school. Don met with the California Superintendent of Schools and learned that there was no curriculum guide for California high schools, giving each school autonomy in setting its curriculum. But the Superintendent's office loaned Don a copy of a high school curriculum that they could review for ideas. A month later, as work was moving forward on designing the academic structure of the school, Don received a large volume of additional materials from the Nevada County curriculum coordinator concerning high-school programs in California. At the same time, Don was fielding inquiries from teacher candidates, many of whom visited the school. Most of the candidates had families, including young children. Some were located in California, but there were also inquiries from other parts of the U.S., including a smattering of Friends who expressed in an interest in being of service in the opening of a new Quaker school. On the other hand, locally there was evidence of attitudes less consistent with Quaker values. Don had made arrangements to host a group coming from the Bay Area for a weekend work party in the basement of a neighbor's house. The following day, a teacher from the Berkeley Meeting called saying that he would like to bring his teenage class for the upcoming work party. Bob Beloof wrote that "as the [teacher is] Negro, we checked with Mrs. D_____. After a few hours consideration she said no, and we have made other arrangements for the mixed group. She expects us to have [only] all white groups in her basement while the weather is cold. I hope the D_____s will become better acquainted with Friends and their point of view."

When the CPFEA sent news releases to announce the new school, the local *Grass Valley Union* newspaper and the *Nevada City Nugget* printed the news release in full. The newspaper publicity worked to a degree. In the weeks just after publication, inquiries about enrollment began to trickle into the school. Don and Harriette created additional promotional leaflets. Because printing was expensive, they used a mimeograph machine that had been donated to the school, and Don observed that they could also use it for other kinds of communications like staff rosters as well as additional promotional materials and materials for fundraising and student recruitment. This low-cost method could be a stopgap until the program was well enough established to justify professional printing costs. Such economies were usual as they tried to accomplish the most they could with limited resources.

February began with unusually warm weather, so work was able to proceed fulltime, including planting two dozen boysenberry plants. However, soon after, winter came back in full force, and the work camp in mid-March endured an all-day snowstorm. The snow held up the planned roadwork, ditch cleaning, and painting tasks. Despite that, the work group almost completed the barn; only the doors remained to be hung, and another coat of penetrating oil needed to be applied to the siding. The recreation hall plans were completed and needed to be approved by the building inspector, and the residence hall design was completed. The original intention was to have two residence halls, but working drawings to be used for construction of the second dwelling were expected to take about another three weeks before they would be completed.

At this point, the CPFEA made a significant decision: because the fund drive was going too slowly and the overall schedule of building was behind schedule, it decided to suspend drawings for and building of the second residence hall, the south house, beyond the construction of footings. Without the second residence hall, it reasoned, it would be possible to enroll 29 students for the first year by putting one extra student in each room of the dormitory. The committee considered other alternatives, but this seemed like the best solution to the funding problem. In addition, lack of the second dormitory building would be a good motivation to potential donors to make additional gifts to the school. At that point, no work had been done on the building.

When the Pacific Yearly Meeting Education Committee met that winter, it received an extensive report of all the progress that had been made on the campus, much aided by the four volunteer work camps that had already taken place. But Don also emphasized that many more work camps would be needed, and most importantly, to be ready to open in September, much more support would be needed from the Meetings. He described the status of progress and delays, noting that the delay in the preparation of working drawings for the buildings was further hampering progress. Building delays are an old story, and adjusting to them was necessary. However, given that the drawings were not completed, and the foundations hadn't been poured yet at the end of March, the residence hall (which also included the Principal's apartment) wouldn't be in livable condition by the summer, when Del was expected to arrive, and therefore he and his family would need to be housed somewhere else temporarily. Don also explained that he was working on developing the water system, calculating the expected needs and determining the requirements for water and sewage disposal. A Friend in Pasadena who was an expert on such systems was helping design a plan.

The constant anxiety about fundraising continued to hover in the background. One concern was that the absolute numbers of donors was fewer than the committee had hoped for. Don thought that it would have been good to have had four times the number of donors making small contributions but showing support. By March, only 80 families had contributed. The good news was that the number of people working on fundraising had increased since the beginning of the year, and it was hoped that they would be more effective going forward. These concerns fueled the discussions of cutting back on the planned construction. The decision to build only one residence hall to begin with meant putting 30 students in a space designed for housing 20, and having one staff family live off campus. Another suggestion under consideration was to omit the kitchen-dining hall and instead use the staff apartment kitchen and social halls for dining. Neither arrangement was ideal. It seemed that if the group didn't go ahead with the kitchen-dining facility, it might never be built, that they might always have to just make do with what they had. Some decision would have to be made soon about the building plans.

Volunteers were essential to the process of developing the campus; using volunteers meant saving money in comparison to hiring workers. But the situation really wasn't so straightforward. In a letter to the committee in late February, Don noted that accident insurance to cover volunteer workers was extremely expensive. He said, "This seems absolutely impossible; we can hardly afford volunteers at this rate. The premium would pay the wages of a worker for over 20 weeks of employment.... I think we and the volunteers will have to take their chances. Certainly that is what we must do this weekend when 30 people are expected. We shall be strict in allowing only certain authorized persons to use power tools and try to exercise other reasonable cautions. I shall bring this matter before the association on March 2." Fortunately, they made it through the weekend with a great deal accomplished and no one injured.

In early March, they were about two weeks behind schedule building the new barn. Dick Bergstrom, the architect, came to the campus to consult on the recreation/assembly hall plans, which were going to be delivered to the county building department. He was still working on the plans for the residence hall, expecting to be done at the end of March. Don expressed his concern about completing the residence halls in time for school to open. Before they could even begin to pour the foundations, they needed to install a culvert to complete the road access to the building site. At the beginning of April, the weather was cold and wet, and there was even a little snow, but the work proceeded despite the weather. Don reported that Dick Pomeroy would arrive on April 6, 1963, to engineer the sewage disposal system before the arrival of volunteer work parties on April 7. The volunteer group included teenagers from Sacramento, families with children, and another party of 10 children and 10 adults. Before the work crew arrived, the sheep had been moved into their new barn, two carpenters were working on the Recreation Hall (where they were running a 220-volt electrical current), and partitions had been removed from the old stock barn so that the work party could bunk there for the week. Don was also in the process of lining up workers for the summer, some paid and some volunteer, in exchange for a place to live. Five weekend work camps took place in the spring, including the Easter vacation camp that included over forty young Friends and twenty adults. They accomplished a great deal despite the less than hospitable weather. In addition to the building work, campers planted and shaded a thousand Douglas fir trees on the property, planted hundreds of fruit trees and grapes donated by the Burchell Nursery of Modesto, CA, put deer fencing around the fruit trees, removed hundreds of feet of old ranch fencing, cleared areas for building, and cleaned a half mile of irrigation ditch grass and mud. The value of this volunteer effort was incalculable.

While work on the buildings continued, Don was also spending time looking for teachers and other personnel for September. He reported regularly to the committee about the people he had spoken to, including a teacher in training from Antioch College. Having a college-age teacher in training would be a financial advantage and would ensure that there was at least one young staff member. In April, 1963, Bob Crichton was hired to teach math and science at Woolman as well as to be on the admissions committee for the school. His Quaker background was strong, including study at Pendle Hill, teaching at the Ramallah Friends School with Del and Julia Reynolds, and working with the American Friends Service Committee in Mexico. Don was still having difficulty finding a Spanish teacher, however.

Support continued from a variety of sources. Berkeley Quakers held another fundraising event on May 4, 1963, sponsored by Berkeley Friends

Meeting. A work party from Berkeley came to campus for a weekend in mid May. They pruned trees in the orchard and finished oiling the exterior of the barn. They also installed windows in the assembly hall, started siding the building, and cleaned up around the dormitory building site. That same weekend, a member of Berkeley Friends (Fred Elkington) donated a trailer large enough to house a whole family. Another trailer was also being set up for a single staff member, though both needed sewer hookups to be ready for occupancy. There were other gifts that, along with various purchases, helped prepare the campus for future occupancy. A water fountain, a small printing press, and a hog feeder were donated. Don bought 100 pullets to provide the school with eggs and (later) chickens for dinner. It turned out to be more chicken dinners than expected, due to a high proportion of roosters in the mix! All these miscellaneous donations and purchases were important to the preparations for the fall.

The dorm foundations and the plumbing system were finally in place at the end of May. The builders started on the floor joists. With the official decision to wait on building the second dorm, the tentative plan was to house three students to a room. It was also becoming apparent that decisions would need to be made about postponing completion of unessential features of as many buildings as possible to spread the available funds around. With limited financial resources, the finance committee recognized that they shouldn't borrow more than they could reasonably expect to repay.

By the beginning of June, 1963, plans were being made to accommodate the incoming faculty. The campus wasn't ready: the sewer system hadn't even been installed. Gifts of used furniture and supplies were expected to help outfit the various living quarters, though Don noted that they still needed quite a few things, including window coverings. The donated trailer with an outhouse nearby would house one faculty member. Another would board with Don and Harriette in exchange for helping Harriette with cooking and laundry for two other summer workers. Because their apartment on campus was not ready, Del, the new principal, his wife Julia, and their five children moved into a house in downtown Nevada City when they arrived. Barbara Shade, the English teacher, and Harue Kanemitsu lived in an adjacent apartment. Frequently, spontaneous staff meetings happened in one of their living rooms. Once the dormitory building was completed in September, they would all move into the staff apartments there.

In mid-July, 1963, the CPFEA formalized its ongoing relationship with Don Smith, whose official job had been to manage all the facets of developing the school. They invited him to become a member of the school staff teaching social studies, supervising the student work program of the school, and supervising construction and maintenance of the buildings. Harriette assisted with secretarial work in the school office. The contract stipulated that the school provided housing and meals in the dining hall in addition to a salary. Soon the rest of the staff of nine was in place, including Don and Harriette Smith, Del and Julia Reynolds, Bob Crichton, Jim and Sally Ceteras, Barbara Shade, and Harue Kanemitsu. Marjorie Wells, an RN and a Quaker who had recently moved to Grass Valley, was enlisted as a health advisor to make regular visits to the campus during the coming school year. About the same time, the Newsletter announced that twelve students had already been accepted for admission, with additional applications pending.

When the staff was in place, and as the work frantically proceeded to make the campus ready for students, the CPFEA published a substantial 24-page brochure to use as a recruitment tool, both for students and for fundraising. The cover showed a photograph of the framed and roofed but as yet unfinished residence hall and advertised "The New West Coast Friends Boarding School for Grades 10,11,12 — Sponsored by the College Park Friends Educational Association, Inc. 1963-1964." The brochure, professionally printed, was very impressive and aspirational; it outlined the purpose, the plan for the school's programming, the staff (including profiles of everyone), academic and extra-curricular opportunities, the work program, fees and expenses, and the school calendar for the first year. On the back was a small map of the campus (see map at the end of this chapter).

As the opening of school drew near, the tempo of work increased.

Every weekend, work parties brought energy and enthusiasm to augment the work of the professional builders. Five tons of hay were stored in the new barn for winter use for the animals. Windows were installed in the new classroom building, and summer school students worked on the exterior of the recreation hall.

Once again, summer school work camp took place, with Harold Blickenstaff as the Director. The monthlong camp was scheduled for July 14 to August 10, 1962. And as this work continued, the CPFEA continued to reach out energetically in the Quaker community for support. At the Pacific Yearly Meeting in McMinnville, Oregon, in August, a slide/tape history presentation was given by Bob Beloof about Woolman, and a dramatic skit was performed by faculty members and students to demonstrate the school's philosophy and academic outlook. Del Reynolds represented Woolman on a panel of representatives from six Friends educational programs.

Students had been accepted, tuition money had been collected, faculty hired, and most of the construction was at a point where it was reasonable to start school—though there is a quote attributed to Mary Jorgensen, who continued as a staunch supporter, raising funds and running programs at Woolman for the rest of her life. She is reputed to have said, "We couldn't afford to open the school, and we couldn't afford not to." There were some big challenges to come because of the pressure to open for business in September 1963.

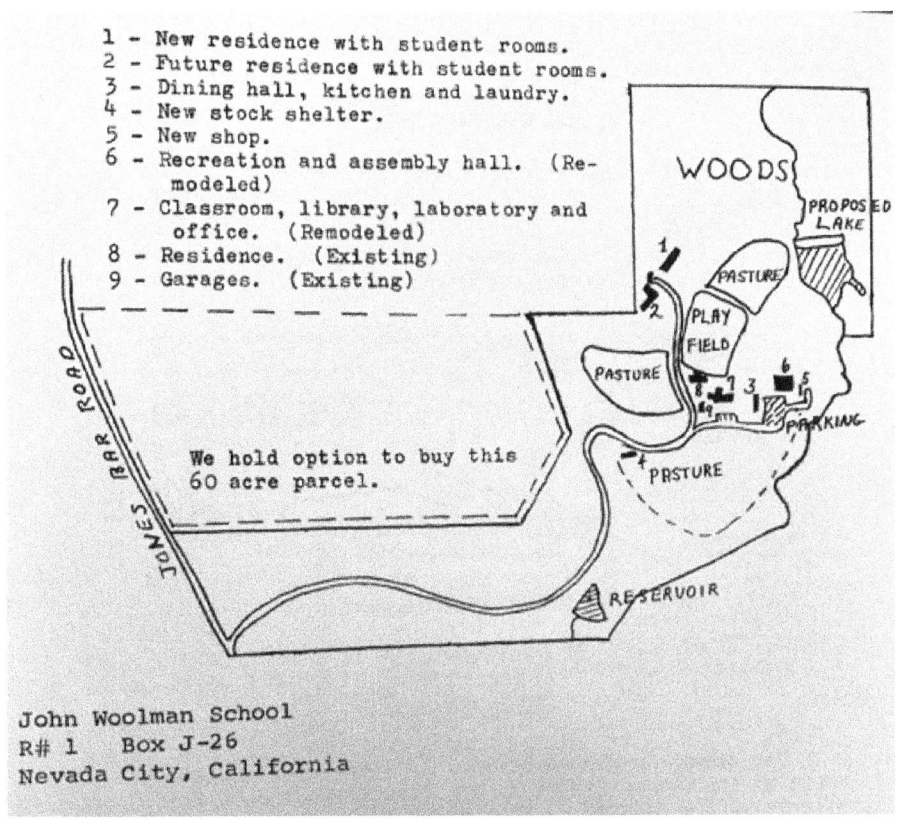

1 - New residence with student rooms.
2 - Future residence with student rooms.
3 - Dining hall, kitchen and laundry.
4 - New stock shelter.
5 - New shop.
6 - Recreation and assembly hall. (Re-
     modeled)
7 - Classroom, library, laboratory and
     office. (Remodeled)
8 - Residence. (Existing)
9 - Garages. (Existing)

We hold option to buy this
60 acre parcel.

John Woolman School
R# 1   Box J-26
Nevada City, California

Map of John Woolman School campus, Nevada City, California

| TEACHING |

4

TEACHERS BUT NO TOILETS

Open they did. The first class of John Woolman School students arrived on September 15, 1963. There was just one slight glitch when school started... Work on the dormitory building had been intense and exhausting during the spring and summer, yet it wasn't ready for occupancy. When the students arrived, their camping gear was stashed in the vacant library room, other belongings were taken to their dormitory rooms, and then they were bused to Camp Augusta, a rustic summer camp facility about ten miles away on Lake Vera near Nevada City. There they began to get to know each other. Work parties went to campus helping to put finishing touches on the living and working spaces, to prepare meals, and to sort out their schedules for academics and work. As the staff assessed the students' academic abilities, they realized the broad range of individual needs and as a result regrouped and re-scheduled many of the classes. Two weeks later, students were finally able to move to Woolman and settle into the first year of school.

Choosing the starting roster of 34 students had taken hours and hours of meetings, interviews, and correspondence with prospective scholars. Eighteen tenth-graders (eight boys and ten girls) and sixteen eleventh-graders (nine boys and seven girls) arrived to take their place in what the school brochure described as "a uniquely promising physical and intellectual environment." (Twelfth grade would be added in the fall of 1964.) The quiet rural surroundings were without the typical distractions of an urban school. The academic program offered team teaching, giving students the opportunity to "rub minds with two or three teachers in

each curriculum area allowing the student to take ideas as far as they can go." It was easy to have versatile and creative spaces for classes in such an intimate academic environment. The plan for which classes to offer was also somewhat flexible, with initial offerings designed to satisfy college entrance requirements of English, Spanish, mathematics, science (including a lab class), and social studies (including U.S. and world history), plus a wide range of electives such as music, art, and craft classes. The classes were what you would expect at a high school aiming for high academic involvement and achievement. The campus had plenty of space, including a cow pasture for recreational activities like soccer, baseball, football, and volleyball. Hiking, biking, and swimming opportunities abounded close to the school grounds, including easy access to the beautiful South Fork of the Yuba River.

One of the most unusual features of being a student at Woolman was participation in the Work Program. It was initially led by Don Smith and described by him in the school brochure for the inaugural 1963-64 school year:

> "Every student at John Woolman School participates in the work of the school community: providing some of our food by tilling the soil and tending the stock; preparing our meals and washing our clothing; caring for and maintaining our buildings. One result of such a program is a lower tuition rate than otherwise would be possible, but the chief value lies in the opportunity to take hold of a few of the basic elements of life at a time when an adolescent feels strongly the need to orient himself; the opportunity to learn to appreciate manual labor and the people who do it, whether or not the student will himself earn his livelihood that way; and finally, the opportunity to learn to plan and work together with others of varying backgrounds for a common and tangible goal."

This philosophy was deeply rooted in Quaker values, which included resourcefulness, minimizing the separation of humans from the natural world, creating community while gathering in service to each other and the land, and living sustainably. In the 1960s, when Woolman opened, there was also a strong "back to the land" movement that transcended the Quaker ideas about community. It was a strong countercultural movement with the underlying intention of living a more sustainable lifestyle, an idea consistent with the values of Woolman's founders, though the inspiration might have been different. The movement began to fade from attention in the late 1970s, a trend that began to influence Woolman's programming, ultimately reducing the size of the farm program in later decades. It was just one of many programmatic adjustments that Woolman made over the years in response to changes in society. In the meantime, the Work Program was integral to the school.

Once everyone got established on campus, it turned out that the new dormitory building was overcrowded and extremely noisy. Activities other than sleeping and studying were soon steered out of the dorm and into the recreation building. There were plenty of quiet places to go on the spacious campus to escape the hubbub, especially in the fall when the days were warm and sunny. Every morning, Harriette and Don Smith opened their living room at 8 am for a bit of quiet contemplation or Quaker meditation and, as the mornings got cooler, a cozy and inviting fire greeted the students and staff.

Throughout the fall, everyone settled in, students and staff getting to know each other, the curriculum, the buildings, and surrounding grounds. It was all new to everyone. Don Smith trained and supervised the student work crews who were responsible for much of the day-to-day cleaning. He, with the help of student labor, was also responsible for the irrigation of the pastures and care of the animals, and the completion of painting and decorating tasks. Though the dorm structure was built, there was still much to be acquired and completed. A wish list of needs went out via the newsletter seeking, among other things, three vacuum cleaners, hand tools, a heavy-duty grinder, looms, a warping stand, ceramics tools, theater lights (including spots, floods, and dimmers), a school bus, and—last but not least—pledges to help finance the kitchen, the dining room, and a second dormitory.

The wish list indicated something of the practical progress of this big experiment. It was also a social experiment. Especially during the beginning months that first fall, it was a place of rugged, independent living. Fortunately, many of the students had previously participated in weekend work camps on campus, so the environment was not unfamiliar to them. However, from a social perspective, the lack of an existing tradition to fall back on magnified the bumps in the road. Everyone was making it up as they went along. The school emphasized personal responsibility, rather than imposed discipline, and students were expected to learn responsibility by assuming it. They participated in the establishment of standards of conduct and governed themselves in most aspects of the school life, with adult guidance. The school brochure listed only a few rules and regulations that students needed to know and follow:

1. No cars allowed (though a Driver's Ed course would be offered); however, in some cases students could drive farm vehicles on the campus.
2. The school must know where each student was at all times. Signing out and reporting in was required when leaving campus.
3. No smoking allowed.
4. To leave for the weekend, academic work must be satisfactorily complete, and parents must give written permission.
5. The school had the right to ask a student to leave in certain circumstances, for instance, if they had harmed others, or were unable to adjust adequately to life at school.

Otherwise, there was no student handbook, and it turned out that even these few rules above were never communicated very emphatically to the students.

At the end of the first semester, the administration dealt with some staff and schedule changes. The American history teacher resigned, and Don was invited to take over her teaching responsibilities. Harriette Smith assumed the duties of developing and managing the library. In January, most classes were changed to the morning, leaving the afternoons for work crews, sports, meetings, and room cleanup. Regular Saturday classes began, but every third weekend was a four-day weekend (Friday through Monday) for field trips and visits home. And Wednesday and Saturday nights were free for plays, movies, singing, dancing, and other social activities.

During this first year, field trips became an important part of the annual schedule. Typical local expeditions included trips to Yosemite for a literature seminar, the San Francisco Bay Area for dramatics, Tulare County for social studies, the California State Indian Museum in Sacramento for cultural anthropology, and desert country for camping and fun. A group of five students and two faculty, Harue Kanemitsu and Bill Copperthwaite, took a long, ambitious field trip to Mexico—25 days in a Dodge pickup truck with a canvas covering over the back. They entered Mexico at Mexicali, traveled to Guadalajara, Toluca, and Mexico City, stayed with two Mexican families, and saw many other sites as they circled around through El Paso, Texas, on the way home to school on March 9, 1964. The Mexico trip inspired future spring Special Projects trips for many years to come, but it was not without some complications. It was an unorthodox arrangement and had less administrative oversight than anyone would expect today. To some extent, it could be seen as a marker of permissiveness that reflected a trend in the culture at large, and certainly permeated the Woolman school right from the start.

The first year ended without a graduation ceremony because the oldest students had just finished eleventh grade. It was good news that by June 8, 1964, there were only a few places left for boys in the class starting in the fall of 1964. The places for girls were all filled. When the first school year came to its end, the administration and staff looked back on the journey. Del felt that the year had been organized (or suffered from a lack of organization) in a way that widened the gap of understanding between the generations. He expressed his concern that because a large group of people (the majority in their teens and with unknown qualities and capacities) were asked to deal with many complex problems and situations, working out the structure of daily living consumed too much time and energy. He felt that it had been unfair to both generations.

He decided that for the coming year, the organization of daily life, as well as the academic schedule, should be set in advance by the faculty. The students would not be without voice or power to effect change, but the faculty should begin by setting expectations and rules. Some of the baseline ideas he offered were to have students participate in two of four fine arts offerings, to be sure that they were in their dorms by 10 o'clock and in their rooms by 10:30 every evening before class days, and to assign them to periods of supervised work in the library if they had low academic performance. When the staff reviewed the year, they offered another set of critiques. They said that in the first months of the school year, too great an effort was made to meet individual student academic needs, for example through special programs for certain individuals. Consequently, staff energy and time were sometimes spread too thin. The existence of major differences in educational philosophy among the staff during the year was mentioned by Del and the staff, though over time those lessened.

The incomplete campus infrastructure certainly had complicated life during the first school year, so it was good news when, in late March, the CPFEA announced the status of the building plans for the much-needed kitchen/dining room/laundry building. Dirk Neyhart negotiated with the unions representing the plumbers, bricklayers, electricians, and tile-setters, and these donated about a third of the cost of labor, bringing the total down from an estimated $68,000 to a hoped-for $45,000. Also, although they originally planned to build a second dormitory building, financial constraints resulted in the CPFEA deciding to build A-frame cedar log cabins at the cost of approximately $40,000 (instead of the dorm, at an estimated $70,000). The cabins would be heated by wood-burning stoves, with the boys cutting their own wood. A three-bedroom prefab faculty house made of the same materials was to be built in the cabin area.

Work on the buildings and grounds was going on all the time, and spring work camps were scheduled on a long weekend in April to construct a Quonset hut for storage. The place was humming with the sounds of hammers, saws, and drills. In early May, work began on the twelve

A-frame cabins, which were described as being assembled somewhat like Lincoln logs. The construction required many hands. The summer was an important time on campus to complete projects and start new ones. In addition to completing the A-frames and the house, summer construction plans included building a prefab toilet-shower building, installing a new sewer system for the new buildings, constructing a road, bringing water and electrical connectivity to the cabin complex, connecting the Ranch House and the Infirmary to the sewer system built the previous summer, and completing the work on the second dorm. Sal Solinas, an active member of the AFSC, a professional plumber, and currently a teacher, provided technical direction for the building program, and again, Mary Jorgensen was the summer work camp director. Norm Cotton, Jim Suddereth, and Thom Heck were crew leaders under Sol's direction, and Reg Paget was responsible for overall coordination and liaison with the Lamon Construction Co., builders of the new dining room and kitchen.

For those employed or volunteering for the summer work camps, the morning cry was "wake up, sleepyheads!" They rolled out of their sleeping bags, dashed cold water on their faces, and crossed the new-mown meadow on their way to breakfast. Up to 25 people per week participated in seven weeklong summer work camps. For anyone with enough energy left after a day of labor, there were evening discussions a couple nights a week, folk dancing, a family sharing night, swimming, and trips to local areas of interest. The cost was $5 per family per week for leadership, $.50 per meal ($.35 for children under 12). Mary Jorgensen coordinated the camp registrations from Berkeley, and ten different families and at least fifty different teenagers worked like mad all summer. With professional but volunteer help from the plumbers' and bricklayers' unions, the dining room/kitchen/ laundry building took shape. It also became clear in the summer of 1964 that the for the next few years, the number of students that could be accepted would be limited by the housing capacity—42 students, plus a few additional day students, could be accepted.

Though there were still unfinished projects, the opening day for the second year was in marked contrast to the beginning of school the first year.

5

······················

BUILDING COMMUNITY

As it turned out, school opened in September 1964 with 45 boarding students and five day students. They got off to a much smoother start than students in the previous year. The 1964 school year began with more comfortable living, working, and playing spaces, and a number of students and staff who knew each other and the campus. Twenty-three girls moved into comfortable dormitory rooms, and 22 boys into A-frames scattered across the campus, complete with woodstoves. The library boasted more than 2,800 carefully chosen volumes, equipment was in place, and everything was nicely spruced up thanks to much volunteer help. Improvements also included the new water filtration and distribution system. The new dining room/kitchen/laundry building was still unfinished, but it was anticipated that it would be ready by Thanksgiving. After some staff changes and additions, a full-strength faculty was ready to lead the planned curriculum.

In the late fall, the new dining hall was completed, and it became the center of community life at school. With its high, wood-beamed ceiling and airy expanse of glass walls, it was an open and inviting space not only for meals, but also for the weekly General Meeting, student-staff meetings, and some student gatherings. From the dining hall windows, one could look across the grass and see the line of A-frame cabins lined up with the pines in the background. At the other end of the building, a shining new kitchen provided a spacious and convenient workspace for preparing meals for 60 people. Art students used the north end of the space as a painting studio under the tutelage of a new art teacher.

Soon after school began, however, Del Reynolds submitted his resignation, effective at the end of the school year, or earlier, if a successor could be found. The Association recognized formally that Del's position was very challenging. He had taken on a very demanding job, from "dealing with unclarified areas in the structure of his work" to the burdensome workload caused when "the school opened before the physical plant was ready." The CPFEA composed a letter announcing the news of his resignation to the students, staff, parents, and friends of the school. The letter also stressed the Association's staunch support for Del and his leadership for the remainder of his time at the school, and the acknowledgment that they were sensitive to his wish to leave sooner rather than later. In the winter of 1965, the CPFEA announced the appointment of Harold Blickenstaff, current chair of the CPFEA, as Principal Elect to succeed Del. Harold was a Quaker and had much American Friends Service Committee experience working with the young people in Europe and in the United States. In addition to all his other involvement with the establishment of the Woolman school, he had been the Summer School director in 1962 when it was held at "the Hedrick's ranch" before the CPFEA purchased the property later that summer.

At Del's request, Harold took over a couple of months before the term ended. During Del's tenure, some tensions occurred around his approach to discipline. Some students resisted his responses to the current rebellious attitudes of teenagers including dress code and hair length, and the casual stance on the rural campus to nudity and personal displays of affection among the students. The CPFEA supported and strongly appreciated all that Del had done as principal for almost two years, but Don Smith noted that shortly after Del left and Harold took over, the atmosphere on campus seemed happier; there was more cooperation, communication, and academic application, as well as "good fun." School activities continued under the new administration, and soon the spring Special Projects period approached. From March 2 to 21, 1965, the students once again left their regular routine. A group planned to go to Mexico again, this time in "Big Bertha," a large and comfortable bus rented from Mr. Andre Hopson of Atherton. Max Parker, an old friend of the school, would be the driver for the entire trip. The plan was to cross the Mexican border at Nogales or Mexicali on March 3 and follow Mexican Highway 15 along the West coast. Those not going on the trip to Mexico were planning individually tutored projects. With modifications in length and destinations, Special Projects time, a change in the usual routine, would become a cherished period of the school year. Some of the students who didn't go on the Mexico trip began a local service project lead by staff members Harriette Smith and Winifred Wright, working with patients at DeWitt State Hospital in nearby Auburn, CA.

After the break for Spring Projects, the students who were planning to move on to college in the fall began eagerly awaiting the arrival of the mail. By the beginning of May, it was confirmed that students had accepted spots at the University of California, Berkeley; San Francisco State University; University of California, Santa Cruz; the Merchant Marine Academy in Vallejo; and Manchester College in Indiana. More college acceptance letters were expected.

Once the school year ended, the campus became a different kind of hive of activity, with an American Friends Service Committee Family Camp in residence for a week in July 1965, and two weeks of High School Work Camp. Only 25 students could come to the two-week-long session, which was very popular. Those who secured a spot worked hard. The summer work plan included grading, landscaping, construction of graveled walks, installing outdoor lighting, cleaning the irrigations ditches, and more. The plan for fun, if you had enough energy left at the end of the day, was swimming at the river, square dancing, evening sings, and discussion groups.

Now, with two years of operation complete, the CPFEA expressed concern about the lack of structure at Woolman. They wanted to move toward more specific codification of the expectations demanded of the students and the duties required of the staff. They did not necessarily want the students to be involved directly in establishing these guidelines. They were concerned enough about this issue to engage a paid consultant to work with Harold to move in the direction they had in mind. This began a delicate balancing act between different philosophies of guidance for the students and staff. The main options were Quaker process (which relied on discussion and an attempt to reach consensus), a Summerhill type approach (which trusted that young people will find a right or good way through eventually on their own), or having the adults make some of the decisions, and these alternatives became part of the internal conflict. As they were deliberating about these issues, Harold reported at the January 1966 CPFEA board meeting that since the beginning of the third year of school in the fall of 1965, there was more emphasis on academic achievement and less student participation in policymaking. At least partly, this was because some of the decision-making had been taken out of their hands.

When the CPFEA held its regular meeting in March 1966, they discussed another big topic, plans for the immediate and long-term expansion of the school. The committee was making plans to accommodate 58 students in the fall of 1968, with hopes of building a second girl's dormitory and expanding the student body to 80 by 1969. The primary motivation for the expansion was financial. Enlarging the student body meant bringing in more tuition each year, but without the need for a proportional increase in staff, due to the economies of scale. The students were aware of the situation and sent delegates to the CPFEA meeting expressing concern about the proposed expansion. They worried about the effects of a larger student body on the educational programs and on school spirit. They were so concerned that they formed a fund-raising committee that met with the CPFEA, who agreed to postpone increasing enrollment next year if the students could raise $10,000-$15,000 by July 1. The students noted that the delay of the expansion, if they could manage to put it off, would also give the school more time to plan for it more carefully. Though the student committee didn't meet its fundraising goal in spite of a valiant attempt, it succeeded in making its point to the CPFEA.

During this same period, the CPFEA did some promotional work of its own. A committee from the Quarter was appointed at the March 12, 1966 meeting of the College Park Quarterly Meeting to visit all the meetings in the Quarter and discuss different educational policies and philosophies.

There had been disagreement in the Quaker community right from the early planning days about the wisdom of putting energy, time, and money into establishing a Quaker boarding school. But there was enough critical mass to get the project going, and it had certainly gained a momentum of its own and a significant following of supporters— including, by 1966, students, alumni, and their families. In addition, there were tireless volunteers who had put in tremendous amounts of work to create the school, reaping the joy of working in community, often with fellow Quakers and their families. Many people had been on the school grounds sleeping under the stars in the summer, singing, dancing, dining together, and working hard to make the school real, with new building and plantings, and dreams for the future.

Counterbalancing these things were concerns of Quarter members, some of whom were solid supporters, some not, and yet they, like everyone, were asked for financial support over and over. Some of them might never have been to Woolman, but certainly some must have been caught up in the wildly changing mores of the late 1960s. There was much rebellion afoot, especially among high school and college students, and awareness of it was inescapable. Changes in the standards for the length of hair and hems, the style of pants, the attitudes toward grooming, the acceptance of smoking tobacco and marijuana, and the attitudes toward harder drugs were very apparent. Dealing with teenagers was never easy and had gotten more fraught during this period. Even civil disobedience, long entrenched in Quaker beliefs and actions, felt menacing to some. For one faction of Quakers, their experience of the Woolman school was primarily through reports to their Meetings and requests for money. It was this group that added weight to the scales when a need for more conservative action was pressed for, and its important voice in the direction of the Quarter had the potential to influence support for the school.

At every CPFEA meeting, updates on the school included mentions of (usually routine) student behavior problems, requests for additional funding for unexpected expenses, changes in personnel, and other issues that could be interpreted either as problems or as the normal challenges of running a school. The CPFEA decided to do some fact-finding to assess the Quaker community's concerns. Members were interested in listening to and gathering ideas for changes to any Quaker educational program, but particularly at the Woolman school. They visited all the meetings in the Quarter asking questions provided by the committee and produced a report at the July 1966 Quarterly Meeting. The summary did not reflect unanimity among Friends, because often there was no unanimity within Meetings; however, the Committee felt that it was a good indication of what the Quarter was prepared to accept and support. From this input, in the fall of 1966, the College Park Quarterly Meeting adopted a set of guiding principles governing the care of John Woolman School. These included a request for more structured and regular communications with regular reports to the Quarter, specifying academic excellence as a primary goal for the school, and establishing a goal of hiring teachers with high personal and academic qualifications. They stressed the necessity of having a director who would exert strong leadership with vision, integrity, and competence. They wanted guidelines for selecting students with good academic potential, emotional and social stability, and variety in cultural and economic backgrounds, and gave preference to students who were close to Quakerism. The Meeting endorsed the exposure of students to Friends' principles for worship, belief, and action, and the cultivation of Quaker character, as regular policies. They also addressed the issue of student behavior. They wanted the school to set and communicate suitable standards of behavior to the students and enforce them. They were willing to allow students participation in decision-making as long as it stayed within the framework of the established rules. They united in urging the continuation and development of the sense of loving community among the students and staff at the school. The Quarterly Meeting intended to help support these guiding principles by initiating joint oversight with the CPFEA. Before the report had been issued, or any practical ideas for implementing them were decided on, the school year came to a close. With all the best intentions, nothing was resolved yet.

Wrapping up the school year, Woolman sent out invitations for Hey-Day, the spring "open house" event on Saturday, May 29, 1966, at which there would be tours of the campus, science and art projects on display, musical and dramatic performances, games, a barbecue, and a campfire; everyone was welcome to camp overnight for the event. Meanwhile, summer plans for 1966 included AFSC family camp, a two-week session of high-school and family work camp to do projects on campus, and a summer music retreat. The projects for the coming summer included building an oxidizing basin, remodeling the staff quarters in the girls' dormitory, construction of an art building, remodeling of the Quonset hut, and work on the road—all ambitious undertakings. During the summer, one group finished damming a creek on the property to create a swimming hole. Another crew painted both exterior and interior areas of buildings, laid cement sidewalks and gravel paths, and still had time for typical summer fun, and evenings with music and dancing. The summer programs provided free labor for projects as well as opportunities for educational challenges, but also brought new people to the campus at the time of year when it was lovely to be there and fun. They proved to be a great recruitment tool.

The 1966 school year started with a slew of enthusiastic new students and a proportionately high percentage of new faculty. New classes were offered, including weaving, guitar, music theory, and drama, and as well as a journalism class that took over production of the *Outsider's Insider* newsletter. Students appreciated the expanded arts programming and even complained that there were more courses that they wanted to take than they had time for. One of the idiosyncrasies of Woolman that continued into the future was that with new staff came new classes. Instead of a fixed curriculum, class offerings were often at the whim of faculty interests and skills.

That fall, the newsletter reported some of the quirky and entertaining stories of the way of life at Woolman. Soon after school started, the whole school traveled to Yosemite National Park for a long weekend. The trip became an especially memorable one when a student was clawed by a bear during the night. The bear was euthanized by park personnel the next day! Also around that time, the wombat was adopted as the Woolman mascot. Tongue-in-cheek speculators remarked that it might have been chosen because it is a nocturnal burrowing animal who was perceived by some to be gentle, lazy, and spending most of its waking hours eating. It proved to be a beloved mascot despite having no actual connection with Woolman. The students were not actually lazy or without convictions, however. In later years, Don Smith recalled (in an alumni newsletter celebrating the legacy of peace activism at Woolman) that in 1966, a group of students with arguably strong convictions drafted a letter on school letterhead opposing Veteran's Day, using words like "killers" and "murderers." Copies of the letter were sent to all the major new services. The first the staff knew of it was when a television crew arrived to do a story on a school that would condone such a letter!

The students returned from Yosemite to take up their regular routine. Visitors to campus, such as the CPFEA committee members, could not help noticing certain aspects of daily life. Observations of student behavior caused Marshall Palley to ask at a meeting in January 1967 what if any limits have been placed on petting and necking. Harold responded by pointing out that "heavy petting is discouraged and that students have been asked to neck in the vertical rather than horizontal position. They have been admonished not to do anything which would embarrass others." This prompted another committee member to say that "perhaps we haven't set limits in the area of sex relations, and that it is time that we do so." It was becoming evident that rules could be made, but enforcement could be challenging.

In addition to wrangling the teenage student body into an acceptable pattern of behavior, becoming an accredited academic institution was an important step that Woolman needed to take in order to attract students to the school. The Western Association of Schools and Colleges (WASC) was (and continues to be) the accreditation commission for secondary schools. They visited the campus in the spring of 1967. The report that they provided after their visit summarized commendations and recommendations to the school. The commendations included the low student-teacher ratio and the strong role of the teachers as counselors; the small class size and flexible scheduling; curricular experimentation, including extended field trips; careful screening given to students before acceptance; the merging of curricular and extracurricular into a fairly cohesive and unified educational experience; individualized study; an impressive library collection of books and periodicals in relation to the number of students; and a general consonance between the school's objectives and the experience that the students were having. All these positive attributes are reflected in the reports of student learning and adventures from the first few years at Woolman. And graduating seniors were being admitted to excellent colleges and universities.

But that didn't mean that the situation was perfect, and the WASC committee was diligent in its observations. The next part of the report was a serious list of recommendations for improvement or the alleviation of problems. WASC noted that the school had a loose and still-developing administrative structure, and that created some issues with regard to the relationship of the CPFEA to the principal and his authority. They also noted that there was a minimum of instructional supervision, leadership, and/or coordination of curriculum development. Some of this was attributable to the amount of time that the administration had available to devote to logistical activities; there was high staff turnover, and in many cases, staff had a lack of academic preparation for the subject they were teaching. In addition, the facilities for science, physical education, and art were minimal. They pointed to these deficiencies as a disadvantage to helping students prepare for college, but noted that because of the high caliber of students, the specifics of their high-school preparation might not be as important. However, another professed aim of the school, to inculcate the religious values of the Society of Friends, might be relying too much on the general climate of the school community and lacking any planned instruction. They did recognize that even though only half the staff was Quaker, all seemed to manifest Quaker philosophy. The final concern was what WASC described as the somewhat "shaky" financial state of the school, especially in terms of having adequate financial resources to address future development that WASC was recommending. Finally, the WASC committee wrote that the school "is a very special boarding school, enrolling special students and having special objectives. More youth want to enroll than can, and few drop out. So far, the venture portends well." In many ways, the report's recommendations reflected the ongoing issues that both guided and plagued the Woolman school in the coming years. A combination of financial pressures and a general lack of clear direction often conspired to undermine the commendable advantages that the report describes. Their report corroborated or perhaps echoed concerns of the CPFEA and the Quarter. At the same time it acknowledged the positive experiences reported by students.

So, the school days flew by. In the principal's end-of-year recap, in addition to all the academic achievements, he reported what happened on the farm during the school year: nine pigs turned garbage into 1,800 pounds of pork chops and bacon; about 15,000 eggs were collected from the chickens; three steers totaling 1,700 pounds were fattened and slaughtered; three sheep were bought, and one was slaughtered; 73 frying chickens were raised and sent to the kitchen; one calf was born. The present stock in the barns consisted of two cows, two steers, one calf, four pigs, two sheep, 125 hens, and 10 ducks. A significant amount of student effort and attention had gone into the farm successes, part of a busy and productive year. Thirteen seniors graduated at a ceremony held beneath the much beloved oak tree in the middle of the playing field. And then it was time again for the summer activities on campus.

The fifth year of operation of the John Woolman School began with optimism. Harold Blickenstaff reported in the fall newsletter of 1967 that the school had reached a new "high water mark" with 62 students: 32 girls and 30 boys enrolled, with 20 staff members, and 17 staff children on campus. The cook prepared food for nearly 100 people at dinner most nights. The increased student-body and staff size meant that the school could offer a wider selection of classes and services. New courses were offered in French, human relations, cartooning, and agriculture. New staff positions included a business manager/fundraiser and a farm manager/biology teacher. Eleven of the staff members were new to the campus in 1967, but they all had experience as educators and some experience with Quaker values, and some had connections to the CPFEA. Twenty of the students came from Quaker families, and ten others came from families active in Friends projects. Most students (26) hailed from the San Francisco Bay Area, with nine from Southern California, seven from Sacramento, seven from out of state, and seven from staff families. In addition to livestock, a flock of 125 laying hens provided as many eggs and stewing chickens as needed, and the community services program was expanded. The new arts center was close to completion and soon would be occupied by the expanded arts classes.

The increased school size also generated some concerns. Robert Heilman, the new business manager, reminded the community that growth meant more income, and to some extent, there would be economies of scale. However, additional services and new facilities meant more expense. Increased tuition made it easier to cover the cost of staffing, but it couldn't be expected to cover the costs of capital improvements and expansion. As the school grew, it needed additional new facilities such as a multipurpose space for dining, classes, and meetings, and it had to purchase equipment such as microscopes, tape recorders, typewriters, an adding machine, and a piano. In addition, students continued to voice their concerns about increasing the size of the student body. They appealed to the CPFEA to come and speak to all the students and staff in a community meeting to discuss future construction, enrollment increases, and possible alternatives to enrollment growth.

Smoking, smoking, smoking — it was an issue that simply would not go away. It was apparent to anyone who visited the campus that the rule against smoking was widely and flagrantly disobeyed. In February 1968, Harold appealed to the Association for help. Many students were either unwilling or unable to stop. Staff were reluctant to turn students in for infractions, and consequently the rule was not vigorously enforced. There were two options: the principal could use the current policy of suspensions and expulsions to enforce the current rule, or the present policy could be modified. Harold suggested that a modified rule might discourage smoking on campus and prohibit smoking in the common public areas, and the school might undertake an anti-smoking campaign. The issue was greater than just the question of enforcing a no-smoking policy. The Friends Meetings were not happy about smoking on the campus; it might threaten their support if the strict no-smoking policy was abandoned. The larger question was how could students and staff be encouraged to support rules they would rather not have? And what would be the effect on the community if rules are flaunted? And how does one keep the issue of smoking in the proper perspective?

In March, the question was moved on for further study by a committee of students, staff, and Association members to make a recommendation. In April, they gave their report. Not surprisingly, they really hadn't gotten very far. Though maybe the most revealing result was that they were no longer talking about punitive measures such as suspension and expulsion for students caught smoking. At the end of an extensive discussion about the influences that lead young people to smoke, including advertising and peer pressure, they arrived at several points to be presented to the school community and the CPFEA. They asked the CPFEA to change the policy from prohibiting smoking to its earlier position of discouraging smoking and limiting smoking to nonpublic areas, as Harold had suggested. They advocated relying on social feedback to reinforce the rules among students and staff. They would take measures to encourage and/or help students to quit smoking and try to mitigate social pressures that encourage smoking. They also recognized and emphasized the necessity of community-wide rules that need to be followed even if some members were not convinced that they are appropriate. This question remained unanswered for years to come and resurfaced in different forms later.

On a more positive note, the school property holdings were being increased and improved. The CPFEA was about to purchase the remainder of the Hedrick's property, 150 acres on the east side of the present school boundary. It had also decided to construct a new combined faculty residence, classroom, social hall, and student residence. The new tasteful and simple arts center was completed, and it hummed with activity: pottery (for which students dug local clays), weaving, wood and metal sculpture, painting, and photography. The dining hall was used for international folk and square dancing that spring. Student activism was not forgotten either; in 1968, students set up an informational picket line in front of the Grass Valley Safeway store supporting the national boycott of California grapes.

In the spring, plans were being made for the 11th annual summer school, which would be directed again by Mary Jorgensen. The emphasis was on a historical and cultural view of China, as well as study of and research on the critical political and social issues of the day. The summer session, scheduled from the end of June to the end of July, would also include creative writing, puppet-making, drawing, painting, weaving, drama, music, pottery, and shop work. As always, students would go swimming at the nearby twin pools, a favorite spot on the Yuba River, do folk and modern dance, hike, and enjoy the spacious campus. It would be another busy summer on campus, with a major building project in progress.

The building project had a rocky start. At the July 1968 CPFEA meeting, members expressed frustration about the lack of communication between various committees of the board. Joachim Leppmann, chair of the Long Range Planning Committee, had two significant concerns. One was that his committee had not been consulted before the decision was made to purchase the additional land from the Hedricks. The second regarded the construction of the new faculty/student house project. He felt that both of these changes were part of, or affected, the master plan and therefore were under the jurisdiction of the Long Range Planning Committee (LRPC). In this case, an ad hoc building committee had adopted Ken Kern's design for the new faculty/student house without consulting the LRPC. The ad hoc building committee members had spent much time with Ken, who was well known for his interest in and experience with owner-built homes. They were particularly interested in his creative design and use of low-cost building approaches. He planned to use natural rock, which was abundant in the creek, and concrete that could be laid by relatively unskilled labor. He had been an architect and designer for many years and could be of great help to the school. CPFEA members also pointed out that the plans and cost estimates were incomplete. The ad hoc committee defended the design, saying that they felt that the authority to go ahead had been granted by earlier decisions of the LRPC, and that they also felt under pressure to move the project along so as to have the house completed for the start of school in the fall. In fact, about $3,000 had already been spent on the project as well as a lot of labor.

Following this discussion, the CPFEA members met with Ken and toured the site, after which they approved continuation of construction according to his design but with some conditions, including oversight by the CPFEA regarding costs, design decisions in the future, and frequent progress reports. Kris Bradwell, who had to leave before the meeting concluded, wrote the next day that although she appreciated that the group approved some decisions, bringing a little more control to the process, she felt unsure that the Association had any vision about the direction it wanted the school to go. One of her concerns was that various projects appeared to have been undertaken impetuously, sometimes very costly and poorly designed, and it was time for that precedent to be reversed. She was not the only committee member with these concerns.

Throughout the summer, Ken led weekend workshops as the construction of Woolman's new faculty/student residence proceeded. Construction had started at the end of June with Harold Blickenstaff as superintendent, Noel White as carpenter foreman, and several volunteers plus Ken on site on weekends to help with construction. In spite of an ambitious work schedule, the building was incomplete when school started in the fall.

The central feature of the building (which came to be known as the Stonehouse) is an elaborate fireplace alcove in the form of a conversation pit with seating for a number of people in a relatively small area. Mariposa slate covers the pit and central room floor. Off the central room of the building are bedrooms, bathrooms, a kitchen, and a living room. The walls are circular and formed in place with concrete and the local rock. Under a common roof, three cylindrical units are arranged in a clover-leaf plan around the inner room with a central fireplace. The outer walls are composed of a thin concrete shell and an outer facing of neutral rock. Rocks used in the fireplace, retaining walls, and exterior facing were broken to size during the Gold Rush by Chinese laborers. Mounds of these rocks lined the stream that cuts through the Woolman property and were an artifact of Gold Rush diggings. These were evident all over the region, where miners dug for gold on land that had long been home to the local Nisenan Indians.

When school started in September 1968, the population count was noted in the *Outsider's Insider* as "66 students, 28 pigs, 25 goats (1 horny, 1 bisexual), one h--- of a lot of sheep, 2 geese, 2 ducks, 7 pigeons, too many cats & dogs, 2 model A [cars], 18 stereos, No dope (we hope)." Things were a bit crowded for the students; 39 boys lived in cabins and in the infirmary, while 30 girls occupied the dormitory and a trailer. Using the Infirmary for housing was not ideal, and as it turned out there were enough students who were sick that fall that the boys living in the infirmary had to move in with the Blickenstaff. Other aspects of crowding meant a lack of good study space. By following the LRPC's recommendation to increase enrollment, more students were admitted than the school had facilities to accommodate. Unfortunately, the necessary developments in the physical plant recommended by the committee hadn't been made in time to accommodate the increase in enrollment. The problem of overcrowding was closely related to the difficulty of raising funds for capital improvements. There also needed to be more analysis of the study space, library resources, and faculty:student ratio, as part of the decisions about enrollment numbers. And all these issues were connected to the need for the Long Range Planning Committee to be clear about the operational realities of their plan.

In spite of the overcrowding, Harold reported the good news that there was greater unity among the staff, and that the staff meetings had been productive and helpful. The troubling news was that the CPFEA was critical of Harold, having some concerns about how he fulfilled his duties, though he was supported by most of the staff and students. The CPFEA was his employer, and it was the role of principal to comply with the expectations they set forth, but it was not clear whether these expectations had been made clear to him. The committee felt that the school needed to be a more businesslike operation and should be cleaned up, both in appearance and for sanitary reasons. At the same time, Committee members experienced pressure from Friends in the Quarter who had issues with the school; many of them felt strongly that Friends values and philosophy should be paramount in the running of the school. This issue was non-negotiable for the CPFEA—they had to honor the priorities of the Quarter to maintain and try to improve that relationship. These political machinations hung in the background as the school year proceeded.

In the fall of 1968, while some students went off for Fall Special Projects Week, another group stayed at school to work on a new pottery kiln, and the Stonehouse construction was nearing completion. Another group went to Ben Lomond to work on the AFSC conference center that was being constructed there, and yet another group went to Kettleman City in the Central Valley to help farm laborers construct their own houses. The Special Project periods were firmly set as an important part of the school schedule. Students could either develop projects following their own interests or participate in organized group projects—like the volunteer work at Ben Lomond that had been going on for several years. Mary Jorgensen noted at the May CPFEA meeting that it might be a good idea to increase the administrative oversight for Special Projects when these took place off campus to ensure sufficient communication between the people responsible for the students during the projects and the school administration. There had been some "unfortunate situations" in the Bay Area in the past year as a result of the lack of adequate communication.

Beginning in the fall of 1968, the journalism class published the school newsletter *Outsider's Insider*. Before that, it was a produced by an ad hoc group of students and staff with a decidedly upbeat tone, mostly reporting enthusiastically on the positive aspects of student activities and new initiatives, as well as accomplishments of staff and students. Once the students took over, the publication took a markedly more critical tone, the students using it as a sounding board to express both positive and negative feelings. Its stated purpose was "to acquaint our friends with the life and thoughts of the school." Whether written by staff or students, it was one of the main ways that the wider community of student families, alumni, and Quakers stayed abreast of the activities at the school. If one of the letters to the editor in the spring of 1969 accurately reflected feelings of the general readership, the students were succeeding in making a favorable impression in spite of any criticism they might have expressed. A reader wrote, "Congratulations on how well your paper reveals your school's development and your students' maturing commitment to values we like to think we share." Mary Jorgensen, who by then had had a long and energetic relationship with the school and the students, wrote expressing her appreciation and encouraging the paper to highlight the student activism and to describe the significance of the work and joy that students experience each year caring for the farm animals. The newsletter routinely reported on the upcoming schedule of events that the community related to the school might be interested in, like summer work camps on campus, summer school, and major school activities. For example, the Spring 1969 issue was devoted almost entirely to the Spring Special Projects. In addition to reporting on the activities of students, it included ads for items that the students needed, such as new mattresses, furnishings for common areas, and even items like new microscopes or (later) computers. This was practical public relations outreach for the school.

The *Outsider's Insider* also served as to reflect the feelings of the students, assuming that the journalism class was a microcosm of the greater school community. From the beginning of school through the end of the the 1960s, talk of students taking responsibility for their actions was a constant thread, and the challenges of living in community (presumably those challenges magnified by members who were not taking their share of responsibility). The stories of student activities reflect the importance of social activism to student experience at Woolman, including joining local Grass Valley High School students at a 1969 peace march, volunteering in the local elementary schools, and going south into the Central Valley of California to help farmworkers build housing during the spring project week. Harold Blickenstaff remarked in the newsletter that "Much of which the students learn in their classes they will find useful, but much will become archaic. It may be that the most practical learning that takes place here is the sensitivity and flexibility that develops from trying to reconcile our differences and live together in harmony. Living here is truly a lab course in human relations." Anyone who has taken a lab course knows that it's a lot of hands-on work.

Around the same time, in the spirit of life at Woolman as a lab course in human relations, the Ad Hoc Committee of the CPFEA Educational Policy Committee prepared a statement on sex to be submitted to the Quarter.

"In consideration of the Association's legal responsibility for the students at JWS and the expectation of Friends Meetings which constitutes the Quarterly Meeting, the College Park Friends Educational Association cannot and does not condone sexual intercourse for students at John Woolman."

The official record of the CPFEA did not record any specific reaction to this statement. Nor was there any comment in the newsletters in the months to follow.

As spring classes and activities proceeded, the student work program followed its regular routine. Daily jobs were performed from 8:00 to 8:50 am. These jobs, which students had been performing all year, included helping with meal prep, general cleanup, farm chores, and janitorial duties in the classrooms, office, library, and dormitories. Every three or four weeks, there were longer work periods, (lasting several hours) to tackle jobs that required more time. From one year to the next, both students and new faculty had to be indoctrinated into the work program, and of course there were always some students who had some difficulty fulfilling their responsibilities and needed to be reminded. The students who were not as likely to get their jobs completed were usually put on jobs which could be checked easily, and if they continued to fail to do them, they were counseled. It was possible, if the failure was egregious enough, that they might be suspended.

In early March 1969, all that remained for the new Stonehouse to be inhabitable was finishing the interior painting and wood trim. Soon, two students who had made the infirmary their home, and the Croninger family, would be moving in. During the Easter weekend work camp, trees were planted, and a considerable amount of cleanup work was done around the new building.

In April, as was the custom, some students took off on various adventurous Special Projects trips including a Baja trip, a trip to the Hopi reservation in Arizona, and a raft trip down the Sacramento River. Others stuck closer to home doing group service work in the local community, and some designed individual projects. Special Projects provided an opportunity for students to move out of the classroom into the community in order to relate learning and living to the life "out there," with some supervision from the school. Looking back on the trips of the 1960s, and reading student accounts of adventures and misadventures, one sees the evolution of parental attitudes from the 1960s to today. Sending an adolescent off to a boarding school in the Sierra foothills in the days when every telephone call to check on their well-being was a toll call (if you could even reach them) was certainly different from today's instant connections. Parents relinquished control; the students were in the hands of the school. Perhaps the possible negative consequences of misadventures were slightly less dire? Or if you didn't even know they were a possibility, you didn't have to worry. However, it is interesting to read the students' accounts, describing how they crossed the Mexican border, hair hidden under their hats to disguise their "hippie" appearances. They wrestled with their truck, stuck in sand for four or five hours at one point, and once they were driven out of their camping place by the incoming tide and, when they eventually crossed the border back into the US, struggled to recuperate from "sunburn, dysentery (one student was evacuated from Mexico by plane with a severe infection), homesickness, and other of the more unpleasant things we had accumulated in Mexico." The eight students who floated down the Sacramento River (on a raft made of twelve surplus oil drums welded together and covered by sheets of scavenged plywood) reported capsizing and fearing they might drown, being stranded on a deserted island for 24 hours with only a bag of prunes, hitchhiking to town and getting picked up by the cops for "looking weird," and various other potentially hair-raising-to-parents stories. And the tales of these adventures were no secret. So it is easy to imagine the seeds of a particular sort of reputation being planted in the minds of some people. There was no question that they were learning and living life "out there" as prescribed, but the question of appropriate adult supervision was an understandable point of debate.

While the students pursued their Special Projects, Mary Jorgensen, continuing to work tirelessly in a variety of ways for the school,, sent out a letter to everyone who had loaned money to the school, giving them an update on the financial picture. The itemized list of outstanding loans included the original loans for the land purchase as well as Friend's loans from the past few years. One item was Hedrick's—New Land. Mary went on to explain,

> "We did not need more land, or want it, but the farm bordering on ¾ of our land was up for sale. It looked as if a gun club or a five acres subdivision would be there where the land would go. This land lies within 300 feet of our main buildings and right across the creek. We couldn't buy just part of it as the owner was not allowed to subdivide [prior to sale], so after much soul-searching, we took the leap. Five acres subdivision has already gone into effect on the north side of our land. We are going to sell 40 acres along the Jones bar entrance road in order to help pay for this. It is really a good thing we bought it as it has a small lake, which is more useful in the summer and fall and allows the school to develop in the natural valley across the creek."

Soon after, an announcement of the land sale was printed in the *Outsider's Insider*. It stated that the CPFEA wanted to offer the opportunity to purchase the approximately 7-acre parcels to the friends of the school before they put it on the open market.

At the end of August 1969, just before school began, Elizabeth Israel, President of CPFEA at the time, sent a letter to the community informing everyone that "the Harold [and Dottie] Blickenstaffs and Dick [and Marguerite] Millers have asked to be released from their posts on the John Woolman staff." The circumstances, though not reported to the public, involved some personal actions and interpersonal activities that some considered inappropriate, and which were generally known and notorious around the campus. It was the sort of situation that really was no one else's business but was difficult to ignore in such a closeknit community. It was also impossible to ignore the sudden shift in leadership at school. Consequently, the academic year began with a new principal, Chuck Croninger, who along with his wife Virginia had been active staff members for the previous two years. Chuck had been teaching social studies, and his style was familiar to the students and staff alike. He immediately instituted some changes in office procedures that aimed at efficiency and improved financial accountability. A newsletter article described his style as emphasizing academics and practicality in comparison with the previous administration's more idealistic approach. There were new staff members, some returning after a short break from the school and some new, including Ted Menmuir, who had been doing graduate work in philosophy and theology and most recently had been working for the Department of Youth in Alberta, Canada. His first teaching foray at the school was American Government and the history of Naziism, World Religion, and Quaker Thought—an interesting beginning to his long and varied association with Woolman.

The farm program had been expanding. It was work as education, and also the opportunity to learn responsibility caring for animals, which was continuous regardless of how you felt or whatever the weather. The work built character and experience for the students. Importantly, the budget incorporated farm production as a supplement to the food costs. The wood to fuel the wood stoves in the A-frame cabins was part of the farming operation too. Students provided their own wood by helping to fell and chop designated trees into firewood. There were costs associated with the farm, however, so it needed an influx of capital each year. It required maintaining a working water system and carefully tended and mended fences. New trees were regularly purchased and planted to eventually replace those that were harvested for firewood. There were also expenses associated with animal care. The program had aspirations in 1969 to acquire two goats, to breed their two sows, and possibly acquire three sheep from a local veterinarian. In addition, they needed new movable irrigation pipes and seed mix. The total budget for the farm program that year was $9,000. It became the subject of yet another fundraising appeal.

The 1969 school year started with a full complement of 65 students and moved forward relatively routinely. The *Outsider's Insider* reported service-oriented Special Projects at the Ben Lomond Friends Retreat in Ben Lomond, CA and in Visalia, CA, students hiking in the Santa Cruz Mountains and doing trail cleanup, and some students staying on campus to tend the farm and help with the continuing kiln construction.

That fall, there was a thread of social justice running through the regular community meetings, strongly influenced by the social and political upheaval in the country as a whole. Discussions among staff and students reflected the political and moral issues of the day and were permeated by the Quaker spirit and philosophy of peace and justice. The concerns continued throughout the year, and during a community meeting in May there were endless ideas put forth, including walking to Washington, D.C. to protest Nixon's invasion of Cambodia (authorized at the end of April). Ultimately, practicality prevailed and the decision of the community was not to sacrifice regular classes, but to devote much time to supporting candidates, holding peace seminars, and going to peace rallies.

As the 1969-70 school year drew to a close, the Long Range Planning Committee of the CPFEA continued wrestling with recurring questions of school size, student body size, and the adjustments in housing and other things that need to happen in order to support a larger student population. More than one committee was working on some of the issues, and this caused consternation among some members. They also asked the staff to weigh in on questions of school size and how student living should be organized. In addition to planning for future expansion, they had to plan for the possibility of a dropoff in enrollment, which could put financial pressure on the school. They would contemplate these concerns over the coming years.

Don Smith had an interesting perspective on the transformation that he observed when he returned to the school after an absence of several years. His efforts were integral to the establishment of the school, and he taught history for three semesters of the first two years once it opened (as well as managing the farm program). Then he left to continue his own education for several years before returning. Many years later, he recalled that the initial years "were difficult and energy depleting ones. The hearts and minds of both staff and students were wrenched and strained as the new school sought to discover how to work together. In the student community the ferment and disagreement arose in part as a reflection of the hippie styles coming into vogue on the UC Berkeley campus, the Free Speech movement and violent confrontations in the college community. Many of our students were from Bay Area homes and naturally wished to try emulating the life-styles of their older peers. For the Staff's part, inexperience contributed to hesitation, false starts, even bewilderment with some student problems. Most of us had never taught in a boarding high school before. Another part of our school community's dissension arose from the remarkably varied both we staff members and Board members had of the school we were building. These hopes and goals literally ran the gamut from a Quaker George School of the West, to a high-powered academic prep school, to an American version of the free-wheeling, permissive English Summerhill. Without a steadying tradition of goals, methodology and standards, each of us felt our particular vision was the legitimate one for the school, and consensus proved elusive. Such staff divisions were naturally exploited by adolescents who had their own agenda for experimental behaviors."

[Don Smith, Autobiography of Don Elton Smith]

In spite of these significant challenges, students successfully completed their high school years, went on to college or other pursuits, with stories of memorable experiences, appreciation of for the satisfaction and dignity of manual labor, as well as intellectual achievement, respect for others, and new experiences in the arts. Some students struggled and might have benefited from a program that was less volatile. At the same time, Woolman was beginning to have some established traditions.

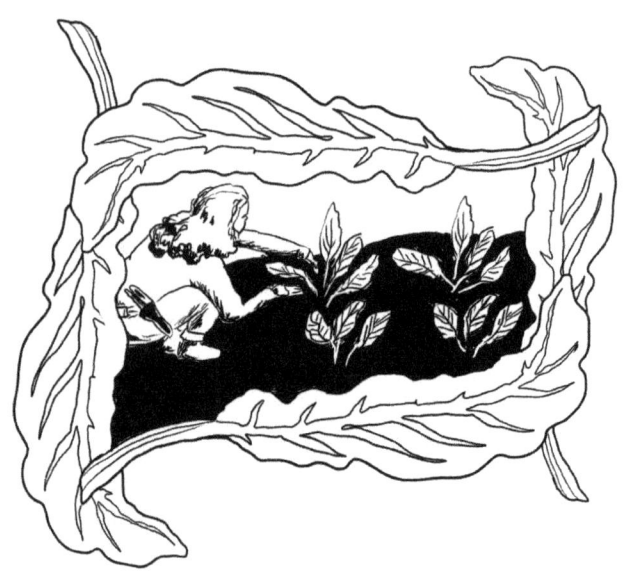

| AGROBUSINESS |

WORK IS LOVE MADE VISIBLE

W hen school opened in September 1970, Chuck Croninger stepped into the role of Principal. His direction prompted new procedures and programs, which overall seemed to have a very positive effect. New systems made each teacher responsible for counseling about six students and communicating with their parents regarding their academic and social progress. He implemented written teacher evaluations, a more systematized administrative office routine, and a college guidance program. Chuck's approach was seen by some as being heavy-handed; however, these changes helped the school to move in the direction of more clearly defined roles, which in turn led to a more cohesive vision among the staff. At the same time, the CPFEA board, which had struggled for so long with its own issues, also made progress on clarifying goals for the school under the leadership of Bob Scott.

In 1971, Don and Harriette Smith returned after several years' absence. Don had been in graduate school, and when they came back, he again assumed a multitude of roles, including teaching history. Harriette returned to work in the library, which had been moved to a new location in the Quonset building near the stream. She had been responsible for the initial acquisition of many volumes. Most books were still in boxes, and Harriette spent almost a year sorting, cataloguing, and shelving them, as well as arranging multitudes of periodicals. Then she created an orientation program for students in the use of the library and began coordinating with teachers to support their needs for books in the classroom. In 1972, she attended a librarian's conference sponsored by the

Philadelphia Yearly Meeting. The conference was held at the Wilmington (Delaware) Friends School and offered ideas about budgeting, innovative use of audiovisual materials, book selection for high-school-student curriculum, and ways to engage faculty with library resources. She also visited several other Friends School libraries in Philadelphia and Maryland on her way back to California. Harriette continued to expand the library. Sometimes she was helped by generous donations of personal libraries, usually from members of regional Friends meetings. She reported in the mid 1970s that the library had accessioned and cataloged about 6,500 books and had received others that had been labeled and shelved for use but not incorporated into the catalogue.

September 1972 marked the beginning of the tenth school year at Woolman. Chuck Croninger reflected on the nature of education at Woolman in a piece in the school newsletter that went out to the Quaker community as well as to families and alumni of the school. Reflecting that part of the Woolman School's reason for being as an institution was to provide schooling for students 14 to 18 years old, he said that it was "...an education for both heads and hands. On the head side are the academic preparatory classes. For the hands (and head) we have gardens, art (drawing, weaving, pottery and batik), and work jobs. Add to this vocal music and you have the outline of our class offerings." The other reason for being was to "be Quaker." He quotes from an unidentified author: "As a way of life, it (Quakerism) emphasizes hard work, simple living and generous giving; personal integrity, social justice, and the peaceful settlement of disputes." He went on to say that "a Quaker educational experience should aim at an experience which would value and include hard work, simplicity and giving, integrity, justice and peace, and the experience of a Friends meeting for Worship. These are our goals and at best they are our experience." And with these words, he launched a new decade of learning at Woolman.

In addition to the academic routine, there was occasional unexpected excitement on campus. Autumn can be critically dry in the Sierra Foothills; it is common for not a drop of rain to fall all summer, and before the first rains of autumn, the landscape is often parched. On October 1, 1973, a fire broke out in an unirrigated pasture on the east side of campus. Fortunately, there was almost no wind, and when the State Forestry Department firefighters arrived with five trucks, one bulldozer, and three airplanes to augment the fire extinguishers, shovels, and picks wielded by the students and staff, campus personnel had the fire under control. The greatest damage done by the fire was to the budget. Almost every fire extinguisher on campus had to be recharged, a significant expense. It was also a reminder of the vulnerability of a campus setting that was surrounded by nature and the challenges of the natural environment, which could be manipulated but not entirely controlled.

Manipulating nature was partly accomplished through the significant energy invested in the gardens. Don Smith took on the role of Head of Farm (he also taught and had responsibility for the school administration when the principal was off campus). In the spring, students began spreading manure and putting up fences. George Burcham of the Grass Valley meeting provided lots of advice and a rototiller. By the end of April, tomatoes, lettuce, melons, squash, corn, and eggplant were in the ground. By July 1, the upper garden had herbs and peppers, mulch, and a layer of black polyethylene film to kill the Bermuda grass. Tomatoes, melons, and summer squash plants were producing heavily by the end of July, when beans and cucumbers were also planted. Fall crops started in August, but except for Chinese cabbage and lettuce, most failed because of bad weather. However, large quantities of tomatoes, cucumbers, and peppers survived and were harvested. The plan for the future was even more intensified gardening, with the expectation that the school could become self-sufficient in its vegetable production. Seedlings were started in early January of the next year in anticipation of spring planting. Another plan was to plant an orchard of at least 70 trees—an assortment of apple, pear, cherry, peach, plum, and prune—in the lower corner of the pasture. Trees planted as bare-root whips, with luck and good care, should bear after about four years. All this was done "freeloading" off the food budget, as there was no special budget for the garden. The gardeners soon discovered that although the yield was excellent, the cost of starting the garden was substantial. They needed at least $50 for seed, which could justifiably come out of the food budget; however, trees, fertilizer, humus, fencing materials, and stakes were calculated to cost about $500, and there was no provision for this in the food budget. Additional basic garden tools like shovels, spading forks, hoes, and sprinklers were also needed, and the big wish list included a large rototiller to replace the one they were borrowing from George Burcham, a compost shredder, and a greenhouse. Working in the garden was an important part of the Work Program in which every student participated, and the extensive garden was unique among the boarding schools on the West Coast. During this period, work truly did seem to be "love made visible" for the students who enjoyed the fruits of their labor, but also the pleasures of working in community.

Plenty of effort went into community work. An article in the *Outsider's Insider* in the winter of 1974 reminded readers that still, after ten years of operation, there was no garbage pickup or school custodians, and the tasks required to keep the campus functional continued to be shared by community members plus students and staff working in crews. A work committee assigned the crews, and assignments generally rotated every quarter. During the school year, tasks included (in addition to garden work) cutting wood, irrigating pastures, managing farm animals (including slaughtering and butchering), repairing the gravel roads, preparing meals, doing various janitorial tasks such as dishwashing and sweeping floors, and picking up and disposing of trash. As much as possible, the assignments considered personal preferences. But all the tasks needed to be done to keep school operations running smoothly. In the process, one could acquire new skills. Some of them were less conventional, like raising (and slaughtering) livestock, while others were more mundane, like washing dishes or windows. But in general, the experience of shared work served to build community. It also became clear that everyone depended on individuals taking responsibility for their assigned tasks. Community meeting notes were full of discussion of how to deal with work assignments, and what kind of penalties might be appropriate when students didn't complete their tasks. Not all jobs were done equally well or efficiently, and over time, the campus infrastructure began to show the uneven attention to maintenance that resulted from minimal professional attention.

The tradition continued of suspending regular classes for a week in October and giving students the opportunity to go out into the world in service to others. In 1972, for example, students worked with Self-Help Housing and the California Rural Housing Coalition, helping with roofing, framing, and foundation-building in the California towns of Winsor, Live Oak, and Orange Grove. In Winsor, students slept on the concrete floor of the Trinity Baptist Church and went to work each day promptly after breakfast. If they didn't know how to drive a nail at the start of the week, by the end they were experts.

Most students took their academic work very seriously. For many students, the next stage of their academic careers would be college. News was trickling into the Alumni News section of the Outsider's Insider that students were graduating from colleges. Many attended schools in the University of California system, and some went to Quaker colleges such as Earlham. They reported feeling well prepared by the academic program at Woolman.

In addition to academic subjects, the arts were flourishing at the Woolman School. Music engaged many students, who participated in community choral and instrumental ensembles. According to the newsletter, the school needed a piano, timpani, metronomes, recorder music, and additional chamber music scores for the thriving chamber ensembles. The arts program was strong, with classes in weaving, drawing, and pottery. Ted Menmuir was working on building a new kiln near the pottery Quonset. All these experiences were woven together with academic subjects to create the fabric of life at the school.

In the background as the academic years progressed, the CPFEA continued to struggle with financial stability. In the early 1970s, the Long-Range Planning committee circulated a Master Plan proposal made by an architectural firm. The scope of the work was ambitious, including ways to improve the facilities to continue attracting and retaining quality applicants to the student body and to the faculty. The plan recommended forming an environmental design team, including geological investigation consultants, and included ideas for generating additional income for the school. The scope of recommendations was:

1. Location of future faculty residences and student housing, learning center/library, recreation/meeting hall, and athletic facilities
2. Investigation of site access from route 49
3. Feasibility of a retreat center
4. Feasibility of lease campsites
5. Recommendation of future expansion and use of present dormitory
6. Investigation of water, power, and sewage disposal facilities
7. Constructing model of site, showing existing structures and future building sites, open areas, buffer, zones, etc.

Though money was authorized for the study, it was never completed in its entirety, and fifty years later several of these recommendations were still on the table for consideration.

In June 1974, Ted Menmuir assumed the role of Principal. He had been on staff for five years in several roles, teaching social studies, religion, and art. Chuck Croninger, who had been principal for five years, moved into the part-time role of Director of Admissions and Development, making it possible to for him to return to graduate school, which he did on a part-time basis.

When the summer meeting of the CPFEA convened in 1974, it brought together familiar faces, many of whom had now been on hand for more than ten years, including the Jorgensens, Pagets, Smiths, Schutz, Leppmans, Israels, Reynolds, and Blickenstaffs. They were there amid the A-frame cabins, the dormitory, dining hall, office, science labs, staff homes, barns, fenced meadows, orchards, library, gardens, greenhouse, art barn, pottery shed, and kilns, all of which were created (in the words of Shirley Tweed) by the "mortar of sweat and caring holding us together." The committee reviewed the needs of the school and noted that at this point the twelve A-frame cabins were ten years old. They had seen plenty of wear and tear and needed refurbishing. They planned to build new beds, buy new foam mattresses, build sturdy desks in the cabins, and cover the floors with durable vinyl. The cost estimate was about $200 for each cabin if the renovations were accomplished with donated labor. An additional $1,500 was needed for essential repairs to the dormitory bathrooms. The request for funds to support this project was on top of the usual appeals for financial donations. In the fall of 1974, with the requested donations in hand, staff, students, and Association members began working on building beds for the A-frame cabins. Construction had begun in late August after the plans were completed and approved, and by October, Don Smith's Special Projects group got things to the point that the student body could varnish all the new beds in one day. The beds had storage compartments with doors, and someone calculated that there was a total of 576 screws for the door hinges—these took a long time to screw in. Once completed, the new beds were installed in the cabins with new mattresses in new covers that were clean and comfortable. The whole assemblage looked nice and was a great improvement.

That fall, other Special Projects continued in addition to the campus improvement efforts. Students worked at the Indian School in Sonora, worked with the Farmworkers Union building self-help housing, helped to refurbish the Friends Center in San Francisco, did maintenance at Ben Lomond Friends Center, and assisted in Palo Alto at a co-op and nursery school. The new staff members helping to guide the students as well as settling into their teaching responsibilities that fall were Doug Tweed (Woolman alum), Olivia Gay (Woolman alum), Jerome Orloff, Lew and Eddie Sitzer, Joan Schneider, and Mary Farley.

In May 1975, the CPFEA reluctantly announced an increase in tuition, from $3,700 to $4,100 beginning in the fall of 1975. In its statement, it mentioned that in the present inflationary times there were only two alternatives to higher fees—wealthy benefactors or underpaid teachers. "We welcome the former but are not willing to have the school carried on the backs of our teachers. Nor are we willing to turn down a student's application for admission because of lack of funds." There was a tuition reduction option for Friends who couldn't afford the full fee. The reduction amount was calculated based on an evaluation of each family's financial resources; going forward, this was to be conducted by the School Scholarship Service in conjunction with the Educational Testing Service of Princeton, New Jersey. The CPFEA gave an example of the pressures on the school's finances; in the current year, one-half of the 52 students came from Quaker families. Many of these could not have attended without drawing from the $45,000 allocated in the budget for tuition reduction. The result, because so much was used this way, was an operating deficit of $4,000 to $6,000. The CPFEA continued requesting financial assistance from the monthly meetings and, in an effort to encourage more support, they gave the meetings a list of suggestions:

1. Encourage applications from students wanting a Quaker-grounded education so the school could maintain a good pool of candidates for admission.
2. Set up (or increase) scholarship aid. (More meetings in Pacific Yearly Meeting were doing this, but not all).
3. Contribute to the operating costs of the school.
4. Help retire no-interest or low-interest school loans that were becoming due by making similar loans to replace the original ones.

In addition to the appeal from the CPFEA, Russ and Mary Jorgensen announced a new fundraising initiative in the Fall 1975. They noted that after several years of calls for fundraising assistance in the community, a group of 35 volunteers, at least five of whom were former students, had finally stepped up to help. They sent out letters to the alumni and the Quaker community asking for financial support for the pressing needs of the school, such as replacing the sewer pipes, repairing the dormitory roof, writing new loans to repay the loans the school had had for ten years, and providing scholarships for students. In unceasing enthusiasm and support for the school, Mary emphasized the beauty of the campus, the excellent news that there were eight students arriving to begin ninth grade (the largest ninth-grade class ever), the expanded food production program, and the generous and meaningful work that students were doing through the special projects, as well as continuing their rigorous academic programs.

When school started in fall 1976, the planning and attention that had been paid to improving food production on campus was reaping benefits. The December 1976 newsletter reported that there had been a fourfold increase in garden production over previous years. The orchard in particular had benefited from an intensive program of care, and about 30 boxes of apples and pears had been harvested. The vegetable garden had been enlarged, making use of some of the fenced area of the orchard. (Everything had to be well fenced to protect the crops from the abundant local deer population.) That year, planting was done with particular attention to crops that would yield late-summer and fall harvests when the demand was high at school. In addition to sheep and pigs, students were raising beef, and almost all the red meat used in the school kitchen came from the resident cattle. In 1978, the farm program, now overseen by Lew Sitzer, expected to raise and slaughter 10-12 pigs (some of which would be used in the dining hall and some marketed locally), five steers, and 10 lambs. All this food production meant that they needed more and better storage capacity. So this was yet another expense—to buy freezers and construct new, secure food storage space in the kitchen.

In February 1977, a committee of the Western Association of Schools and Colleges (WASC) visited Woolman for three days to make an appraisal of all academic departments, the student body, library media services, counseling and school-community relations, extracurricular programs, and the school's physical plant. A few months later in June, the school was notified that it had been accredited for the maximum five-year term by WASC. Their report commended the school for the "exceptionally low pupil teacher ratio (8:1 in full time teacher equivalents), for the development between staff and students of a great degree of mutual respect and personal commitment to the philosophy and goals of the school," and for "conducting a highly individualized almost tutorial, education program within a family-society relationship."

Much effort went into preparing for the WASC committee visit, which was the culmination of a long process of self-evaluation on the part of the administration and staff. Everyone was justifiably proud to know that the accreditation was for the full five-year term. They were also happy to read the news reported in the Outsider's Insider in June 1978 that graduating seniors had been accepted at colleges throughout the country, including Vassar, Bryn Mawr, Antioch, Earlham, Scripps College, Chico State, Reed College, and Mills College. This seemed to be another indicator of the overall success of the Woolman program.

The beginning of the 1978 school year brought several staff changes as well as Ted Menmuir's announcement that he would retire as principal in the summer of 1979. The plan was that once he stepped down as principal, he would assume a new position created to promote the school, recruit new students, and raise funds. In the spring of 1979, after a six-month search, the CPFEA named John (Jack) W. Hunter as the new principal for the coming school year. Jack had a strong Quaker and education background and he, his wife Ruth, and their four children would be coming to campus in July to settle in before the start of the academic year. Ruth would also be employed at Woolman, primarily doing library work, replacing Harriette Smith, who was retiring.

The spring newsletter in 1979 announced significant upcoming construction plans. The improvements were made possible because of a major gift of $110,000 to the school from the Palo Alto Friends Meeting (from the Pentler Estates funds, which they managed). The gift carried no specific restrictions on its use. The CPFEA asked its finance committee to review the school's needs and make a formal recommendation at its July meeting. Decisions about using the funds were made in accordance with a Needs Committee study carried out the previous year by the CPFEA. The report had noted that the buildings and grounds were shabby, and it spelled out a detailed $300,000 improvement program. In addition to maintenance and repair issues, it called for new housing facilities for students as well as more adequate classroom and library space. Some of the refurbishing work was already underway, funded by a $10,000 loan from a friend of the school. Utility and drain lines were repaired, and grading and installation of culverts was being completed to improve water runoff around the dining hall, where a larger deck for outdoor tables was being added to the west side of the building. Retaining walls were also being constructed at the dining hall and in front of the dormitory. On the docket were repairs of the A-frame porches, painting of the art barn, and a new outside stairway for the dormitory. A new mower that could be drawn by the Ford tractor was bought, making it possible to cut the grass much more quickly in the orchard, pasture playfield, and around the office.

Possibly the most significant part of this project was building a complex of new cabins and bathhouses. The present dormitory arrangement no longer met the requirements of the state fire marshal. In addition, there was strong support for more decentralized living arrangements, which were preferred and seemed to work better for the students. The funding for all the recommendations of the Needs Committee was being raised in stages to supplement the Pentler funds, and the CPFEA initiated a $45,000 fundraising campaign to help pay for the new cabins and the central bathhouse. After the cabins were completed, the third stage of the project was the conversion of the dorm to additional classroom space, learning and study centers, major improvements to the science facilities, and a major renovation of student recreation space, library, and office facilities. The newsletter described the upcoming work:

> "The design of the new cabins incorporates concern for energy efficiency. The walls were planned to have six inches of insulation, double glazed windows, and heat provided through airtight wood stoves. Solar heating of hot water and radiant space heating were planned for the central bathhouse. The four-person cabins will provide a variation in small group living arrangements as contrasted with the two person A-frames which have been in use since the second year of the school. The new cabins will have more complete facilities than the A-frames. Generous desk and countertop space will be provided closets drawers and shelves will be built in. Bunkbeds will be located in an alcove that can be shielded from the lights of the main room."

The construction area was directly south of the existing dorm building, to the west and across the road from the new athletic field, referred to as the "rec field." Once again, much of the work was done by volunteer labor during the three summer camps planned for 1979, directed by the very experienced Russ and Mary Jorgensen. They recruited volunteer leader/teachers to receive work assignments from the construction foreman and then direct and teach work campers. In the usual tradition, a variety of activities, discussions, construction seminars, music, and dancing would take place in the evenings, with time set aside during the day for swimming and other recreational activities.

By June, after two years of planning and design, construction of the new cabins and bathhouse was underway. The cabin foundations had been poured and subfloors installed in May, and the bathhouse rough plumbing was complete and ready for the slab floor to be poured. Fundraising for the project had so far amounted to $11,300, a sum that would pay for the cost of two of the eight cabins that were being constructed, but contributions were still coming in. Mary Jorgensen reported that they were getting a good response, with plenty of signups for the volunteer work camps scheduled from June 29 to July 19, and they expected to finish the cabins in time for the opening of school in September.

The 1979-80 school year began with Jack Hunter, a new principal, at the helm. In addition to the student body, there were 140 farm creatures in residence. There were three garden plots, the orchards, and pastures to tend as well as the animals. Many students and community members helped the productive enterprise, which produced 400 pounds of fruit, 416 pounds of beef from the steer slaughter, 25 pounds of rabbit, 60 quarts of milk, and more than 100 eggs. There were also many vegetables harvested from the fall garden. It was hardly self-sufficiency, but it represented a lot of food, work, fun, and learning. Academic classes, work jobs, field trips, political action, special projects, regular extracurricular activities, and community meetings filled the students' days.

The two person A-frame cabins which have been in use since the second year of the school, photo by Dave Worley

The Woolman orchard

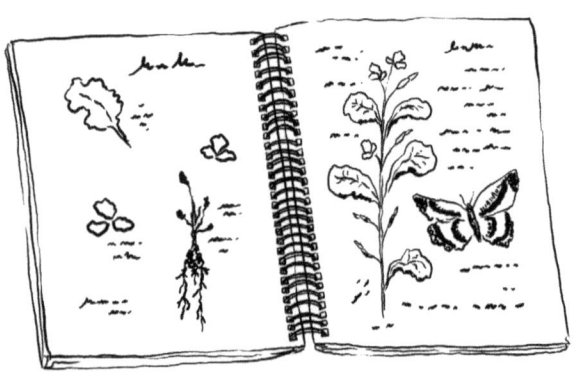

| SCIENCE |

7

....

STUDENTS IN ACTION

As a new decade began, the outside world was in flux, while the sheltered beauty of the Woolman campus was mostly constant. It was inevitable that these opposing dynamics would bring change and even conflict. Ronald Reagan's election in 1981 reflected a conservative shift in the nation, with a focus on morality and the character of young people, particularly a crackdown on drugs and a lessening of tolerance for recreational drug use. To some parents of prospective students, drug use was perceived as a great evil and a problem potentially lurking at any boarding school. And a few kids whose drug use had gotten them thrown out of more conservative schools landed at Woolman, sometimes bringing their habits with them. There was no denying the presence of drugs on campus. The seriousness of the problem fluctuated, but the concern about it by the outside world grew over the course of the decade.

At the same time, respect for the Quaker values of peace and justice were not lost on this new crop of students. These values were reflected in the campus community, which generally rejected the conservative and often war-mongering actions and attitudes pervasive in the country. In 1979, three students who had been commended in the National Merit Scholarship program joined students protesting the death penalty outside a maximum-security prison. On April 26, 1980, Woolman students participated in the March for Survival in San Francisco, a joint effort by groups concerned with foreign policy issues, nuclear energy, and the military draft. At the same time that the San Francisco march was taking place, thousands were gathering in Washington DC for a similar

event where protesters carried signs saying, "No Nukes is Good Nukes" and "Down with the Draft." And again in 1981, students joined a silent protest vigil opposing conscription, sponsored by the Nevada City Anti-Draft Coalition at the post offices in Nevada City and Grass Valley. Later, on May 3, 1981, they joined a peace march in San Francisco protesting U.S. involvement in El Salvador. The actions, and many similar ones before and after, were supported by the school administration and were consistent with Woolman Quaker values.

The opening of school in September 1980 brought 61 students to the campus, 44 of whom were new to the school. The community had grown from the previous years' opening enrollments of 43 in 1979 and 42 in 1978. It was a younger group: half were ninth and tenth graders. The staff of 15 had four new members. Principal Jack Hunter remarked in the fall newsletter that the young students seem to have brought a lot of energy to the community meetings and to the campus in general. There was a great deal of searching discussion. Trust, communication, and what it was like to live in community were hot topics, but community spirit was high.

When school started in September, students were greeted with campus improvements outdoors and indoors. The soccer field, a much-appreciated improvement over the rough and rutted pasture playing field, was completed. Also celebrated were new student cabins ready for occupancy when students arrived. Tucked within the stand of ponderosa pines just south of the old dorm building, each cedar-planked cabin housed four students. The units were well insulated and tightly sealed, heated by woodstoves, and needing little PG&E power. The matching central bathhouse had a solar water heater system for the showers and sinks. A timed electric radiant-heat lamp provided space heating that switched off automatically ten minutes after being turned on. (The idea was to warm the person, not the room itself, and then only on demand.) The new cabins were being used by the girls. Reports from the cabins were mixed; they were snug and warm, and the stoves were great, but their fire alarms seem to go off every time a fire was lit, and the space was a bit cramped for four people. They were irreverently referred to as "the condos" by the residents.

For the first time in 17 years, because of the new student cabins, no students were living in the two-story board-and-batten dormitory that had been built for the school's first year. The vacated student-housing sections of the dorm building were being remodeled into a science facility with new classrooms, several staff offices, student study centers, an additional staff apartment, and a textbook storage room. The project began the third stage of the three-part development plan that had been initiated by the CPFEA during the 1978-79 term. Remodeling was scheduled to begin in the winter, with some internal framing changes and the installation of sheetrock to replace the old wooden paneling on the walls, as well as electrical rewiring and installation of handicapped ramps. The new classrooms brought the building up to current fire-prevention standards and building codes. Not surprisingly, the whole project was more involved and costly than anyone had anticipated. The work was completed in the nick of time for the opening of school in 1981. The building was now set up for some serious academic endeavors. The science department settled into the downstairs classroom/laboratory. New study and classroom spaces were available on other floors.

The school began to experiment that fall with a new schedule, allowing students more opportunities to choose different courses during the year and giving teachers a chance to divide the subject matter of their courses into smaller units. By December, students and staff gave the new schedule a thumbs-up. In a more challenging area, Jack was dealing with the continuing matter of student commitment to the minimal school rules. Rebellion—evident on issues like nudity, student sexual activity, and smoking—seemed to be entrenched in the school culture, though the rebellion of the young was certainly not confined to the Woolman campus. Another source of conflict involved former students who returned to campus unannounced. Some individuals flagrantly disregarded the school rules by bringing alcohol and drugs on their visits. The archives contain huge notebooks of Staff Minutes from meetings during the school years in the early 1980s at which all these topics were discussed over and over. There were no easy solutions, and sometimes the only viable one was to expel a student.

Another very common topic of conversation at staff and community meetings was "work jobs." The (slightly awkward) name, used throughout the era in all the staff notes, applied to the work assigned to every student. This was integral to the goals of the school and essential to keep the campus clean and operational. Woolman and its community relied on students taking their responsibilities seriously and performing their assigned tasks. An interesting example of how important work jobs were to the ethos of the school involved a few students who were struggling academically and in danger of failing. The staff was trying to work out an arrangement that would enable them to graduate. One proposed solution for two particular students was an option to do a greater number of work jobs and pass with a D (at least) for 5 units or, if they could manage it, do the usual number of jobs and get an A or a B. If the students couldn't stick to the plan, the staff would "lower the boom" and they would not graduate. In this situation, work was considered an alternative to academic success, but with standards of accountability for the jobs that were to be used in lieu of academic achievement. The students would have to show up and complete their work assignments.

At a meeting in September, the staff also discussed the student work jobs as they related to coursework. There was a request at the meeting that a group of 18 students be freed from their housekeeping jobs so they could participate in a new section of Algebra I. Meeting attendees pointed out, however, that many staff had been given additional class assignments and yet they had not been relieved of their housekeeping responsibilities. Participation in housekeeping was significant and important. If they were to excuse students from work jobs, housekeeping might be seen as being devalued. As an alternative, they decided that some students could participate in a self-paced Algebra class so they could continue their work job responsibilities.

This was also a time when the school was looking at the relationship of the program to the school's Quaker roots. Student attendance at Silent Meetings became lax enough that the staff was compelled to remind them that Silent Meetings, a regular occurrence, were an occasion that students and staff were expected to attend. Students were told that even if it seems hard to accept,

> "It is important for you to examine what it means to be going to a Friend's school. Staff are clear on their commitment to Meetings being a time for the community to gather together, to think, to appreciate each other, and to share things about our common life that are problems and those that are good. All of us need to be part of this effort."

To show the seriousness of this position, they began to take attendance at Meeting and to give students feedback on their community participation.

Despite these thorny issues, in June 1982, the group of 21 graduates represented one of the largest graduating classes that the school had ever seen in its 20 years. About 250 people gathered on the lawn and the patio next to the principal's residence. Alumni at the ceremony reminisced about their past experiences at Woolman, recalling that in 1965, boys were suspended for offenses such as shoulder-length hair or wearing an earring. Others remembered pranks and pratfalls, as well as the ways that Woolman had inspired their teaching careers or successful business ventures. It also turned out that the gathering and reminiscing at graduation inspired a group of alumni to begin organizing an official alumni association for Woolman. Former students and the administration were noticing that it was becoming harder and harder to maintain connections. In later years, the alumni had a more official presence on campus for events, including graduation.

In 1983, the Western Association of Schools and Colleges (WASC) came to evaluate the school again in order to renew the accreditation. Ninety-six percent of the evaluation relied on the self-study process undertaken by the school. The visit by the WASC team added another 3%, and the review by the WASC commission constituted the remaining 1% of the process. Generally, the judgment of WASC was based on how well the school accomplished its stated goals. One whole academic year was devoted to the evaluation process, culminating in a visit from the WASC committee in May. The final report included many positive commendations, including recognition of the following: members of the community practiced Quaker values of simplicity, peace, and community to an extraordinarily high degree; Woolman provided a highly personalized learning situation for students; and the staff, in the spirit of understanding and friendship, routinely extended themselves with hospitality, support, and counseling to the students, and did a good job of teaching students basic and critical skills needed for success in college. The report also recommended ways in which the school could improve. Woolman should consider strategies for presenting itself to prospective students, emphasizing the importance and excellence of the school's academic preparation and college acceptance statistics. The informality and closeness of teachers was an important tool for the development of wisdom and restraint in matters concerning drugs and alcohol, and that should be highlighted to families of prospective students. The board and staff could benefit from studying ways to expand the drama, foreign language, physical education, and practical course offerings, and it was important to find ways and the means to strengthen the college and career counseling services. They also recommended conducting a survey of graduates to determine their achievement levels following their time at the school, especially to identify their success at colleges and universities. The WASC recommendations were important because future accreditation evaluations would pay attention to whether the recommendations were followed. Consequently, the administration and the CPFEA needed to take them to heart as they planned. In early June, the school received the good news that WASC had again renewed the school's accreditation for five years.

During this period, economic recession and higher inflation in the wider world added to the pressures on Woolman's finances, which had always been strained. Across the country, private secondary schools experienced a decline in enrollment, while tuition was rising. Ted Menmuir reported to the CPFEA that he had checked with fourteen boarding schools in the Western U.S. and determined that the Woolman School had one of the lowest tuition rates of any of them, while providing about twice as much financial aid as the next most expensive school.

Despite this, rising costs were making it increasingly difficult for families to afford tuition. The school was hoping to establish a loan fund for prospective students to assist them with tuition payments at very favorable rates. The call went out for contributions to the fund, which would be tax-deductible and bring a good return on investment. There was greater and greater economic need as a result of the recession, and in the 1982-83 school year, the school granted $95,000 in financial assistance to families.

Other changes that marked the 1983 school year included the arrival of a Heath Digital Microcomputer donated by a supporter, ushering in the computer age. This was the beginning of changes in, among other things, bookkeeping, correspondence and outreach, scheduling, remote library access, and so many other features of the digital age to come. Along with a dot-matrix printer, the computer became the basis for a newly organized computer class. Also, for the first time, the staff included a Dean of Students, a role filled by Ted Menmuir, in which he would help "acknowledge student's emerging self-direction and the insistence that students be held accountable to the guidelines of community life."

The ever-evolving condition and needs of the campus, the WASC report, and the overall economic climate prompted the CPFEA to look to the future. A Long-Range Planning Committee had been appointed by the CPFEA in 1982. The committee, consisting of Jack Hunter (principal at the time), Paul Niebanck, Judy Phillips, and Nickie Garmin (clerk), met nearly every month from January 29, 1983, until June 29, 1984. Their task was "to remember accurately" the growth of the John Woolman school and "in that light, to frame our vision anew, clearly and realistically, for the next decade of the school's life." After almost 20 years, they needed to take a long and serious look at the capacity of the school to meet the goals that had been set out at the beginning regarding social development, academic skills, methods of inquiry, citizenship, and self-sufficiency. The CPFEA asked the committee to look at what was "sound and satisfying" about the school now, what were the internal and external concerns about the school, what would an improved situation look like, and what could realistically be accomplished in the next few years. They sought advice from past and present staff and talked to experienced educators from other institutions. They looked at every aspect of the school's operation, the good and the bad, and thought hard about what could realistically be done to solve problems. In September 1984, the committee presented its report to the CPFEA. The report began by restating the philosophy adopted by the CPFEA in 1971:

> John Woolman School was founded by the Religious Society of Friends (Quakers) in 1962 as [a] rural Quaker boarding high school. Friends attempt to follow a way of life which emphasizes personal integrity, social responsibility, reverence for truth and the peaceful settlement of dispute. Woolman is an educational community designed to encourage its members to participate in the values and practices of this Quaker tradition.

The plan that resulted from this work was intended to act as a framework to assist the management in running the school for the next five years. The plan addressed several core issues including curriculum, enrollment, staff, school facilities, and finance.

Curriculum issues identified in the Long-Range Plan would be addressed by the newly formed Educational Policies committee of the CPFEA. From the very beginning (and sometimes to the frustration of staff members), the curriculum at Woolman was driven by more by the interests of the current staff than by an overarching educational philosophy reflecting the stated curricular goals of the school. The new plan stipulated that the school must have an established curriculum set by the principal, staff, and the Educational Policies Committee. The curriculum would in turn guide the choice of staff members, making sure that they had the appropriate knowledge and experience in their chosen fields. The plan also identified three specific areas that needed to be covered in the curriculum design. The first was that compliance with University of California entrance requirements should serve as a minimum standard for graduation from Woolman. Establishing a curriculum meeting these requirements was also the standard for membership in the California Association for Independent Schools, an organization that the Woolman School aspired to join. The second was expansion of the curriculum in certain existing areas of study, including Quaker philosophy and history, physical education, drama, art and music, foreign languages, computer technology, and farm and garden. And the third was developing or expanding creative approaches to learning, including intersession courses, creative projects, summer workshops, exchanges with other schools, and adjunct faculty arrangements such as Friends in Residence.

The issue of enrollment, which was also linked to school size, presented a most intractable problem. The CPFEA decided to table the related issue of the student-to-staff ratio until they could fill the school to its current capacity. The enrollment question was not only about numbers; the makeup of the student body was also an important factor. Increasing enrollment would be good economically, but selectivity and intimacy were both important to maintaining the greatest strengths of Woolman. The committee recognized that the closeness of a small student body made it possible to "affirm and maintain the values of community and the nurturance of the individual" in a way that became more challenging as the school size increased. This dynamic was very important to the committee, but members also recognized that the school was currently under-enrolled, with only fifty boarding students in a campus with a capacity for sixty. Without enough applicants, the school was forced, by economic necessity, to accept students who were known to have what the committee delicately expressed as "problems of adjustment." Woolman was developing a reputation as a school where you could send a "problem student" who had been asked to leave another institution. Adding additional day students was a plausible strategy that the committee suggested. They also wanted to increase the number of students from Quaker backgrounds, encourage more racial and ethnic diversity, and encourage students with special talents and interests. Their goal was a more selective (according to these newly defined criteria) student body of sixty boarding and ten day students, at which point they would have a period of consolidation and assessment before making any decisions about expanding the size of the school. The committee recognized that if Woolman did decide to grow, it would need a detailed architectural plan as well as a focused fundraising drive.

Once again, the report noted the desire not to turn away students for lack of funds. "Scholarships" had always been available, but in practice, Woolman simply reduced tuition for needy students, with the financial consequence that funding wasn't secured in an amount corresponding to the lower tuition payments. In contrast, a model that raised scholarship money and granted those funds to needy students would be necessary to avoid the funding gap. And as the report noted, Woolman's tuition reduction approach "places a drain on the school's ability to function." Planning had to take this situation into account.

The reputation of the school was another important factor addressed by the long-range planners. It affected the number of students applying and the ability to fundraise to support programming and scholarship assistance. The early years of what some committee members had described as "free-wheeling lack of discipline" had taken their toll on the school's reputation. Although the committee worked to address the concerns of both the Quaker and the local community, it was difficult to change established perceptions. Because the school was not very well known outside the Quaker community, maintaining a good reputation was essential to attracting a new pool of student applicants. The committee thought that a development director could help address the problems of perception by increasing and improving outreach, and that position could also do fundraising, recruitment, and public relations. The new position could be supplemented by the efforts of board subcommittees as well as outside PR consultants as needed.

Staffing issues presented a host of challenges. Warmth and mutual appreciation between the staff and students had always been a hallmark of the school. For several years, there had been an abundant supply of good teachers, but signs pointed to a shift in the job market. And whatever the situation, it was time to review the extent to which the school was nurturing the staff, as well as the students. The committee expected the staff to be professionally competent, know and feel comfortable with Quaker values, have reasonable energy and good health, be interested in serving as surrogate parents, be willing to perform and supervise physical work around the school, and possess a certain flexibility to deal with situations when things went awry. To continue to attract good teachers going forward, they needed to provide adequate housing—something better than the trailers on campus, which were often in need of repair and maintenance. The solutions were either to build more permanent housing and/or to allow some staff members to live off campus. Staff salaries, low in comparison to similar schools, needed to increase to attract the kind of candidates to which the school aspired. If they could meet the goal of increased enrollment, the additional tuition income would help support raises for staff.

Money was only part of the compensation problem. Teachers needed opportunities for professional enrichment and personal refreshment, and meaningful feedback on their performance at regular intervals. The committee strongly recommended that the school join the California Association of Independent Schools and the National Association of Independent Schools. Both organizations offered staff development opportunities to member schools. They also suggested planning for teachers and administrators to visit other schools, to help alleviate feelings of professional isolation inherent in a remote rural setting. The isolation of a boarding school in the country, where not only the students but almost all the staff lived on campus, inevitably resulted in a situation where the teachers seemed to be on duty 24/7. Not only did they prepare and teach, but their responsibilities included overnight supervision, participation in campus work jobs, and "parenting" and emotional support for the students. The staff homes were used for meetings, and students often stopped by on a casual basis. These routines brought the staff and students close together and built excellent rapport, but it was exhausting for staff members and "eroded their capacities to serve themselves and the school throughout the years," according to the report.

The poor condition of the campus contributed to negative perception of the school. Woolman needed to be upgraded to appear orderly, and well-kept to project the image of a serious academic institution. Many goals of the 1978 Needs Committee Report had been achieved, including the new student housing and the renovated classroom facility with science lab. A full-time maintenance program was making progress toward improving function and appearance on campus, but much more needed to be done. A campus development plan was needed to guide all future decisions about the physical plant in a cohesive way. Such a plan would include landscaping and locations for any new facilities that might be built. Beyond that, there was an urgent need to repair and remodel the A-frame cabins, upgrade the A-frame bathhouse, provide an outdoor blacktop area for games, improve the paths around the grounds, and provide more directional signs on and off campus. And if this list wasn't long enough, they also needed to pave the main road from the entrance to the top of the hill, make the library a more visible feature of the campus, enlarge the dining area, provide a student lounge or activity center, replace the trailers with permanent faculty housing, remodel the Stonehouse to make better use of the central fireplace room, and construct a covered athletic facility, which would also serve as a venue for programs and plays.

The plan was ambitious and predicted that if enrollment increased substantially, as they hoped, there would be a need for even greater expansion. Future development would necessitate obtaining a revised "use permit" from Nevada County, which might be more difficult to secure in the future, so trying to do so now seemed expedient. They also mentioned the Quaker expression "as the way opens," meaning that if you hold steadfastly to a vision, a way will open despite apparent impediments and roadblocks. "In the development of this campus, as in all respects about the school, we will proceed as the way opens."

Just as the Long-Range Planning Committee report was published, William (Bill) L. Moon, Jr. arrived to replace Jack Hunter as principal for the 1984 school year. Though a native of California, Bill and his family had been living in Europe for the past 16 years, where he worked as an administrator in European schools, primarily in France. Bill's graduate study was theater arts, and all through his time as an administrator, he continued to make time for writing and directing plays. When he arrived at Woolman, he taught a popular theater class in addition to his administrative work. Bill and his wife Mary felt that it was time their children spent a period living in the United States, and Bill's father and stepmother lived nearby in Auburn. They liked the idea of living in the country near his family, so the position of principal at Woolman was appealing. An even stronger magnet was Bill's affinity for the values and aspirations of the school. After reading the long-range plan and the school files about curriculum, enrollment, staff support, and school facilities, he could see the obvious strengths, as well as some significant weaknesses. He hoped that the flexibility of approach, the patient attention to everyone's concerns about the school, and the warm Woolman commitment to the community would make it possible to overcome the weaknesses. Some of his optimism and enthusiasm was fueled by listening to eloquent testimonials when he attended the memorial service for Marshall Palley, who died September 22, 1984. Marshall (whose role is discussed in Chapter 2) served as the Chairman of the CPFEA in the formative years of the school, and had strong ties to Woolman, from his early days working to establish the school, to the years when his children were students there, to the recent days when he had walked the woods on campus and prepared the Woolman Forestry Plan. At the service, which was attended by more than 200 people, Bill got a sense of the depth of Woolman's legacy. He heard many stories that illustrated how the school had endured and thrived in difficult circumstances and continued with great commitment to improvement.

Bill had an idea. Based on the desire to improve the academic focus of the school, he proposed establishing an International Baccalaureate (IB) program at Woolman. The IB is a comprehensive and cohesive curriculum of general education administered by the IB office in Geneva, Switzerland. It encompasses a traditional course of study incorporating multicultural perspectives and internationally based standards of achievement. The CPFEA approved the establishment of the IB program, and in February 1985 the school's application to participate was officially accepted. The John Woolman School became the first boarding school on the West Coast and one of two Friends schools in the U.S. authorized to prepare students for the IB exams. Offering the IB courses would result in an expanded curriculum and hopefully lead to increased student enrollment. Geri Stout, who had been teaching science at Woolman since 1978, was appointed IB coordinator.

The IB program had the potential to address one of the most critical goals for Woolman's future: increasing enrollment. Now, with the new program available to incoming students, a concerted effort was planned for recruitment. Brian Fry, Director of Admissions, met with supporters and counselors in public and private schools around the state to promote the program. The school revised its advertising strategy and pushed to attract foreign students and Americans living abroad who might want to send their children to the U.S. for high school. In 1986, thirteen juniors participated in the IB program. Five of the thirteen were taking the full course work for an IB diploma; others were preparing to sit single-subject exams at the end of the year. For Woolman to offer the program, teachers had to attend training workshops from a few days to a few weeks in length. These programs informed teachers about the IB exam process and how to prepare students, and it gave them opportunities to work on curriculum development and to network with colleagues.

That year, important improvements were in the works on the physical plant. Following the recommendations of the Long-Range Plan, in February the older leaky woodstoves in the A-frame cabins were replaced with new airtight stoves, greatly increasing the ease of heating the cabins and decreasing demand on the wood supply. The A-frame cabin area shower house and bathrooms were remodeled to make them easier to ventilate, heat, and maintain. And several basic plumbing changes were made, including adding a restroom to the administrative office space. (Previously, visitors who needed to use the lavatory had to be directed 50 yards away to the basement of the dining hall.) A big push was underway to raise funds to pay for an outdoor athletic area for basketball, tennis, and volleyball. Many prospective students and their parents had commented on the lack of a place for sports. By the spring of 1986, they had raised some of the funds, but about $6,000 more was needed to make the athletic area project a reality.

By the mid 1980s, there was a clear societal trend toward more structure and away from the laid-back attitudes of the 1960s and 1970s. But the norms of the earlier era had, to some degree, been institutionalized at Woolman. The school attempted to recognize the concerns of the parents of prospective students who referred a more traditional culture by establishing more rules, more explicitly stated, with more clearly enumerated consequences (even if they weren't always enforced). In this vein, in the spring of 1986 the ad hoc Substance Use Committee was formed to make recommendations to staff regarding serious concerns about certain student behaviors and their relation to the survival of the school. The new committee felt that educational program rules and social behavior were intrinsically linked, so the rules governing them needed to take both into consideration. They wrestled with how much supervision was needed, and in particular how to deal with the pervasive issue of alcohol and drug use. Were these values and behaviors simply deeply embedded in youth subculture of the day, and if so, how much tolerance was appropriate for a Quaker boarding school? What should be done about it? There were no easy answers, but clearly the issue was affecting the institution and, in some cases, creating barriers in student/staff relations. This conflict would persist.

After three years, the school abandoned the IB program. The goals, including the international approach to curriculum and the quest for excellence in education, fit very well with Quaker educational goals and philosophy. However, in year three, a careful yearlong evaluation by the staff and board concluded that the program was extremely expensive to administer in relation to the small student body size at Woolman and the even smaller number of students enrolled in the full IB curriculum. Too many staff resources were going into supporting too few students. The evaluators felt that putting more energy into the advanced placement program could provide most of the same academic advantages. Though IB did not continue, it yielded some positive benefits. Overall academic standards were raised, and the school continued to benefit from the quarter-time Academic Dean position that had been established for the IB program. Now that position could focus on assisting all the students' progress toward meeting graduation requirements and college admissions and administering the Advanced Placement program. Following the discontinuation of the IB program, in August 1986, Bill Moon resigned his position and became the director at the French-American School in Houston, Texas. Ted Menmuir stepped back into the position of principal that he had left in 1979.

The next year, there were low-tech and high-tech changes to note. The success of a fundraising campaign earlier in the year enabled the completion of new outdoor basketball and tennis courts. The courts were located south of the art barn, east of the orchard, in the lower end of the pasture. This low-tech addition to the campus pleased the students and was also a visible enhancement that prospective students and their parents would notice. The high-tech addition was a network of IBM Dash PC computers, donated and installed by a former graduate. This system gave the staff access to a wide range of programs, from word processing for English classes to accounts payable and data management for the office. It also offered the potential to eventually tap into research and library information from other sources that would otherwise have been out of reach for such a small school. One other significant change was that the school moved from a six-day to a five-day academic program. The two-day weekend was intended to provide more refreshment from the demands of academic work, although the total amount of class time would remain the same. This new schedule also made the academic program more attractive to day students. New student activities programs were created, and two new staff members were hired to run the program and to assist with evening supervision.

At the end of the 1986 school year, the CPFEA, after much internal board discussion, directed the staff to develop corrective measures to deal with the school's image problem. They asked the staff to consult with the board and the students to deal with the adverse impact of lack of cleanliness, inappropriate dress and nudity, and the students' insensitivity to the impact these issues were having on Woolman's spiritual life, image, and student recruitment efforts. An all-school meeting convened to discuss the topics of student dress, offensive language in public places, nudity, order in and around student cabins, excessive noise, public sexual expression, and a mechanism to maintain standards. At the meeting, they came to consensus on every point except nudity and created a set of reasonable guidelines to follow. A final version also included the explicit prohibition of drug paraphernalia and alcoholic beverage containers. Whether or not consensus was synonymous with total buy-in on the part of the students, at the direction of the CPFEA, the guidelines became codified in a new, more detailed and directive Student Handbook.

As always, in addition to discussions of policy and procedure, the real purpose of school—the academic regimen—continued throughout the year, enlivened at times by some of the less routine activities of the farm. That spring, the farm class raised and slaughtered a lamb that was served at supper for the whole school. And it not only provided food, but the hide was also tanned and used for moccasins, and the fleece was handspun into weaving wool. Spring Special Projects period also punctuated the regular routine. Groups of students were scattered across California and southern Oregon doing physical labor, and working with small children, the homeless, or senior citizens.

Once the school year ended, attention shifted to campus improvement. Painting, construction, repairs, projects for the summer work camps, and other volunteer work parties were all on the docket for the summer. Also during the summer, a big push was underway to fill the space for incoming students in the fall. The school encouraged parents, students, alumni, and other supporters to make use of new outreach resources, including a 16-minute video about programs at school and a new school brochure.

School opened in 1988 on a hot note. On Saturday, September 11, orientation day, ominous smoke welled up in the sky to the north, and by Sunday the entire school had been evacuated. As firefighters battled a nearby blaze, the home of board members Harry and Lois Bailey became the school headquarters, and the administration made the decision to send all the students home. For three anxious days, everyone who was left in town wondered whether the school would survive the largest wildfire of the year in California, dubbed the 49er Fire. Fortunately, no one was hurt and there was no damage to the school property. Everyone returned to campus on September 18 to start over again.

In early 1989, the WASC Visitation Committee report was published. In the previous cycle, WASC had granted a five-year accreditation to the school. The new report itemized the progress on the recommendations from the 1983 report. A few items from the report reflect the changing times. For example, in response to recommendations to improve the farm program, the school reported that there had been a significant decrease in the program's popularity, and consequently no improvements had been made to the farm infrastructure except maintenance of the existing facilities. Along with the near demise of the farm program, the Special Projects period had been reduced to one week. The days of the extended free-wheeling trips to Mexico, or floats down a river, had passed. Despite that, the week was much loved, and, through it, students took part in a wide variety of service projects.

The WASC report raised the continuing concern that the school often adjusted the curriculum to the strengths of the teaching staff, instead of establishing a curriculum and hiring the necessary staff to carry it out. Further, the report underlined the recent concern that the curriculum had been too frequently dictated by the University of California entrance requirements and the various interests of individual faculty members instead of reflecting a more systematic attention to the fundamental goals of the school. Fortunately, despite these critiques of the curriculum, alumni enrolled in colleges and universities informally reported that they felt adequately prepared for further study.

The report mentioned finances yet again, and also reported staff comments that included concerns about maintaining the facilities. They said "In the maintenance department, more money is needed in the school budget to attend to some pressing repairs and hire an occasional helper. The need for more money in the school budget is a well-recognized need, which the school is currently addressing in its planning for next year."

Ultimately, the report listed the same strengths that had been the hallmark of the school since the beginning: small school size and excellent student/teacher ratio, committed staff who care, a commitment to Quaker values, and a spacious and beautiful setting. The areas that needed improvement also were familiar: stabilizing enrollment (which in turn would help the financial situation); remodeling, maintenance, and expansion of the facilities; and expansion of the curricular and co-curricular offerings.

By the time the WASC report was issued, the enrollment numbers had declined from earlier highs of 60+ students. The school year began in 1989 with 48 students enrolled, down from 57 in 1986 and 71 in 1987.

In the fall of 1988, Ted Menmuir announced that he would be stepping down as principal at the end of the school year but staying to teach. After an extensive search, in April the CPFEA announced the appointment of Barbara Bradshaw as Principal, to begin July 1, 1989. Barbara was a Quaker and most recently had been a principal-level coordinator in St. Louis County, Missouri. Previously she was a faculty member at the Harris Stowe Teachers College in St. Louis. The announcement said she would arrive in California on April 1 to begin a three-month period as Principal Elect before she started her official role in July, and that her husband Vaughn would also be a part-time staff member.

At the beginning of the 1989-90 school year, Barbara Bradshaw found herself leading a school that was $400,000 in debt. This was a familiar but now dire situation, and in response, the board took some emergency steps so they wouldn't have to close the school. They decided, after much deliberation, to subdivide and sell 70 of the original 320 acres of property owned by the school. Seven ten-acre lots were sold, mostly in the area of Jones Bar Road. The acreage was not part of the central campus, and the change of ownership had little effect on school operations. The sale brought in enough money to retire the $400,000 debt and leave a reserve of about $100,000.

The property was first offered for sale in the Quaker community, and among those interested were Susan Hopkins and her husband. They were Quakers who lived in southern California but had been coming to the area to camp for many years. As soon as they learned about the property sale, they came up to visit and immediately put down a deposit on one of the parcels. By 1994, they were living in their newly built home on Woolman

Lane. They were not the only Quakers to move to the neighborhood, and as it turned out, some of these new neighbors had a special relationship to the school in the coming years.

During this time of trial and uncertainty, the school, along with the CPFEA, developed new goals for financial stability, and for social and educational renewal. In the past, they had optimistically budgeted and staffed for 60 students each year, but enrollment consistently fell short of that goal. As a result, tuition could not support the number of staff on the payroll. Therefore, the board decided to plan the budget based on a reduced student population of about 30, leaving open the possibility of increasing enrollment to as many as 60.

The board, the administration, and the alumni association had all recognized the ways the school's reputation had impeded its ability to attract the desired student population. Everyone was aware that some students who were academically and emotionally secure thrived on this freedom. Others with more scholastic and emotional challenges floundered without structure. Clearly, a change in the school's image was needed, and they decided that the school needed a more rigorous academic program, more stringent policies regarding the use of drugs and alcohol, and clear, enforceable rules regarding interaction between the sexes. To realize these goals, they put in place new rules and procedures, including making the campus nonsmoking for students and staff, having a positive lights-out at 11 PM, carrying out random bed-checks, restricting the times that students of the opposite sex were allowed in the cabins together, and encouraging students to spend their evening hours in the Stonehouse, which had been converted into a student center. Everyone hoped that these changes would have positive effects on the success of all students while moving the school's reputation in a more positive direction.

At the end of the decade, the essential beauty of the landscape remained unchanged and enchanting to many who visited, but on closer inspection, there were ever-growing signs of maintenance needs. Maintenance and repairs had been referred to in reports in the 1980s, and by now much upkeep had been deferred. Often the deferred work resulted in fixes that were more expensive than regularly scheduled maintenance, especially when breakdowns triggered emergency repairs. At this point, there we a total of 35 permanent buildings on campus, including two student-housing areas, the west cabin section made up of eight four-person cabins and a central bathhouse, and the east cabin area, made up of twelve two-person A-frame cabins and a central bathhouse. On-campus staff were housed in five residential-type homes, three apartments, one trailer, and one A-frame cabin. Fortunately, the active Buildings and Grounds Committee of the board, which included three staff members, worked constantly to prioritize maintenance needs. They had the usual long list of planned improvements, but finances always seemed to be the limiting factor. The 1989 WASC report generously remarked that "the campus has been developed in keeping with the Quaker commitment to the value of simplicity."

The 1989-90 school year had some contentious moments. Barbara had financial concerns to deal with, as well as whatever pressures the board exerted on her. A combination of her leadership style and board directives resulted in some staff dissatisfaction. One example of conflict that year involved some staff members who had gotten permission in the spring of 1987 from Bill Moon to move off campus. Before that time, the expectation was that staff, many of whom had families, would live on campus, especially because regular responsibilities included evening and night-time supervision. Those who were given permission to move off campus continued teaching, and were, by that time, well settled in their new living situations. When the board told them that they needed to move back to campus or lose their jobs, they all refused, and they were soon let go. CPFEA meeting notes from that year are not in the archives, and anyway, the decision to let staff members go during the school year would likely have been in confidential Personnel Committee notes not available to this history. However, without speculating on the possible motivations for the Board's actions, it's apparent that it was a difficult time for Barbara Bradshaw, who left Woolman soon after.

Student sawing

Student doing some heavy lifting

Driving a tractor on the John Woolman School farm, 1972

8

TRIALS AND TRIBULATIONS

W hen Barbara Bradshaw left, after leading the school for less than one year, Ted Menmuir stepped in again as principal. He had helped to shepherd the school through the financial crisis of the previous year. Using funds from the sale of the lots, the current operating budget was balanced, and some of the school debt was repaid. The school reached its enrollment target of 35 students by early August for Fall 1990. Educationally and socially, the school had searched deeply to renew its vitality through emphasis on personal integrity, social responsibility, and academic rigor. It had implemented new social guidelines and policies stressing these values, with the all-school Meeting for Worship regarded as central to the life of the school. The first school newsletter of the 1990-91 school year even had a new name. No longer *Outsider's Insider*; it was now Essay, Volume 1, No. 1.

A visitor to campus that winter who knew the school well remarked on the seemingly eternal beauty of the setting, but also said that she felt the rigor and commitment to Quaker education from the staff and students. There seemed to be appreciation for the solid academic program, the responsibilities of community life, and the school's support for rules and consequences. Whatever daily reports of the darker side of life and pervasiveness of social problems were circulating in the wider world, Ted felt optimistic about the positive atmosphere on campus. The students were committed to social justice and Quaker values. And proving the point, in April students once again went off to do a wide variety of special projects for a week, including helping to build a children's playground

in St. Helena, doing trail maintenance at Pt. Reyes and along the Rogue River with the Bureau of Land Management, aiding a program for single mothers in Mt. Shasta, helping the American Friends Service Committee in San Francisco, and working in the organic garden at the Green Gulch Zen Center in Marin County, CA. When this week of service was complete, students returned to campus to finish out the year, culminating with the twenty-seventh graduation ceremony on the first of June.

Woolman had never had a formally organized alumni association. In 1990, Michael Hartman and Lisa (Hubbell) Mackinney, alumni who were both on the CPFEA board, recognized that without an alumni association, an important voice was missing from the community that cared about the school. They put together the first mailing list and began publishing a newsletter, *Wombats in the Real World*, in 1991. It took some effort to get the fledgling organization on its feet. Members discussed the needs of the school, what was going well and what was problematic, and what kinds of support the alumni could give the school that would be most helpful and effective. Among the ongoing problems they recognized were the perpetual shortage of funds and the frequent turnover of staff.

The campus hosted the first Reunion/Business Meeting of the new John Woolman School Alumni Association on July 12, 1991. The campus was beautiful when they gathered, even though it was hot and dry, typical midsummer weather in Nevada County. Only 15 people showed up for the festivities and the meeting, but this group included members from the first-year class through the graduating class of 1986. Ted gave his principal's report on the state of the school, reiterating that the most pressing financial issue was planning for the future to prevent getting into the same situation that they had faced in 1989-90. He explained that there were two sources of income for the school: tuition and donations. Most desirable would be for tuition income to cover the cost of running the school; however, as with most nonprofit educational institutions, it was generally accepted that donations would be essential to make up a portion of the budget. Ted reminded the alumni that decisions about staffing had to be made before each school year started and enrollment was known. Therefore, each year the budget was based on the assumption of a full complement of students. The alumni listened attentively and, taking these comments into consideration, they began with optimism and enthusiasm to set their group's fundraising goals. In addition, they recognized the opportunity to help the school with recruitment of the 30 students sought for the coming school year. They intended to communicate the state of the school, keep alumni connected, and provide supportive voices out in the world to promote the school to prospective students. They also planned to serve an important role as mentors to newly graduating students, helping them find their way by networking and offering encouragement for their future activities.

When school started in 1991, Ted was the only faculty member staying on for the new year; otherwise there was a complete turnover of teaching staff. Though the staff was new, other aspects of life at Woolman proceeded as in the previous year, including continuing students, the expectations and routine of classes, meals, social activities, Community Meeting, and Meeting for Worship. The curriculum for the year continued to focus on creative problem-solving and independent thinking. The farm program had shrunk to a negligible size, though a popular gardening program remained.

That fall, as always, there were important maintenance projects. Woolman inherited its water system when the school bought the property in 1963. The system was based on a series of surface ditches left over from mining days. Relic ditches were still maintained in the Sierra foothills and provided most of the agricultural water for Nevada County, and this was the case on campus. The school had always filtered and chlorinated the water for domestic use, and tested regularly for bacteria, but it was almost impossible to filter out all the fine sediment. It was definitely time to improve the system. Workers dug and tested a new well, and installed a 10,000-gallon water tank. It took until the end of the year to complete the project.

The students were busy with academics, though not to the exclusion of all else. In 1991, the school continued its tradition of an Intersession after Fall-quarter classes and exams. During the week preceding Christmas vacation, guest instructors and regular staff led "hands-on" classes, such as ballroom dancing, cross-country skiing, sculpture, a wide variety of other art classes, bodywork/massage, creative writing, and sometimes field trips such as marine biology trips to the coast. As in past years, the 1991-92 class had a wide variety of options available. Later in the year, other nonacademic activities included a winter project that engaged a group of students and volunteers planting 500 pine trees on the campus. And in the spring, a group renewed the nature trail with new labels for native and non-native plants, physical repairs to the walkways, and the creation of a self-guided trail brochure.

Following the close of the school year, 16 alumni gathered on campus in July 1992, mostly a different group from the previous year. Before they began their serious work, they trekked to the Yuba River for a dip, a longstanding tradition for anyone visiting Woolman in the warmer months. During the weekend, they began planning a 30-year anniversary celebration for the following summer. When the anniversary gathering took place at end of July 1993, it included "feasting and dancing." The alumni group continued to discuss and define how its role as an organization could have a positive influence on the school, including through fundraising, raising awareness of the school, and helping recruit new students at events such as the Pacific Yearly Meeting. Also, Ted Menmuir announced his plan to step down as principal in the spring of 1994, and the alumni offered to help with the search process for a new principal. After the official meeting, several attendees stayed on to help during a weeklong work camp. They helped get cabins ready for the incoming class by painting, cleaning, and generally sprucing up the grounds. In the process, they had plenty of time to reminisce.

After 30 years of history as a school, not only the alumni but also the CPFEA and the school itself could look back with some perspective. The days of the wild '60s, along with the counterculture and the mantra of "never trust anyone over 30," were long gone. The graduates of those early years were well past 30 themselves, and many of them were parents of young children. Woolman had made many changes in the past 30 years but was still having some difficulty leaving behind its reputation as a "hippie boarding school" out in the woods run by a bunch of Quakers.

Woolman had been suggested to one student's family in 1989 by a Bay Area psychologist who held that impression of the school. There was no doubt that the school enrolled a fair share of misunderstood, rebellious teenagers who were struggling with their sexuality or identity. The remote setting lent a certain aura of mystique and suggestion of permissiveness, whether or not that was true in the same way it had been in the past. In the July 1994 *Friends Bulletin*, Vanita Blum reflected that the the school had been seasoned (the Quaker process of mulling over the facts before making a decision) by the '70s, '80s, and early '90s, but that students were still encouraged to find their own gifts and strengths. However, now there was a conscious effort to offer a "firm framework of responsibility to the [school] community."

The program at Woolman had always encouraged the use of Quaker process for decision-making. The work program as well as the academic classes offered a path for students to follow as they developed skills and learned to navigate their way toward adulthood. The degree of "Quakerliness" at the school had fluctuated throughout the years, but at this point, for the 1993-94 school year, six faculty members were Quaker, and leaders hoped this would provide a stronger Quaker emphasis and influence than in the recent past. A daily "Settling In" gathering was part of the regular schedule and, at the Staff Institute just before the 1993 winter holidays, the time of Settling In was changed to later in the morning so that day students could also be required to attend. Attendance was also mandatory at Meeting for Worship once a week. As recently as 1989-90, it had been referred to as "Silent Meeting," and attendance had not been compulsory. The school handbook described it as a central part of community life and, although it was called "worship," it was explained as neither prescriptive nor dogmatic, but instead meant as a time to allow community members to "authentically consider their own values, beliefs and attitudes within the experience of community living."

Issues addressed at the December 1993 Staff Institute reflected changing times in the wider world. The staff endorsed the idea of allowing students to have computer modem access installed in their cabins. The details still needed to be worked out, and they mandated that the modems be solely for data transmission, not for phone calling, that all costs associated with them be borne by their parents, that they could not be used after "lights out," and that misuse would result in disconnection. All of these rules would be in writing and agreed to by the parents and the students.

Elee Hadley took Ted Menmuir's place as principal in 1994 after an intensive search process. She had a strong Quaker background and considerable experience in educational administration, most recently working as a Staff Development Specialist in Douglas County, Oregon, after many years of teaching. She and her family relocated to Woolman from Eugene, Oregon, where she had been a member of the Eugene Monthly Meeting and active in the North Pacific Yearly Meeting. They moved into Cedar House, and her husband taught biology during their first year at Woolman. They were both avid gardeners and, after the first year, he took on responsibility for maintenance and the garden, happier not to be in the classroom.

Elee's tenure began with the dogged issue of financial instability. In 1994, the Alumni Association began a scholarship fund in an attempt to lift some of the burden of aiding needy students from the shoulders of the school budget. In typical school years at that time, the school was giving out about $100,000 of financial aid in the form of reduced tuition, and that generosity was a significant strain on the annual budget. If some of those funds could be raised from the community, and specifically from the alumni who, from their personal experience, were well aware of the value of the investment, the money could help move the school budget toward a more stable financial footing. At that point, the Alumni Association had matured, and six alumni served on the CPFEA board. This high level of alumni involvement, and positive energy on the board as a whole, meant that 1994 began with high hopes for financial solvency and solid academic achievements.

As it struggled with financial issues, the board also revisited the discussion of the fundamental values and goals of Woolman. At the end of his most recent stint as principal, Ted had noted that, when alumni returned to campus, they would often remark that nothing had changed, while at the same time, students complained that the school was changing too rapidly. Perhaps the truth was somewhere in between. Their comments referred to the physical surroundings and also to the aspirations and directions of the school. To help clarify Woolman's goals, he suggested turning to the school's mission statement; it had evolved over the years but still reflected the same basic values the school had when it was founded. The version in place in 1994 was as follows:

> "JWS is an educational community founded on Quaker values of truthfulness, simplicity, nonviolence, and listening to the spirit within. Our mission is to provide an environment in which inquiry and creativity flourish, physical work is honored, and academic skills develop fully. As students learn to respect people and nature, they are guided on to lives of service in the world."

Under the umbrella of this mission, the board directed Elee to use her professional educator's expertise along with her Quaker background to set goals that would bring renewed Quaker influence to the school. She changed the name of weekly Meeting for Worship to Meeting for Reflection, perhaps to be more inclusive to non-Quakers in the community while still preserving the spirit of the gathering. She emphasized that there were also other ways Quaker processes could be implemented. She maintained an open-door policy with the students, but she was hard-nosed about the rules when necessary, including expelling students or making it clear to families that the school was not the right place for a particular student. At the end of the first year, she reflected that the school had managed to stay within budget, and that financial procedures were being streamlined. When the board hired her, she learned that the school had been given a one-year probationary accreditation by the WASC, including feedback that needed to be addressed immediately. She had the background to respond to the WASC concerns, and with the help of the staff, the school succeeded in getting a full three-year accreditation the following year.

In 1995, the school year started with 49 students. Two things were especially noteworthy: Woolman was about to join the internet age, and the big infrastructure project of the year was converting the old tractor barn into a Student Center. Brian Fry, who had returned to campus as Admissions Director (he had previously worked at the school from 1979 to 1988 in a variety of roles), observed that the Alumni Association had pulled itself together into a strong organization. Several alumni were serving on the CPFEA board and working hard to move the school into the future with vision and some fundraising support. However, in spite of their efforts, in 1996 Elee Hadley more or less begged for money in the summer alumni newsletter. As often happened, there was a summer cashflow shortage exacerbated by an unusually large number of tuition reductions. Full tuition with room and board was $16,000 for the school year. The practice of granting tuition reduction to many students continued to play havoc with the annual budget. The school still had not succeeded in building a separate fund for scholarships, and continued to simply collect less tuition money from families who needed assistance. On a positive financial note, $80,000 of long-term debts had been paid back, and at that point there was no longer a mortgage on the property. Meanwhile, classes continued. As usual, students went into the community to do service work during the spring Special Projects period. They participated in various activities, including an Alternatives to Violence project workshop involving some students, staff, and community members.

When the 1996-97 school year came to a close, the traditional summer work camp took place on campus. The A-frame cabins, originally built in 1964-65, got a major overhaul. A formidable group did the work, including former principals Ted Menmuir and Harry Blickenstaff, Harry Bailey, and volunteers from the county jail work-release program, summer work campers, and others who assisted with bits and pieces. They replaced old louvered windows; insulated the cabins; repaired broken hearths, floors, subfloors, doors, and porches; and installed new desks, beds, dressers, and bookshelves. It was a major endeavor and wasn't finished when school started. Students in the Construction Class worked on painting and installing the furniture units in some of the cabins in the fall to complete the job.

One other new space was almost completed: a Student Center that had been in the works for a few years. It started out as a tall shed-roof that remained from the days when the Owner-Builder Center leased the campus during the summers. It was near the climbing kiln (for more about the kiln, refer to Chapter 22 - Crafting Clay in About the Memoirs: Wombats in the Real World, the Second Section of this book) between the library (formerly the art barn) and the pottery building (Quonset hut). A concrete floor was laid, and eventually windows and doors were framed in with volunteer labor from students and board members. A little more work still needed to be done when school started, mainly painting. With couches gathered from around campus, a brand new ping-pong table, tapestries on the walls, throw rugs, teapots, and other touches added by students, the center was a comfortable spot for gathering. Yet another space, the Academic Building, still needed refurbishment. A call went out for contributions to install a new heating system in the 33-year-old building, which was originally the dormitory and then repurposed as lab and classroom space, and which still sported a single-zone ancient propane heating system. The project was labeled the "Ted Menmuir Heater Project," with a fundraising goal of $9,000 to cover the cost. Ted suggested the project when the school asked him how they could honor him for the upcoming anniversary of his 30 years of service at the school. He knew the campus inside and out and knew very well the needs of the school, so this project was an apt tribute.

New staff members in 1998 included alumni from the 1980s who returned after college and graduate school to teach. Among the new staff were a few with Quaker backgrounds. The year also saw some additional long-awaited improvements to the campus. Restoration began on the Stone House with a professional re-roofing job. The building consisted of three almost circular pods built around a central room that had originally been conceived of as an all-school meeting area. It turned out to be impractical for that purpose because the central stone fireplace did not draw smoke well and blocked people's view of one another in meetings. The fireplace had become a passthrough and storage area. For a long time, the building served as a staff residence, overflow student housing, guest rooms, or classroom space. During the previous year, a huge improvement project involved cleaning up the center room, replacing old flooring, and installing new carpeting in the living room and kitchen areas. The newly painted walls made it possible to turn the space into a bright art gallery. The massive unused fireplace was filled with water and became a koi pond, and the room itself was transformed into a quiet meditation spot open for students, staff, and visitors' use.

After the 1998 school year began, Principal Elee Hadley wrote a column for the fall newsletter that focused mainly on the financial pressures on the school. Echoing her message in the previous June's alumni newsletter, she suggested strategies, leading with the need to become less dependent on tuition income as a key to attaining financial stability. Again and again, this issue had been identified as crucial to stabilizing the financial situation. Now, the CPFEA set aside a sum of $30,000, with a goal of $100,000 by 2005, to serve as an "endowment" to provide student scholarships. This was a start in the right direction. In the meantime, the money that had been raised by selling off the subdivided lots had reduced the school's debt, and designated contributions had partially paid for the recent improvements to buildings and grounds. Ever frugal, volunteers had done a tremendous amount of the work, but there were always administrative costs, including all the normal office expenses, staff medical and retirement benefits, and loan interest. More than 60% of students received financial aid in the form of reduced tuition in 1997, bringing that cost to 28% of the budget. Elee pointed out that Woolman was not frugal with financial aid, a figure that was typically 10-20% at other independent schools across the nation. They were generous because it was so important to the mission to assure a diverse learning community with students from various nationalities, races, religions, and economic backgrounds. Doing so was possible only through generous financial aid. This same need had required tremendous generosity from school backers since the beginning. After 35 years, the number of supporters had grown but so had the expenses, including increased debt. The supporters included some of the hundreds of former students and staff and their communities, plus dedicated Quakers who felt strongly about founding a Quaker school on the West Coast. They continued to provide support in so many forms, giving money and volunteering time, labor, and guidance throughout the years. But it was never enough; there was always a shortfall. Contributing to the financial problem, enrollment was unusually low, further decreasing income from tuition.

Elee's assessment was true and timely. The late 1990s became what might be described as a crisis time for Woolman, not just financial, but existential. For more than thirty years, the school was supported by monetary donations, but also by the dedication of so many. The staff, who often worked for low wages, were mostly all earnest, committed individuals who loved the students, loved the place, and believed in Quaker values. Many people went to board meetings and retreats, and showed up for volunteer work year after year, doing hard physical labor to build and improve the facilities. It all added up to the whole that was the school: a school that had been educating students for three and half decades. There were so many students with so many memories, and they had Woolman to thank for what they knew and who they were as they moved on.

However, there were also students for whom the academic environment and/or the living situation was not ideal. In the best scenario, a school has the resources to respond to all students' developmental needs. Ideal boarding schools create a supportive learning environment and coordinate its practices across the classrooms, the living community, and the students' families and communities, to enhance all students' social, emotional, and academic learning. To accomplish this kind of intensive support, students with learning problems, behavior problems, or substance misuse issues benefit from access to a multidisciplinary team of well-trained counselors, teachers, and mentors and a very low student/teacher ratio. Woolman never intended to be a school for at-risk teens but, driven by the need to meet enrollment targets, it accepted some students in that category. It had the best of intentions to deal with student problems but lacked the financial resources to provide the professional counseling and intensive communication systems necessary to offer such support. There were students at Woolman who were well-adjusted and thrived in an atmosphere of intellectual inquiry and Quaker values. The subset of students who were struggling for a variety of reasons seemed to be having a disproportionate influence on the reputation of the school—mainly relating to student misuse of drugs and alcohol. By 1996-97, the school's Community Handbook contained pages of rules addressing behavior and describing the disciplinary consequences. Under the category "Alcohol and other illegal drug use," the handbook stated:

> "Students are not permitted to possess, use, be under the influence of, sell, or otherwise distribute, produce or cultivate any illegal substances (alcohol, marijuana, LSD, methamphetamines, or other substances), while under the supervision of the school. A student is under the supervision of the school, both on campus and on field trips, and while away from campus when school is in session, except when under the supervision of his or her parents. Students sometimes have an idea that staff say that alcohol and drugs are not permitted, but they don't mean it. Some students believe that if they are good students and can maintain using drugs it's OK. IT IS NOT. The school takes a strong position against illegal drug use."

The endlessly supportive CPFEA board, which always had shouldered the brunt of the financial pressures and now had more alumni participating, struggled to understand the current problems and the intractable issue of the school's reputation. One of the board members, an alumus himself, took a trip to Southern California and visited Quaker meetings there to see what they knew and thought about Woolman, to better understand what might be impeding the school's ability to recruit a more robust student body. He reported to the board that the school was not perceived as a strong learning institution. He was told that it had a reputation for serious behavioral issues, and a lack of discipline and academic rigor. He felt, and he was not alone, that these issues made recruiting quality students and families with financial resources very challenging, since they had other choices for their children's education.

This was not new information, but it was discouraging, especially in light of sincere and constant improvement efforts.

The negative factors that threatened to bring this situation to a head were as complicated as the positive actions that had created and sustained the school for so many years. Inadequate financial resources were certainly one of the root causes contributing to the school's now being in a very vulnerable position. For many years, the positive results outweighed the downward pull of the financial issues. It could be argued that the precarious financial position had its roots in the 1960s, from the days when Mary Jorgensen uttered the often remembered statement, "We couldn't afford to open the school, and we couldn't afford not to." Perhaps this was the future challenge she envisioned as a result of the pressure to open for business in September 1963, and the consequent necessity to play catch-up financially. From the very beginning, the fundamental Quaker values required a form of generosity that challenged the economic foundation of the operation.

The commitment to give reduced tuition to families who needed it fit the values of the school. However, as a board member from the 1990s pointed out, in the 1960s and '70s the shortfall was smaller and more manageable, but as inflation and interest rates increased, government support for student loans was reduced, and Woolman's debt grew, the magnitude of the shortfall became life-threatening. The sale of some of the property was meant to solve the problem, but the plan for how those funds would be used, or perhaps simply the insufficiency of the amount, wasn't enough to address the accumulated seriousness of the situation. There had also been less of a pressing need for sophisticated financial management at the beginning. Compounding the historical issues, less rigorous enforcement of the admission standards in the interest of keeping enrollment up was damaging the school's reputation and feeding the downward spiral.

During the 1997-98 school year, in view of the ongoing economic pressures on the school, questions of reputation, the high cost of a private boarding-school education, and all the topics that had resurfaced repeatedly during the years, the CPFEA gathered together to visualize the school's future . With a new century coming, there was talk of a new or renewed direction for the school. On Valentine's Day weekend in 1998, 27 students, staff, past and present board members, alumni, and interested parties met for a weekend retreat at the home of board member Susan Hopkins, just up the hill from the campus. Some board member felt that outside guidance would be helpful, and the group invited Martha Bryans from the Friends Council on Education and Clerk of the Philadelphia Yearly meeting to facilitate.

Discussion during the weekend focused on the idea of putting Quakerism, spirituality, environmental concerns, and social activism at the forefront of Woolman's education program, and to that end, possibly beginning each school year with a workshop on these topics. Further, a clear consensus emerged that the academic program at Woolman should be focused on preparing students to attend a four-year college. The group recognized that planning had often been sidetracked by concerns about the school's financial stability, and sometimes by recriminations over problems of the past. Recently, board members who had gone to Friends Council workshops had heard over and over that a Quaker school is not a Quaker meeting; it must have an administrative hierarchy and can't survive if it isn't run like a business. The concept of meeting, discussing, and waiting for "a way to open" might not be the most effective approach for a business. Out of the meeting came specific recommendations for a focus on personal spiritual growth guided by Quaker tradition; the environment and global systems; and on activism and service. The retreat produced a vision for new directions, but not solutions to the financial problems. From the newsletter:

> "…some of the ideas that came forward were a whole school workshop on Quakerism and Quaker practice at the beginning of each school year, a summer program with an environmental focus, a meeting House on campus, creating more family oriented housing for freshman and other students that might be assisted by it, create more possibilities for seniors to be involved in community activities off campus, more student involvement in local community radio broadcasts, involving the junior class in topic selection for activist focus in the coming year, and many more."

The results of the gathering were to be presented to the Board at the next meeting for consideration. The board was poised to assemble the next phase of long-range planning, and these ideas would be incorporated.

On Saturday, September 12, 1998, Woolman celebrated its 35th anniversary. Returning students, new students, alumni, current and former staff, and many longtime friends of the school gathered to celebrate and reminisce. It kicked off a year of anniversaries that punctuated the regular curricular and co-curricular activities. The Spring Projects week in April was the 25th in the history of the school. Some students ventured all the way to Utah in a "van with no radio!" to the country's largest animal sanctuary, Best Friends, for a rigorous week of service. Some returned to project sites in Mexico. A few stayed close to home and worked at a shelter in Oroville, while others volunteered at the Ben Lomond Quaker Center. And as a indicator of a successful academic year, by the time the school year came to a close, the nine graduating seniors had all been admitted to four-year colleges and universities, and all but two, who were postponing attendance for a year, were college bound.

The school declared April 29, 1999 "Ted Day," honoring Ted Menmuir's 30 years of dedicated work at Woolman. He had served as principal (three times), dean, fundraiser, admissions director, teacher, and head of maintenance, and he was teaching again—algebra, geometry, drawing, and pottery. He helped build the hillside kiln in 1972, hired and fired staff, worked with many boards, been revered by students, expelled students, and celebrated years of graduations. The completion of the "Ted Menmuir Heater Project" had been delayed due to budget constraints, but the Palo Alto Friends Meeting was spearheading efforts to raise the $9,000 to finish it. The alumni association continued working hard at fundraising activities. In spite of a smaller than normal attendance at the summer gathering of alumni on campus that year, it kept the momentum going on the project to develop a communication infrastructure for the organization. One element of that was the newly announced website at www.jwsaa.org.

Once again, in 1999, summer work camps gave a great gift to the school. It was the 20th summer of the camps. Most had been organized and attended by Mary and Russ Jorgensen. It was hard to turn around on campus without seeing a feature created, enhanced, or repaired by the Woolman workcamps. Mary noted in the newsletter that the formal camps had been going for 20 years, but that was just the formalized version of a tradition that had built the school from the ground up. An Arbor House wall was replaced and the whole building painted, the academic building stairs and ramps were rebuilt, the interior of the west cabins' bathhouse was painted, a new tile floor was laid in the office bathroom, cabins were oiled, hearths were rebuilt in the A-frames, the pasture fence was repaired and painted, bridges were oiled, paths were cleared to Mel's Pond, and much care was given to the garden. This work was essential to the upkeep of the campus and always had been.

When school started, Elee Hadley, principal since the beginning of the 1994 school year, announced her future departure. She and her husband Neal would be leaving at the end of the 1999-2000 school year to move back to Oregon. In anticipation of her departure, a search was underway for a new head of school. Along with her day-to-day running of the school, Elee continued to devote her energy to many diverse activities, including creating new meeting spaces, designing and building benches, working with staff to develop curriculum, and starting an endowment fund.

Perhaps the most intensive and continuous project at Woolman, other than physical maintenance projects, was articulating the mission and vision of the school in the form of strategic planning. The goals in the current version of the long-range plan were: to achieve a firm school identity through changes; to assure the school's financial stability; to further develop expectations for students in academic and personal growth; to implement a curriculum that supports students, recognizing increasing maturity as they progress through the years at Woolman; to improve staff commitment and professional development; to implement a six-year rotation for the maintenance, improvement, and beautification of the campus and facilities; and to cultivate the alumni as essential members of the learning community. The goals included a wide range of issues, but "the devil is in the details." The next steps would be under the direction of the new principal, with the guidance of the board.

The board held a retreat in early July 2000 to continue discussions about planning for the future. To frame the discussion, board member Harold Blickenstaff gave a brief and selective history of the school. Hardly anyone was in a better position to tell this story. Harold had had many important roles at Woolman since the earliest days, including succeeding the first principal in the 1960s and remaining actively involved for years after that. He reminded the group that Woolman had been reassessing goals for a long time. The original planning envisioned 160 students, a goal that was quickly scaled back by necessity. Harold said that among the issues with which the school had contended since the beginning was the lack of a well-defined decision-making process, particularly "boundaries between what is decided and by whom." To illustrate this, he told a personal anecdote. When he was principal, he decided that the location of the duck pond should be changed, and on his own initiative, without consulting anyone, he bulldozed a new pond. His action inspired the board to create a committee to oversee such matters and gave rise to a Woolman expression, "Giving the principal the keys to the bulldozer." He revisited many of the issues that had been debated over and over for the past 35+ years—for example: is Woolman really a "Friends school?" This was a question that first arose in conjunction with the issue of drug use in the 1960s. At that time, some Friends perceived that drugs were particularly a problem at Woolman, not realizing that the problem was faced by American society in general. This view caused a division in the Quaker community and among those whom the school looked to for support. In fact, Quaker kids had no more nor fewer drug problems than their non-Quaker peers. Woolman's drug-use issues were not caused by a failure to be a Friends school. Harold touched on the topic of discipline, noting that many systems had been tried over the years, but none had succeeded in eliminating student misbehavior—and again, this is a common problem among adolescents, in no way unique to Woolman. He reminded the group that some of the reputation of the school grew out of the early years, when there was no dress code at Woolman and the community reacted negatively when students looked very different from public-school kids. He also addressed programmatic history, noting that the farm program had been a strong and important component of the school, but was now discontinued, mainly through lack of student interest, and yet the longstanding Special Projects program, which was closely tied to the school's Quaker values, remained strong and effective. He also recounted some of the historical aspects of the finances, reminding his listeners of the days when the school benefited from government-surplus food and equipment, and the labor of conscientious objectors.

Mary Jorgensen spoke next, another voice from the earliest days who had worked tirelessly raising funds and was still doing so. She talked about the importance of a dedicated fundraising position at the school. She understood better than anyone that fundraising is a long-term relationship-building process, and there are consequent difficulties when a new person is brought in and expected to be successful overnight. On a positive note, Russ Jorgensen felt that there was still much goodwill out in the community on which to capitalize.

Mary Jorgensen also introduced the subject of living in community. She spoke in a general way about the concept, and then more specifically about the John Woolman school as an intentional community, an environment with a uniqueness that can sometimes come as a shock to new students and staff. The social milieu was accepting, and generally did not demanded a high degree of conformity. While nonconformity had always seemed integral to the school culture, its downside was often a negative judgment by the outside world about the eccentricities that the school community took in stride. The intimacy of the school community also was sometimes a source of instability when individuals refused to conform at all. In that close-knit environment, it was essential to have a trusted, equitable, but explicit system of accountability to which everyone on campus adhered.

The board used these thoughts to prompt further discussion about how to move into the future. They distilled all of the conversations at the meeting down to the question, "what must we do to manifest our vision and mission so Woolman thrives?" After identifying the central question, they itemized specific goals and tasks. They emphasized keeping values in the forefront of their actions, including honesty, accountability, integrity, and "right action." Then they moved on to articulating the on-the-ground work, like updating the long-range plan (including a finance plan), strengthening school programs, nurturing and supporting the staff, and widening outreach efforts to bring the gifts of Woolman to others and bring others into Woolman. Even in the minutes of this meeting, where they acknowledged the complications that result from long deliberation over issues, some cautioned against moving too fast, while others suggested that Amy Cooke, who was at the meeting in advance of taking the helm as principal in the fall, "would do well to keep her eye on the clock and the calendar being mindful of what decisions are needed by what date or time." Finally they noted their intention to improve relations with Friends. Their final words: "All board and staff members will take up this matter." These were not new topics, but this was the group that would carry the problems, and hopefully their solutions, into the new century.

The end of the decade also found Woolman renewing a focus on the environment as it considered a forest management plan for the campus. The 230-acre property consisted of about 50 acres, developed with buildings, the central campus area, and irrigated pastures. The rest was divided between forest, meadow, and chaparral zones, interspersed with a few riparian areas. In the Forest Management Plan (FMP) that had been prepared in 1982 by Marshall Palley (a professional forester and early founder of the school), he suggested harvesting a carefully chosen area for timber sale to raise money for the school. When this idea was brought up, it was met with resistance in spite of the sound scientific arguments for some careful timber harvest. The purpose of the harvest plan was to address issues of fire safety, controlling overgrowth of the understory trees and shrubs, and liability for fire spreading to (or from) neighboring properties. Marshall's original plan recommended review and update in 10 years. After extended discussion, the board agreed to update the FMP and to identify and clearly state objectives, including preserving the natural ambience, reducing the fire hazard and potential liability, facilitating firewood collection for the student cabins, and seeking to be good stewards of the land. A further goal was to maximize the educational potential for this project not only for the students but for the wider community, with the intention to provide a model for responsible land and resource management.

Amy Cooke assumed the role of Principal at Woolman for the 2000-01 school year. She came to Woolman from Visalia, California, where she had founded and run the Venice Hill School. She moved onto campus with her husband Chamba and daughter Nora and officially began working in the summer before the start of school. Amy had visited Woolman several times since she accepted the position in January 2000, working with Elee Hadley to ensure a smooth transition. As a result of her previous visits, she was familiar with conditions on campus. However, she brought a fresh eye that saw the shabbiness of the facilities. Although so much effort as was expended doing maintenance and building projects, there was always more repair and renewal to be done. The couch in the office was falling apart, held upright with a piece of plywood nailed to its side, the cushions spewing their stuffing under a fabric shroud. The original tables in the dining hall, installed in 1963, were losing their metal trim, the dining hall linoleum was so worn that water seeped under the tiles when the floor was mopped, and many corners of the grounds had old odds and ends piled up in them. The physical condition of the facilities could not be disguised or ignored when parents and prospective students came to visit.

In addition, there were ongoing concerns about the school. Factors like the housing arrangements, challenges of supervising teens in such a facility, student drug and alcohol misuse, and the impact of returning students who were accustomed to a relatively permissive environment—all these made it very difficult to change the reputation and culture of the school. Discontent simmered among the staff who had to enforce the penalties for rules infractions, a situation that contributed to an adversarial attitude between students and staff. Amy, who was made aware of the issues, took the first year of her tenure as a time to assess the situation before making any big changes. Dorothy Henderson joined the staff that fall, and she and her husband Doug Hamm, both Quakers, moved into the back of the Ranch House where the cook lived. Dorothy had been teaching nursing, and was hired as the Health Coordinator, and Doug took on the role of Garden and Orchard Supervisor. Amy and Dorothy were new to the community, so Susan Hopkins, the CPFEA Clerk, worked closely with them and provided much support.

At this point, it seemed that the daunting challenges were multiplying. Yet many people were committed to the vision for Woolman's future and to finding a way to create and sustain a quality living and learning environment. At the same time, a cacophony was coming from factions of the Quaker community who were especially concerned about the state of the school. That fall, the CPFEA once again formed a Long Range Planning Committee (LRPC). The committee was charged with the task of bringing the school's mission more powerfully into the next decade and creating a new strategic action plan. The committee began by reviewing the visioning and planning documents of the past, including the 1984 Long Range Plan, the 1998 Valentine's Day Retreat reports, the 1999 WASC Action Plan, and the report of the board meeting the previous summer. The LRPC intended to complete a unified strategic plan by July of 2001.

The April 2001 newsletter, which had changed its name back to the *Outsider's Insider*, went out to the whole community, and included a series of soul-searching articles from past and present administrators of programs, including Susan Hopkins, the current Clerk of the CPFEA; Brian Fry, Admissions Director; and Sheila Harrington, Dean. An article written by Mary Jorgensen entitled "Why a John Woolman School? An Early History & a Bridge to the Past" recollected the ambitious dreams of the founders:

> "We wanted an alternative to all the war propaganda being pushed in our public schools.
>
> We wanted our children to realize that more than their parents have passive pacifist beliefs.
>
> We wanted classes structured so that the students could go as fast as they wanted to go in any subject regardless of what year student they were.

We wanted a rural school where there could be gardening and domestic animals. Students can learn much from taking care of plants and animals. Some can find companionship, and give and receive affection, which they aren't finding elsewhere!

We wanted a school where they (students) serve themselves and each other, and that housekeeping, eating and groundskeeping were desirable and maturing responsibilities. Also, the school would be more affordable.

We wanted the arts to play an important part of the program: pottery, drawing, weaving, music, etc.

We hoped to develop service opportunities, off-campus that would also expose them to societal problems. We wanted to be interracial and international in staff and student body."

The action goals in the 1999 WASC Accreditation Plan outlined the current challenges, many of which had already been discussed by the board. The first goal, "to achieve a firm school identity through changes," indicated that the school identity was currently on somewhat shaky ground. The second, "to assure the school's financial stability," was a familiar one, echoing years of economic challenges —and the situation had not improved. "To further develop our expectations for students in academic and personal growth" and "to implement a curriculum which supports students recognizing increasing maturity as they progress through years at Woolman" seem appropriate for any school, but also suggest a ongoing situation in which curriculum was adjusted to the interests and needs of students and the talents of teachers, rather than being set in advance and followed consistently by everyone. The last goal, "to improve staff contentment and professional development, and to implement a six-year rotation for maintenance improvement, and beautification of the campus and facilities," reflected staff discontent and the much-deferred maintenance, which by anyone's reckoning was a big problem. When school started, the board was gripped by these issues. In addition, there was the distressingly pervasive question of drug and alcohol misuse. Monitoring and regulating student behavior was rightfully the responsibility of the staff, but the CPFEA could not help being aware of public and Quaker community opinion on the matter. As a result, they worried about the situation even if they were not directly involved.

While the board and administration wrestled with these problems, the students got on with school. In December, the school applied for a grant and received a donation of computer networking equipment from Hewlett-Packard. Using the new equipment, the computer network could be expanded from the office to the library and academic buildings eventually.. The traditional intersession week, now moved to March, offered a variety of classes allowing students, faculty, and guest teachers a chance to share their hobbies and avocations. The spring Special Projects were as varied as usual, sending students all over the West to do a week of service before the seniors graduated at the beginning of June. Following graduation, there were two sessions of Summer Workcamp, now a 22-year-old tradition.

When Amy took over in 2000, she intentionally spent the year observing the state of the school and not making any dramatic policy changes. Based on her experiences the first year, she and trusted colleagues worked together over the summer of 2001 on changes for the new school year, including replacing some staff. They also made revisions to the student handbook. They removed penalties for undesirable behavior and replaced them with a system of community agreements and commitments that were voluntary and included behavioral expectations around sex, drugs, and alcohol. They established a Ministry and Oversight committee of students and staff, with the goal of governance structured as closely as possible around Quaker principles. To set the stage for the new approach, at the end of the summer, they contacted every family by phone to get a commitment in the form of a signed contract from students and parents to respect and follow all the school rules—including a zero-tolerance policy for drug use.

A core group of students arrived committed to getting a good education, and to studying and learning, but some students returned not so committed. In spite of the pledges, during long discussions at Community Meeting, these students stood up and voiced their opposition to the policies, claiming that the behavior the school wanted to eliminate was just part of the culture of the school. It seemed that these students didn't believe that the zero-tolerance policy for drugs would or should be taken seriously. A few students left when they heard the attitudes of the students rebelling against the school policies. By early October, only about 16 students remained, posing a critical financial problem; losing any more tuition revenue was going to devastate the budget.

The board was trying valiantly to rescue Woolman's reputation by creating a long-range plan for a stellar school, one in which all the problems Woolman faced were solved. While all the important issues were on the table, the root of the problem was the financial situation. Without adequate revenue, there could be no realistic solutions to any of the challenges.

It was a moment of true crisis. Woolman's leaders had to make a quick decision about how to avoid further damage to the organization. In preparation for an emergency board meeting, the Finance committee met and concluded that, financially, there was no viable way to go on operating as a boarding school. When the full board met and heard their report, with heavy hearts they elected to close the school the following Saturday, six weeks into the school year. Over the next few days, while all the students were away on a camping trip, the school notified parents of the decision to close and asked them to come and pick up their children. More than a month into the school year, parents faced a scramble to find new schools.

Closing John Woolman School was a devastating, yet probably inevitable event. But the closure still came as a shock to many people connected with the school—families, faculty and staff, long-time supporters. No one was happy. Unfortunately, the problems that Woolman faced had been somewhat siloed. None of the problems that led to the closure were secrets. However, as with many institutional crises of long gestation, it never seemed to make sense to detail the most serious problems to the Quaker community, donors, volunteers, alumni, parents, and the local community. First, to do so would have shaken faith in the institution and eroded support. Second, there had always been great belief, hope, and effort toward turning the situation around. Unfortunately, because leaders had mostly shared optimism with supporters, the closing of the school came as a shock as well as a disappointment. For some, there was a profound sense of loss, and others felt their trust had been betrayed. Many Quakers from the Quarterly Meeting and locally who had given money and time to the school were distraught about the decision. The same was true for alumni and former staff members who had worked so hard in spite of the challenges. Very few people could see the whole picture.

In the fall of 2002, Don and Harriette Smith visited the campus, after the closure of the school and before any new programming began. It was a rare opportunity for one of the mostly deeply involved founders of Woolman to weigh in on the present situation. Don attended the morning Meeting for Worship of Grass Valley Friends in the Library and afterward spoke to Susan Hopkins, Clerk of the CPFEA. Don had stayed involved with Woolman as a founder, teacher, administrator, and volunteer over a period of forty years. During his visit, he acknowledged the extraordinary and ordinary roles that the school had played in the lives of so many people, but he also expressed his firm belief that "...we are now in different times. Families cannot afford several years of private school in addition to college expenses. The needs of students are different as well. We have to change and grow in order to meet the current needs and challenges." Susan noted the great wisdom and long experience that Don's view brought to the CPFEA's discussion of the future as the committee worked on finding a way to carry on in a new form. Don's view of change was not shared by everyone. Amy Cooke pointed out that with change, especially the change of old ways, comes grief, uncertainty, and sense of loss, and for some even anger. And that was certainly true for many who had been associated with the school over the years.

| ENVIRONMENTAL PROTECTION |

9

....

WE'RE LIVING LIFE IN LIGHT
AT THE END OF THE ROAD

It was clear that the doors of the John Woolman School were permanently closed. But the Quaker-inspired vision and mission of the past 40 years were still alive in the minds and the hearts of many people, and the facilities were still there. Where should they and could they go from here? The CPFEA immediately began an 18-month period of discernment to try to answer these questions. In the context of Quakerism, discernment is a process of seeking "a sense of the Meeting." It involves no voting, but rather is used to try to reach unity about the wisest course of action by remaining open to new ideas while listening respectfully to the experience and knowledge of others.

The CPFEA formed a steering committee, which reached out to a wide community to help with the process. In 2002, the steering committee renamed the campus the Sierra Friends Center (SFC). The name change reflected a synthesis of ideas from several sources: the discussion among 75 people who attended a gathering on December 8, 2001, the mailed-in responses to a survey sent to John Woolman School supporters, and other interested parties (including contributors to the annual fundraising campaigns, and more than 350 people who responded to an online survey).

Other ideas were generated in addition to the name change. The board developed three program concepts to help guide future planning: Pathways to Sustainability, Pathways to Wisdom, and Pathways to Learning. Pathways to Sustainability focused on incorporating sustainable economic, ethical, and ecological practices as a guide to

energy use, food production, land and resource management, and community living in an onsite learning community. Pathways to Wisdom would sponsor multi-generational programs at SFC, including sojourns, retreats, courses, workshops, and/or mentoring opportunities. Pathways to Learning envisioned a program for juniors and seniors in high school emphasizing service learning in the context of friends, values, environmental principles, and global awareness. They established two educational programs for the learning path, a summer camp, and the Woolman Semester.

The planners modeled the summer camp on the Quaker summer programs of the Baltimore Yearly Meeting, which for many years had focused on wilderness camping and hiking "as a means of community building and development of personal strength and skills, helping young people build self-confidence, and the life of the Spirit." For the Woolman Semester, they planned a single-semester program for high school juniors and seniors. As with a semester abroad, students would earn a semester of high-school credit that would transfer to their home schools. Some people resisted the idea of continuing the school in any way, but over time, and with the input of new people and ideas, the new venture went ahead. The fundamental purpose of the program was in-depth study of political and social issues, intended to give students a strong foundation from which to build a lifetime of service in the areas of peace, justice, and sustainability. The program was not entirely unique; other, similar concept programs were being launched across the country around the same time.

The campus had a new name, the program was new, and the newsletter got a new name too, *The Woolman Witness*. The first set of newsletters (1962) was simply entitled Newsletter and was initially directed at the many constituencies of supporters of a Quaker school. Even after Woolman opened, it served as a general outlet for news about the school. In 1966, it was renamed *Outsider's Insider*, making it clear that it was aimed at parents, donors, alumni, and other friends of the school, and was intended to help them feel connected with the current life of the campus. Brian Fry wrote in a brief history of the newsletter that in the late 1970s, the possessive "s" in "Outsider's" was dropped when Ted Menmuir produced a new banner that graphically implied the blurring of separation between insiders and outsiders. In the early 1990s, the name was changed to *The Essay*. Don Smith, who had been one of the authors of the first newsletters in the 1960s, was the volunteer editor of *The Essay*. In the mid-1990s, nostalgia prevailed, and when Brian Fry returned to the staff and took over producing the newsletter, the name changed back to *Outsider Insider*. And for one issue only, the newsletter had yet another new name, *The Woolman Times*, the one and only time (Brian believes) that the newsletter was almost entirely written and produced by students rather than staff, in an issue filled with student stories, poems, and artwork.

In fall 2003, despite significant promotional efforts, only four students enrolled for the inaugural semester, much to everyone's disappointment. Optimistically, the board delayed the opening to January, hoping for a larger group, but no rush of enrollees materialized. A tremendous amount of work had gone into preparing for the opening, so they decided to go ahead and open in January with just a handful of students. On January 23, 2004, the Woolman Semester program launched with a commitment to the same ideal as the 1962 Summer Program that preceded the opening of John Woolman School 40 years before, "Service in a World of Need." Three main classes made up the students' schedule: Global Issues included social studies, Peace Studies satisfied English credit, and for the Environmental Science class, the neighboring Yuba River watershed provided a setting for fieldwork as students researched environmental issues. The curriculum also included Nonviolent Communication (NVC), a technique for conflict resolution and a tool for social change, and Garden, working on the land. Students had an active role in caring for the school's animals and garden, helped prepare food, and, as always at Woolman, chopped wood for heating their cabins. This opportunity for analysis, examination, and real-world application stood as the hallmark of the experience of the Woolman Semester. The program attracted students who had a desire to create change in the world, whether their particular focus was peace and justice issues, environmental sustainability, or other related interests. Some of the students were recruited from the Quaker community by Admissions Director Kathy Runyon, who routinely went to Quaker meetings, including the Yearly Meeting, to rally support. Much of the study and discussion during the semester involved exploring creative solutions to effect change in the students' communities. Despite low pay, good teachers came to work with smart, motivated juniors and seniors who were activists and intended to go to college. The U.S., and particularly California, was still recovering from the 2001 economic downturn, so jobs were somewhat scarce, and this helped the staff recruitment process.

Initially, Amy Cooke was both the Head of School and Director of SFC. In addition to the Woolman Semester, the Center offered summer camps for children, the traditional summer work camps for families and individuals, and a schedule of workshops offered in partnership with other organizations. Of course, the never-ending needs of the physical plant required continued planning, elbow grease, and above all, funding. The low enrollment numbers for the semester program did not help the budget and in fact moved the bottom line in the wrong direction. Efforts to find new donors increased, and as time passed, the semester program did benefit from a new crop of supporters. The board began to recognize that the job of running the semester program and SFC was too much for one person. They split the job, and Amy was given the position of Director of SFC. Shana Maziarz, a Woolman alumna who had been teaching Peace and Global Studies during 2004-05, became the Head of School. After a semester directing SFC, Amy decided she wanted an entirely new but less stressful challenge and stepped down to become the school cook until 2006, when she left the Woolman staff. Bob Runyon, a Quaker who had served at length on the board and whose wife Kathy was the admissions director, was appointed as the Interim Director of SFC.

During these years, SFC and the Woolman Semester continued to suffer the legacy of challenges from the John Woolman School days. The financial situation became so dire that there was a constant rumbling about closing the whole program. When Bob Runyon was the Interim Director, he wrote in the spring newsletter about the desperate fundraising needs of 2006. At this point, the future of the Woolman Semester and SFC was uncertain. SFC faced a debt of $1.25 million, and projections showed increased indebtedness over the coming years. At the meeting on March 11, the board threw down the gauntlet: raise $150,000 in pledges within two weeks to guarantee the Woolman Semester for the fall, and raise an additional $150,000 in pledges in the following three months to guarantee the Woolman Semester for the following spring. If either goal was not reached, the pledges would not be collected, and the Woolman Semester would be suspended. If the fundraising effort succeeded, it would give the Center a year to devise and activate a plan to continue programming and build long-term financial health. Once again, friends of SFC responded generously. Pledges for $150,000 came in with six hours to spare before the March 25th deadline. In addition, $80,000 had been pledged to secure the spring 2007 semester, and though SFC had a shortfall of $70,000, it would continue fundraising efforts to fill in the gap. In May 2006, six students graduated from the program, and by fall of that year twelve students from across America were enrolled, a good sign for the future.

Though the Alumni Association floundered during this period, many former students and staff still helped in various ways. Del Reynolds, the very first Principal of the school, was active in the Grass Valley Friends Meetings and was often around the campus. Ted Menmuir, another long-serving principal, taught ceramics for the Woolman Semester. Amy Hunter, daughter of former principal Jack Hunter, joined the board of the school, and Amy Cooke, no longer on staff, was building a yurt with her husband Chamba on land adjacent to the school, where they planned to live.

After a couple of years, Shana no longer wanted to continue as Head of School and asked Dorothy Henderson, who had fulfilled various roles after her stint as Dean from 2000-2001, to share the job. Dorothy's preference was to take on the job herself, rather than job-share, and she took over as Head of School in 2008, the position Shana had held for three years. About the time that Dorothy became the Head, Colman Watts was hired to teach. He came up with the ingenious idea of creating an internship program for recent college graduates to come and mentor the students for a semester. Shortly after the internships were started, the Great Recession of 2008 began, and jobs were scarce once again in every sector of the economy. The internships looked attractive to new college graduates, and candidates from Yale, Columbia, Antioch, Oberlin, and other colleges jumped at the chance to work for room and board. This was an opportunity to have a Quaker experience, living what you believe, speaking truth, and working through conflict using the principles of NVC. At the beginning of the internship program, places were allocated for six interns a year (later increased to eight), all of whom worked in the kitchen and in the garden along with the students as well as acting as mentors. Free rent, free meals in the dining room, and the opportunity to work brought in energetic participants, and the internships benefited both the interns and the school.

The Woolman Semester was a lively, eccentric, creative, and demanding program. Descriptions touted it as a place to question assumptions, explore viewpoints, understand the ideas of others, and act on beliefs, and according to student feedback, it was living up to its billing. It also transpired that the accomplishments of the Woolman Semester inspired some Quaker supporters. The program did much to embody the Quaker values of peace and justice, and the students stepped up to support these ideas with their activism every semester. What was missing was diversity in the student body. Not surprisingly, the typical applicants were white and came from relatively privileged backgrounds. Recognizing that having a more ethnic and economically diverse student body was consistent with the overall goals of the program, some donors stepped in to make this possible. They gave money to pay tuition for two students each semester from Oakland, California. Diversifying what had traditionally been a largely homogeneous student body required a significant cultural shift for everyone. It was critical to acknowledge differences with sensitivity and live the values of the program to make it work. For the next few years, the Semester Program maintained its momentum and flourished.

After five years as Head of School, Dorothy Henderson stepped down and Marjorie Fox took her place. In fall 2013, she presided over the largest class of the Woolman Semester, 24 students and eight community interns. The large and lively group seemed to be a testament to the original spirit of the John Woolman School. Among the interns for the class were former students of the program who had enthusiastically returned to serve as mentors. In the meantime, the summer camp program, Camp Woolman, continued to be popular. Camp was extended to five weeks and filled up with campers each week. It was a financial boon to the struggling budget. In addition to generating needed income for SFC, it provided young people with opportunities to play, work together, and push beyond what they may have thought physically possible. Some of the programs were challenging wilderness hiking and camping experiences, building campers' confidence and competence as they learned to be comfortable in the wilderness.

Marjorie's tenure as Head of School was short. In 2014, Dorothy Henderson was back as Interim Head of School when SFC celebrated the 50th anniversary of the founding of the John Woolman School and the tenth anniversary of the Woolman Semester program. More than 150 former staff members and students from all corners of the United States returned to the Woolman campus to reconnect with old friends. Dorothy commented that "the sizable attendance is a testament to the impact the school has had on its former pupils." On this occasion, Amy Cooke observed that the original spirit of the school had carried forward into the semester program. The format was modified, but the mission was the same, with students and staff coming together to find their way as a community. That fall, the Semester Program welcomed 16 new students, ushering in its 22nd semester.

The board knew when Dorothy Henderson returned as Interim Head of School for the Woolman Semester in March 2014 that she was there temporarily. They formed a committee in the fall of 2014, composed of Board, staff, and community members, to begin searching for a new Head. After advertising and interviewing candidates and a careful discernment process, they offered the position to Gray Horwitz, who had been teaching Environmental Science in the program. He had just completed his second year as Director of Camp Woolman and was clearly very committed and dedicated to SFC, and he seemed to be undaunted by the challenges that he faced.

On September 14, right after the start of school, many old friends and Woolman supporters gathered to celebrate the life of Mary Jorgensen, who had died peacefully on July 23, 2014, at her Nevada City home at the age of 98. Her memorial took place under the great oak tree outside the dining hall at SFC, on the campus she had helped to found. She embraced Quaker values and lived her life with boundless, passionate, principled action, committed to family, community, education, peace, and social justice. The ongoing programs at Woolman carried on her vision of a school where young people from diverse backgrounds, socioeconomic levels, and cultures met and engaged in a radical experiment in learning, living, and being. In addition to being a tireless supporter of John Woolman School and the SFC, she was an extraordinary role model. She and her husband Russ were "Freedom Riders" in the early 1960s, they were avid lovers of the outdoors, and together they worked for social justice all over the world, as well as supporting groups like the American Friends Service Committee and the local Peace Center in Nevada County. Her efforts had been instrumental over the years in keeping Woolman moving forward.

Elusive enrollment targets plagued the Woolman Semester. Full enrollment meant 24 students per semester. Sixteen students enrolled in fall 2014, fourteen in the spring 2015, and fourteen in fall 2015, despite creative efforts made by everyone, including Emily Wheeler, the admissions director. Board and staff members were encouraged to contact and inform progressive educators, to take literature to meetings and events, and tell young people about Woolman. Woolman Semester alumni, the best spokespersons for the experience, were ready and willing to talk to prospective students. With the continuous and faithful support of donors and friends, many of them Quakers, SFC met the fundraising goal for 2014. They were making progress reducing debt through scheduled loan-principal payments and loan forgiveness. But the budget didn't work if they were under enrolled. Reaching full enrollment was critical for long-term sustainability. The board understood once again that they were in a precarious situation. They had cut salaries and some benefits for staff, who were working at well below comparable pay for their positions. It was getting harder and harder to hire new qualified people. Though staff members continued to love SFC and wanted to work there, they felt more and more of the strain. In this taxing situation, conflicts and dissatisfactions became harder to deal with, and conflict resolution, challenging in the best of circumstances, could become elusive.

In fall 2015, the board planned yet another visioning meeting with Board, staff, and concerned community members for the weekend of December 4-6, with a facilitator from Friends Council on Education. Among the questions on the agenda were how to bring in more students and possibly new programs, more tuition income, and contributions from new donors. As always, the financial aid and operational obligations, including the need to renovate much of the campus infrastructure, stood front and center for the board to consider. They made plans for future improvements to the facilities and brainstormed ways to increase enrollment, but by the end of the spring semester, Gray Horwitz, Head of School, was pleading on Facebook for financial support. A big push was made to increase donations before the end of the fiscal year on June 30.

By August, the news went out to the public that the CPFEA had made the difficult decision to suspend operations of the Woolman Semester for fall 2016. The issues were more complicated than the financial concerns; the spring had been a challenging semester, with students delving deeply into concerns about racism entrenched in institutions, including at Woolman. The ensuing discussions strained the already tattered nerves and energy of the staff and board and added to the burden of making the decision about continuing the program. With all these pressures in mind, the financial situation first and foremost, the difficult decision was made to suspend the Woolman Semester after more than 300 students had passed through the program since its inception in 2004.

The Semester Program started in the Internet era, and much evidence of student projects, feelings, and even graduation speeches are preserved on YouTube videos and still accessible today. These primary sources showcase the enthusiasm of the students for the program and are documentary evidence of the effectiveness of the curriculum. For instance, if you search for "Woolman Semester" on YouTube, you will find a video entitled "Peace Studies Banner Drop," depicting Woolman Semester students painting a huge banner and then, on a rainy and apparently quite chilly day in November—students were bundled in coats, hats, scarves, and gloves— taking the huge banner and hanging it from the railing on a local freeway overpass. It said, "Happy Thanks Taking—Ask Native Americans What They Think." Other videos depict students exploring issues of gender and the environment and expressing joyful memories of place. A video of the fall 2009 graduation ceremony features three students joyfully singing the Woolman Lane Song with the refrain, "We're living life in the light at the end of the road."

Woolman's trials and tribulations were not unique. Other Quaker schools with similar missions and goals had many of the same challenges and the same fate as Woolman. For instance, the Meeting School in Rindge, New Hampshire, opened in 1957. Like Woolman, it aspired to be a school where Quakerism could be a way of life for students, embracing simplicity, honesty, mutual respect, the dignity of physical labor, care for the earth, and the nonviolent response to conflict. The school was housed on two farmsteads, and classes were held in the living rooms of the faculty. Like Woolman, the economic downturn that began in 2008 brought what turned out to be insurmountable financial challenges and, after taking a sabbatical year in 2011-12, it closed permanently. It had intended to reopen in September 2013 as the New England Friends Semester at The Meeting School, a semester-long Quaker and farming immersion program for high-school juniors. In January 2012, the Board decided against continuing. What would it take to run a program that could survive in the modern world? Before the Woolman Semester started, Amy Cooke researched other similar programs. She looked at the Mountain School in Vermont, which is not a Quaker School but has many philosophical resemblances to the Woolman school and the Woolman Semester. A Farm and Food program— Eat What you Grow, and Grow What you Eat—is an integral part of the program, and justice, equity, and inclusion are important components of the school's philosophy. However, many differences help to explain why this program continues while schools like The Meeting School and Woolman have been unable to survive. The academic program is designed to ensure that students don't miss any of the academic requirements for graduation in their regular school programs. When the school was on shaky ground in the 1980s, the founders were able to negotiate an arrangement with the elite Milton Academy, a Massachusetts boarding school, to buy the school and maintain the program. Today, the Mountain School receives around 225 applications each year and can enroll 90 students each year (45 per semester). Tuition is more than $32,000 for a semester. Although it operates independently from Milton Academy, it enjoys the prestige of its affiliation, among other benefits. It survives because it has a powerful support structure, including substantial financial resources.

The CPFEA remained undaunted. Amy Cooke was hired as Director for the SFC, and she and the Board set out to establish benchmarks for viability as an organization. Once again, through a discernment process, they planned to reassess whether and how the mission of peace and justice through learning and service could be carried forward with new programming, and to find a way to put the organization on a sustainable financial footing.

Road to John Woolman School, 1960s

| DANCE |

....

THE PHOENIX METAPHOR IS APT

In August 2016, the CPFEA Board meeting opened with a worship-sharing question, a tradition of Quaker meetings: in this case, an existential question of whether and how Woolman would exist in the future. Former and current staff members were also present, including Grey Horwitz, who was still the Head of School, and former Heads Dorothy Henderson and Amy Cooke, to help begin the deliberation (or as Quakers call it, the discernment process). The decision not to offer a fall Woolman Semester was certain, but many other programming alternatives remained on the table, including the option of resuming the semester program in the future. Among other ideas, they discussed the possibility and complexities of "laying down" SFC completely. "Laying down" is a Quaker term used to describe the termination of a committee or an entity, recognizing that the work of that group has come to an end; there was still much discussion as to whether they were at that point. They were considering renting out the campus for a variety of uses, thinking about what kinds of staffing configurations might be needed in various scenarios, and what opportunities there might be for collaboration with other organizations. Without the Semester School, there were likely to be fewer donations, a key consideration for all the alternatives.

The meeting was long and intense, and along the way they realized that they needed to form feasibility committees to evaluate and report to the Board about the many possibilities. Over the next few months, they began to establish benchmarks for viability as an organization, reassessing how the mission of peace and justice through learning and service could be carried forward with new programming. Underlying the discussions lurked the crucial question of how finally to establish a sustainable financial footing.

In October 2016, Amy Cooke was appointed Director for the SFC. She knew Woolman and she certainly knew the challenges they were facing. In mid-October, the College Park Quarterly Meeting held its fall gathering on the Woolman campus. The CPFEA gave a thorough report, recounting recent challenges and decisions regarding the suspension of the Woolman Semester. Friends gathered for the Quarterly Meeting responded with love and support for the CPFEA and the Woolman staff, but they were equally clear in in expressing a strong opinion that if Woolman could not be turned around, made strong fiscally and sound organizationally, it should be laid down, closed for good. Amy said poignantly after the meeting, "Once again, the autumn rains came down on an empty campus, with a board and tiny staff in discernment." In 2001, when the John Woolman School was laid down, she had been in this same situation. At that time, she was instrumental, though not alone, in coming up with the vision, research, and plans for creating the Semester School. Once again, she set out to lead the Board and staff forward, considering scenarios to realize the newly restated mission, "to steward diverse learning communities and educational programs that weave together spirituality, peace, sustainability and social action," of SFC. However, creating programs represented only part of the process. The aging infrastructure might now be one of the biggest obstacles to future programs' success. As always, it needed a lot of work. Any plan to generate income by renting the facilities to like-minded groups for workshops and retreats, and succeed in a competitive market, would require a lot of improvements. One vision was to develop programs for a variety of audiences that built on the strengths of the Woolman Semester curriculum, Camp Woolman, and the organic garden. All these possibilities required careful assessment of the capacity of every aspect of the organization's resources, work that would be done partly by the feasibility committee and reported to the Board.

The CPFEA invited Irene McHenry, who at the time was the Executive Director of the Friends Council on Education and had led several planning processes for the Woolman Board and staff in years past, to come back and guide the board as they established benchmarks. Irene recommended that the group set goals for funding, building the Board, and evaluating the organization. As the months passed, the Board and staff moved through the goals, and gained some stability and clarity about how to evaluate the program options.

Amy worked with the feasibility committee to hash out ideas for the next steps and to establish some aggressive targets for actions. First, it would work on drafts of business plans for an initial review, and then in early January create the overview plan for the maintenance of the property through 2017. It needed comprehensive plans, including staffing needs and any capital improvements required to run the programs envisioned for 2017-18. It needed timetables and effects on cash flow, and a plan for housing staff, nonstaff residents, and participants for rentals, events, and programs. The Board intended to present the plans to the CPFEA for approval by February 1, 2017. These were very ambitious goals.

In early 2017, the planners began considering an outdoor school model, building on the strength of the summer camps. Outdoor school programs typically involve sending urban or suburban youth to a multiday program, like summer camp, but during the school year. Often, the programs focus on environmental education. They hadn't yet worked out the possible outdoor-school curriculum when they learned that Sierra Streams Institute (SSI), a local environmental nonprofit focused on watershed research, education, and restoration, with a strong citizen-science focus, was seeking a home. Together with SSI, they began a conversation about the possibility of Woolman as an environmental center, with SSI housed on the campus. If Woolman started an outdoor-school program, they might be able to partner with SSI's existing education programs.

The academic building, which had originally been the dormitory, looked like a good option for renting to SSI. A couple of apartments in it were rented, but the rest of the building was mostly unused except as a repository for anything that had no other place. Everything about the building was out of date and in extreme need of renovation, but it was spacious and had a science lab area, which was something that SSI needed. Plans moved forward to renovate the building and rent it to SSI for its offices, water-quality monitoring and macroinvertebrate-identification labs, classrooms, and a small environmental center for the public. The organization had a large volunteer base, and its presence could greatly expand SFC's exposure in the community, as SSI volunteers visited the campus. The first order of operations was the costly renovation of the building, which was renamed Madrone Hall. The idea appealed to donors, and several people stepped up with funding for the work. In February 2018, SSI moved to the newly renovated 4,400-square-foot space amid 230 acres of meadows, forests, streams, and ponds, perfect for scientific studies in which community members and students could be involved.

While renovations of Madrone Hall progressed, the strategic planning efforts moved forward with the help of a consultant who interviewed Board members and staff, donors and lenders, student alumni, and campers. It was apparent that the community strongly wished to keep Woolman in existence, to maintain its unique message of authenticity, simplicity, and community. Social activism, part of the Woolman experience for over fifty years, emerged as a strongly supported element of Woolman's mission. Planners suggested a pilot program to support youth activists in designing and implementing nonviolent direct action for social change. The Board approved the concept of creating the Jorgensen School for Nonviolence, named for Mary and Russ Jorgensen. A committee worked on designing the program. During the spring, two pilot sessions of the nascent Woolman Outdoor School took place on campus in partnership with the North Oakland Community Charter School. City kids dug in the dirt and gazed at the stars as they participated in activities ranging from invasive-species removal to astronomy. Yet even as these new programs emerged, serious questions remained about the overarching viability of Woolman. Supporters, who expressed both skepticism and hope, were exhausted from years of struggle.

In August 2018, after almost two years of discernment and planning, the CPFEA met to consider adopting the strategic plan called "Woolman Rising!" The goals of the plan included fiscal health, site improvements, a strong staff and Board, mission-driven programs, and work grounded in Quaker faith and process. The plan contained no magic bullets to solve the financial problems, and executing it would require dedication and hard work, with continuous attention to fundraising and wise spending. The alternative was to begin the process of shutting down the organization. With both trepidation and excitement, the Board adopted the plan. With a 55-year history of extraordinary labor and commitment behind it, it knew that the way ahead held many of the same challenges on which Woolman had stumbled before, and that skepticism would dog their path, and yet, it was willing to try again.

Throughout the planning process and before any final plans were made, work began to make the facilities more functional and attractive. This work required a constant stream of funding, and the Board needed to raise money immediately to make necessary repairs. During the strategic planning period, Amy enlisted Marty Coleman-Hunt, former Executive Director of the Nevada County Land Trust and an experienced nonprofit consultant, to help create a major fundraising campaign. Marty began with a possible campaign target goal of $2.5 to $3 million, the estimated amount needed to overhaul the physical plant and launch new programs. Amy, a small staff, the Board, and Marty worked toward the goals outlined in the strategic plan.

Suddenly, in March 2020, with planning underway for the spring outdoor-school programming and summer camp, and many months of rental reservations on the books, the COVID-19 pandemic shut down SFC, along with the rest of the world. While the campus was shuttered, Marty and Amy continued to meet with donors to generate the support they needed to weather the additional stresses of the COVID shutdowns and get commitments for funding for the new programs when they finally resumed normal operations. During this period, Amy stepped down from her position and left SFC. The board asked Marty to take on the role of Interim Executive Director. She was a logical choice, since she had been learning about the operations and was very aware of the fundraising needs.

In May, Marty and the Board still held out hope for a shortened camp program of three weeks instead of six; however, the decision was finally made to cancel camp completely. Families had already paid tuition for camp, and those fees had to be refunded. Some families declined the refund and gave the money to Woolman; others optimistically rolled it over to the 2021 camp season. The budget for running camp included paying staff early in the year as they worked to prepare for the summer. Staff salaries that had already been paid during the first few months of the year had come out of regular operating income, much of it from camp fees already paid and now needing to be refunded to many families. By the time the decision was made to cancel the summer session, this became a significant drain, pushing the organization toward serious financial instability. Marty and some Board members met with lenders regarding the financial situation. At that point, Woolman's long-term debt was $1.13 million. The lenders were understanding and generous. SFC received a Federal Payroll Protection Program (PPP) loan, and funds from the first COVID CARES Act issued by Congress to help businesses and nonprofits keep people employed. With those funds, the Board hired camp staff to do general maintenance work on the campus and a general contractor to continue work on the Ranch House, which it had been readying to rent at current market rates, part of the strategic plan. It also received an Economic Injury Disaster Loan of $150,000 from the Small Business Administration at a favorable interest rate; this allowed it to retire some higher-interest debt.

Despite the unexpected support, as summer approached and COVID-19 shut down all income opportunity—rentals, camp, retreats, weddings, etc.—the Board realized that it would not be possible to hold out much longer with the cash on hand. One alternative was bankruptcy, and no one wanted that option. Instead, it engaged a real-estate broker who specialized in selling large properties like camps and ranches throughout the west. He suggested marketing the property for $2-3 million and started holding buyers' meetings in July and August with interested parties. Possibly a buyer or a group of buyers could be found who would be interested in owning the land and leasing it back to the CPFEA for programs. The Board planned to report on its progress at Quarterly Meeting in October.

On August 17, 2020, lightning struck, literally. It had been hot and windy, and already a problematic fire season in California. Everyone was on edge. A lightning strike in the canyon of the South Yuba River started the fire, dubbed the Jones Fire. The first reports came in before 3am. Amy and Chamba Cooke, who lived on a small lane adjacent to the Woolman campus, woke up at 4:30am to the smell of smoke and knew immediately that they needed to leave. After packing up as many important possessions as they could, they left; soon after, the entire neighborhood, including the Woolman campus, was evacuated after shifting winds spread the fire. Access to fight the fire was difficult, as no roads led to the bottom or the sides of the blaze. The fire map stayed stable overnight, but as temperatures rose and winds shifted, wider evacuations were ordered. The fire burned 705 acres over 12 days and destroyed 21 structures. It forced over 4,000 residents to evacuate, including the fifteen residents of the Woolman campus.

While the fire raged, no one knew the conditions at Woolman. Marty posted updates as news became available. On Tuesday evening, she learned that the firestorm had blown through campus while strike teams and two water tankers worked to save buildings. On Friday morning, Marty and Chris Benfield, the maintenance supervisor, went to the Incident Command briefing to find the crew in charge of mop-up at SFC. Later Marty described the experience:

"We walked through a sea of orange jumpsuits with 'PRISONER' printed their backs — mostly worn by people of color holding axes and shovels. They looked bedraggled but ready. I smiled and mouthed 'thank you,' but they were not allowed to engage with me. We talked to the captain in charge of Woolman operations, Jack Kane, a tall, broad-shouldered man in his well-pressed navy blue CalFire uniform. He told us of the heroic efforts of fire fighters keeping flames off our buildings while allowing the fire to burn through the campus from one end to the other. He personally held the hose that protected A-Frame #12 and Redwood House where Chris lived. We fought the urge to embrace him in tears (Covid concerns) as he described the scope of their efforts almost nonchalantly. He arranged for an escort, and we finally got on campus to tour the damage."

They learned that fire entered SFC at the north end. It was about 300 yards wide and moved south across the west side of the campus, burning everything from the soccer field to Dorothy Henderson and Doug Hamm's property adjacent to the school, on the south side. Their home was fully defended and was untouched by the fire. The fire was also turned away from the main buildings and the east side of the main campus by the green, grassy interior meadow and soccer field. The orchard was also untouched. Many other buildings were gone—turned to mounds of ash. The burnt structures included newly renovated Madrone Hall, the home of SSI. The building was a smoldering pile of rubble topped by the twisted remains of the metal roof. The firewood barn, Tree Frog trailer, six of the eight cabins, the westside bath house and showers, Cedar House (a residence), all the garden buildings, the animal barn and the storage barn—all were gone. The well and a main sewer line collapsed, which meant that there was no potable water or wastewater system, so restoring the water system would be the first focus of the emergency recovery plan. The forest around Mel's Pond was burned for about 150 yards on either side. Marty estimated that about 150 acres of forest had burned, including much of the understory. Blackberry, buckbrush, toyon, scotch broom, and small trees had also burned, though this was beneficial to the health of the remaining forest. Luckily, the main buildings, dining hall, meetinghouse, office, Ranch House, Stone House, Fern House, ceramic studio and kiln, all 12 A-frames, Redwood House, Arbor House ,and the three homes on upper campus (A-frame in the Pines, Hedrick House, and Cypress House), plus the maintenance shop and Quonset hut, were all saved. But it was a tragic loss for the two tenants who lost everything; the residence had housed a family of three, and Madrone Hall.

In September, the campus was closed while frantic work focused on getting the critical utility infrastructure up and running so tenants could return with full services. PG&E and CalFire worked hard removing dangerous debris, along with many damaged trees that endangered roads, powerlines, trails, and other buildings. Some days later, assessing what was lost and what was left, it was clear that the fire had truly changed everything for Woolman. One of the first orders of business was to work with the insurance adjusters. SFC's insurance policy through Church Mutual provided excellent coverage, though it would take some time to finalize the settlement. In the meantime, the County Disaster Relief Fund awarded SFC a $15,000 grant, which was used primarily to provide rent relief to the tenants who were all displaced for several weeks due to water and power issues, and damage to some homes. The CPFEA Board members had their hands full and appreciated Marty's strong background in land and site management. She knew where grant funding could be obtained for some of the recovery operations. Finance Committee member Doug Smith and longtime supporter Peter Trueblood assisted Marty in wading through the fine print of more than 600 pages of the insurance policy as they prepared to make recommendations to the Board about the future. Money also began pouring in from supporters. Unsolicited donations from Friends and supporters for as much as $5,000 arrived in the mail.

It quickly became apparent that the fire had turned into the most unlikely opportunity to save SFC. The real estate agent they had been working with to sell the property was clear that it was not the time to try to sell. Because of the level of damage to the land and buildings, it would literally be a fire sale. So, accepting this recommendation and seeing the outpouring of financial support from donors, the Board announced that the land was no longer for sale. There might not be enough money to rebuild some of the buildings, but there would be a substantial amount to invest in the infrastructure. They intended to use the money responsibly and with an eye to the future.

In fall 2020, the College Park Quarterly Meeting met virtually because of the COVID-19 pandemic. Had the group been at Woolman, as in normal times, they would have seen the devastating results of the fire. The Quarterly Meeting was traditionally an opportunity for the CPFEA to present an annual report on the status of SFC. Sandra Schwartz, CPFEA Clerk, had the job of delivering the update. However, before she spoke, a special guest was introduced: Shelly Covert, the tribal spokesperson of the Nisenan Rancheria of Nevada City. The Nisenan are the original inhabitants of the land around the SFC. Early accounts of the Woolman property from the ranching days mention Nisenan presence on the land.

In recent years, as the local community in Nevada County became more aware of the presence of the Nisenan people and their history in the region, Woolman staff and the Board began to recognize their responsibility to acknowledge and respect the local indigenous community. Before the fire, Shelly and staff members had walked the land, observing landmarks that her people knew as Yulica (you-lee-chaw), the name of the Nisenan town where Woolman sits today. The fire exposed ancient grinding rocks and an important spring, and Shelly reminded the gathering that the land would endure whatever the human impact. She shared a sacred song and spoke about her people's beliefs.

After thanking Shelly, Sandra reported to the meeting on the impacts of the fire. She recapped the progress that had been made, recounting the timber-salvage plan and the hazardous waste cleanup, which needed to be completed by FEMA before any rebuilding could be started. Her message emphasized that before land-restoration efforts could begin, they needed management plans for the grounds, the farm, and the forest that would make the best use of current knowledge and practices for healthy forests, watersheds, and land management, all supported by financially stable business plans. Above all, she emphasized that the Board needed to be expanded to help do this work "to protect the investment that our donors and lenders have made in Woolman, to care for the land, and to bring mission-driven programs to Woolman."

Marty had her hands full managing the day-to-day cleanup and salvage operations. She was skilled and knowledgeable about land management and facilities projects and fundraising. During 2021, many operational details occupied everyone's time. As repair and maintenance work went on at SFC, the staff and board worked on clarifying objectives and creating timelines to implement the Strategic Plan. They assessed the plan to make sure that the goals were still appropriate to the circumstances and then identified the action steps needed to achieve them, including staffing requirements. Marty planned to step down as Interim Executive Director. She felt strongly that soon a different type of leader, someone visionary and not as occupied with operations management. would be needed to move forward with the goals of the

Strategic Plan. The search began for someone to replace her. In January 2022, after a long and intense interviewing process, the CPFEA hired Coleen Hedglin as Executive Director of Woolman at SFC. Coleen came to Woolman with more than twenty years of nonprofit management experience, a degree in Education, and a passion for social justice. For several months. Marty advised her on the operational issues at Woolman while wrapping up projects and transitioning the financial management to a new Director of Finance and Operations.

At the Fall 2022 College Park Quarterly meeting, Coleen reported for Woolman at Sierra Friends Center, described the activities that had taken place so far that year and others still in the planning stages for Camp Woolman, Woolman Outdoor School, Woolman Arts, and Jorgensen Center for Activism, as well as retreats and stays. Students from San Francisco Friends School and International Montessori School came to campus for the Woolman Outdoor School program. Plans were in the works for contracting with three to five schools to participate in the onsite outdoor program each year. Woolman Arts recruited artists and crafters to give workshops. Major repairs and renovations had been made to both indoor and outdoor spaces, and retreat and workshop rentals had increased because of the more appealing and functional facilities. Three hundred people had attended seven group retreats. New flooring and sound paneling to improve acoustics were installed in the Meeting House, roof leaks were fixed, and workers installed heating, ventilation, and air-conditioning with high-efficiency particulate air (HEPA) filters in all the main buildings. The outdoor dining area had been expanded and equipped with handwashing stations. Many of these improvements had been made since April.

Achieving financial stability still loomed as a challenge. The Board made the prudent fiscal decision to use the insurance money to pay off previous debt and establish an emergency reserve account. Fundraising efforts had increased, but spending continued to outstrip revenue, and more income was needed to balance the budget in the coming year. It was important to build program income. The local community was a potential source of additional revenue through arts and children's workshops during the school year. To realize this potential, program staff promoted these programs through social media and advertising.

Both summer camp and the Woolman Outdoor School programs required new accommodations for children. Even if the cabins hadn't burned in the fire, best practices in lodging children in groups had changed quite a bit over the years. After much consideration, the Board decided to build seven platform tents in the flat area near the dining hall, instead of rebuilding the lost cabins. The improvements included plans to add showers to the bathrooms in the lower level of the dining hall to meet the needs of summer campers without having to build an entirely new bathhouse. The new tent circle would also make it possible to increase the size of school groups that Woolman could accommodate during the year. As always, financing was the challenge: each platform tent cost approximately $10,000 to build. This plan bore a remarkable resemblance to the time 50 years ago when money was raised to build the A-frame cabins, which still serve today as a source of economic support for Woolman. In April 2023, a familiar call went out; volunteers were needed to mount platform tents and assemble bunk beds. Other volunteers were assigned to tasks such as carpentry, painting, or landscaping, depending on their skills. A few people helped to prepare and serve coffee, tea, and lunch as a hardworking group of volunteers set up the tents.

Woolman was a busy place in the spring of 2023, with Woolman Outdoor School in full swing. Seventh graders from San Francisco Friends School and 11th graders from Oakland High School each spent a week of learning, exploration, creativity, and fun. Malaika Bishop, whose grandparents helped found Woolman, ran Bluebird Farms on the campus, growing food and flowers and participating in food-justice education with students. Other activities included ceramics, forest restoration, native-plant walks, indigenous acorn processing, basketry, collaborative mural painting, and more. A youth ceramics program and an after-school arts program, weekend arts workshops for adults, the open pottery studio, and a weekend writer's retreat were among the activities.

Plans for the summer of 2023 include camp for children ages nine to seventeen. On the website, Camp Woolman is described thus:

"...a non-religious organization that draws inspiration from its Quaker roots. We look to the Quaker values of integrity, equity, simplicity, community, stewardship of the Earth, and peace as pillars for creating a safe and open community. Camp Woolman is a place of acceptance, where staff and campers are welcome regardless of race, ethnicity, religion, sexual orientation, gender identity and gender expression."

And, in the oldest tradition of Woolman, Family Work Camp is scheduled to take place in early June with playing, cooking, cleaning, singing, working on projects that benefit the Woolman campus, and celebrating together.

In September 2023, Woolman at SFC plans to mark the 60th anniversary of the founding of John Woolman School with a celebration. When visitors arrive for the anniversary weekend, many will likely find it both very familiar and very different. It will probably still feel like "home." There is still a farm, an orchard, and a smell characteristic of the Sierra foothills, especially when the warm summer sun shines on the pines and pungent kitkitdizze. On the other hand, visitors will see changes. The fire altered the landscape, but many beautiful old trees remain. Some old buildings are gone, and there are new structures. The campus has a clean and neat appearance, and many of the buildings are more comfortably appointed than ever before. What remains to be seen is whether the organizational challenges that repeatedly threatened Woolman's past survival remain or have finally been surmounted. Financial instability and sometimes a lack of clear goals haunted the programs of the past. The insurance proceeds from the fire, the kind of large cash infusion that Woolman could have used in the 1960s when the founders were preparing to open the school, help a lot with the present transformation. Is it enough? Is the Phoenix metaphor apt? The current resilient Board and staff, and everyone who has come along the "Woolman Way" throughout the years, will also be the key to the future success.

One thing that hasn't changed for sixty years is the spirit that brought John Woolman School into being. The dreams of the founders to create an institution providing an education for both heads and hands, a way of life emphasizing work, simplicity and giving, integrity, justice, and peace have been realized over and over. When you read Catherine Lenox's portion of the book, "Wombats in the Real World," you will see the legacy of this dream in the stories that she has collected. Woolman has already influenced almost three generations, many of whom were activists during their education and went on to carry the values they learned and lived at Woolman into their adult lives. Today the programs at Woolman continue to embody that spirit.

John Woolman School barn and dining hall

NOTES
By Lisa Frankel

Introduction
By 1885 the property included...
    Forest Management Plan John Woolman School Property, Nevada County, CA.
    Prepared by Marshall Palley, June 21, 1982 for the College Park Friends
    Education Association.

SECTION ONE (1)

Chapter 1 - Rooted in Quaker Tradition
They believed that a distinct way of life...
    https://www.friendscouncil.org/resources/quaker-curricula/quaker-education-a-
    source-book/chapter-1-the-rise-of-q-ed-early-schools

The principles of early Quaker educational philosophy...
    Galusha, Debbie K., "The Impact of Previous Schooling Experiences on a
    Quaker High School's Graduating Students' College Entrance Exam Scores, Parents'
    Expectations, and College Acceptance Outcomes" (2010). Student Work. 20.
    https://digitalcommons.unomaha.edu/studentwork/20

In 1982 Douglas Heath wrote the pamphlet...
    Page 3, The Peculiar Mission of a Quaker School, Pendle Hill Pamphlet 225. 1982.

General note:
    For a comprehensive book about Quaker education, see:
    https://leonardkenworthy.files.wordpress.com/2014/06/1987-quaker-education.pdf

**Chapter 2 - Toward A Friends Secondary Boarding School in
Northern California**
Several dozen people, mostly families from the College Park Quarterly Meeting...
    Regional Quaker Meetings are often referred to as "Quarterly Meetings" because
    they usually meet at least once a quarter to make decisions about issues and concerns
    that affect the local group.
    Report to College Park Quarterly Meeting from Friends Secondary School Conference
    at Hidden Villa Ranch, April 16, 17, 1957. From the JWS archive.

At the end of the weekend of discussion, the group established a committee, the College
Park Friends Educational Association (hereafter referred...
    The College Park Friends Educational Association became the governing body of

the school and later, subsequent programs held on the campus. Over the years in the documents produced by the school and referring to the school, the College Park Friends Educational Association is referred to as the "CPFEA," the "Association," and the "Board." In the text, all these names are used depending on the time or circumstances.

During this period there was an interesting twist that involved the Bureau of Land Management (BLM)...
https://www.blm.gov/sites/blm.gov/files/Media_Library_BLM_Policy_h2740-1.pdf

In the past some surveying had already been done...
The Hedrick's property was adjacent to BLM land along the South Yuba River.

Chapter 3 - Making the Dream a Reality
No Notes

Chapter 4 – Teachers But No Toilets
Ken Kern who was well known...
Ken Kern wrote numerous books on sustainable building. Many articles by Ken Kern have been reprinted over the years in *Mother Earth News*.
https://www.motherearthnews.com/contributors/Ken+Kern/

Chapter 5 – Building Community
No Notes

Chapter 6 - Work is Love Made Visible
Chapter title: Work is Love Made Visible, From *The Prophet*, Kahlil Gibran (Knopf, 1923)

Chapter 7 – Students in Action
No Notes

Chapter 8 – Trials and Tribulations
In the July 1994 *Friends Bulletin*, Vanita Blum reflected that the JWS had been seasoned...
"Seasoning an issue" —Quakers make decisions based on a sense of the meeting. Sometimes an issue is important enough and possibly controversial that it requires "seasoning." This process may take months. It may involve gathering relevant facts and speaking to Quakers both within and outside the Meeting. After allowing open inquiry and discussion, Quakers believe they are better positioned to come to a spirit-led sense of how to proceed. That sense is called the "sense of the Meeting."

It started out as a tall shed roof which remained...
The camp was started in 1980 by the Owner Builder Center, a Berkeley-based

nonprofit group that offered building and remodeling classes. These were mostly one-day seminars and ongoing night classes in the Bay Area all year around. Its mountain camp ran from mid-June through late August at Woolman. Richard Drace, who ran a residential design business in Nevada City, directed the camp.

Some board member felt outside guidance would be helpful…

The Friends Council supports Quaker education, offering publications and experiential trainings on various subjects, and providing consultants to help schools with issues like board development, professional growth, and maintaining their Quaker identity and ethos.

Chapter 9- We're Living Life in the Light at the End of the Road
No notes

Chapter 10 – The Phoenix Metaphor is Apt
There is still a farm, an orchard, and…

Kitkitdizze, Chamaebatia foliolosa, is also called bear-clover, bearmat, tarweed, and the colonizer's deprecating "mountain misery."

SECTION TWO (2)

The paragraph from an article written by Kerry O'Regan on April 1, 2019, "Finding Friends in the Light" for *Friends Journal* is used with permission from Martin Kelly, Senior Editor of Friends Journal, who wrote and said, "Catherine Lenox has permission to use "Finding Friends in the Light" from the April 2019 issue of *Friends Journal*. You have our blessing and thanks to use the paragraph."

"Fly Away" by singer/songwriter Kate Wolf, is used with permission from Max Wolf, Kate Wolf's son, who wrote Catherine Lenox and said, "You are more than welcome to include Kate's lyrics from "Fly Away" in your book about John Woolman School. This seems immensely appropriate since Kate visited the school and wrote about it in her song."

PHOTO
GALLERY

THE EXPERIENCE

Woolman poster from 1969

Ceramics/Pottery

Tambores/Music outside, photo on cover

Horseback transportation around campus

Choir performing in the dining hall, 1972

Campus garden, photo by Dave Worley

Mel's Lake, 1960s

Climbing kiln

OUTSIDER'S

Vol. 6 No. 2   *JOHN WOOLMAN SCHOOL*   Nevada City, Calif.   Jan. 1969

we caught the sun
thru our whistles
wooden bamboo burnt
and sand scorched

we laugh softly
not wanting to waken
all the whispers
hidden in
the darkness of our
souls
but i told you—
we caught the sun
(knowing only that
instant was ours)

—hina leshan

Newsletter, 1969

The kiln, 1971

Student, 1970s

Student throwing a pot on the kiln, 1969

Student partipating in class, 1970

Student painting sign for a recycling event

Peaceful setting, barn

Banner/Artwork

The Dorm, photo by Dave Worley

Prepping the land for seeding with
the tractor

Poster

Dorm

Ted Menmuir with a student in front of the science building

Staff housing under construction

School office, 1960s

Exterior of the dining hall

Interior of the dining hall

Exterior of
A-frame cabin

Interior of A-frame cabin

Interior of small cabin

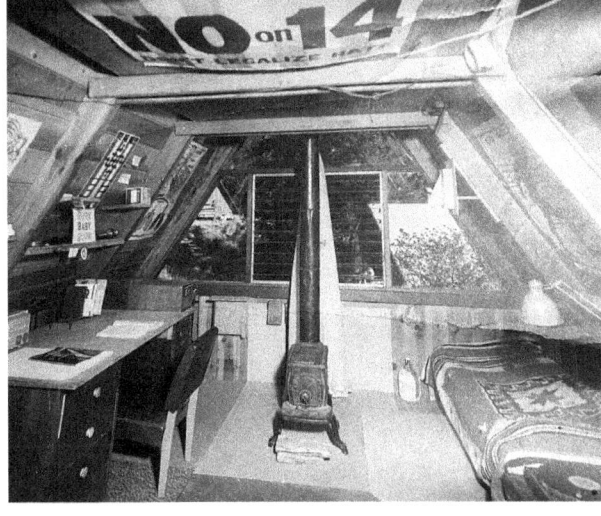

Tinky's Cabin,
circa 1969

Interior of the greenhouse

Recreation
near campus

COMMUNITY

John Woolman School, near Grass Valley, California, illustration by Earl Thollander

Harriette and Don Smith, two of the founders of John Woolman School

Russ and Mary Jorgensen, two of the founders of John Woolman School

Marguerite and Harold Blickenstaff

Hoyt McCurley, with students, 1960s

Friendships

Friendships

Kitchen manager/cook, 1970s

Kitchen manager/cook, 1970s

Students at work

Student playing harmonica

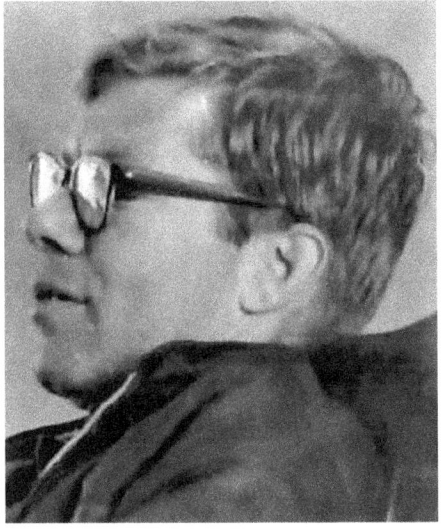

John Woolman School former principal,
Chuck Croninger, 1970s

Student, 1970s

Student playing piano, 1970s

Student typing, 1960s

Student, 1960s

Student life and culture at John Woolman School

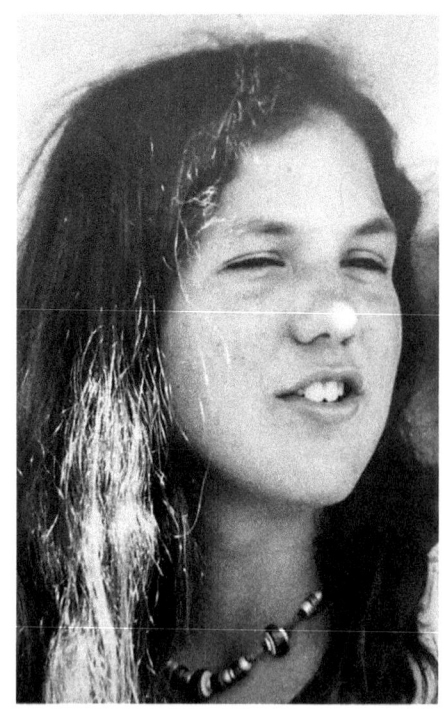

Student life and culture at John Woolman School

Alumna Nina Hoffman

David Russell with the JWS goose, circa 1965

SPECIAL PROJECTS

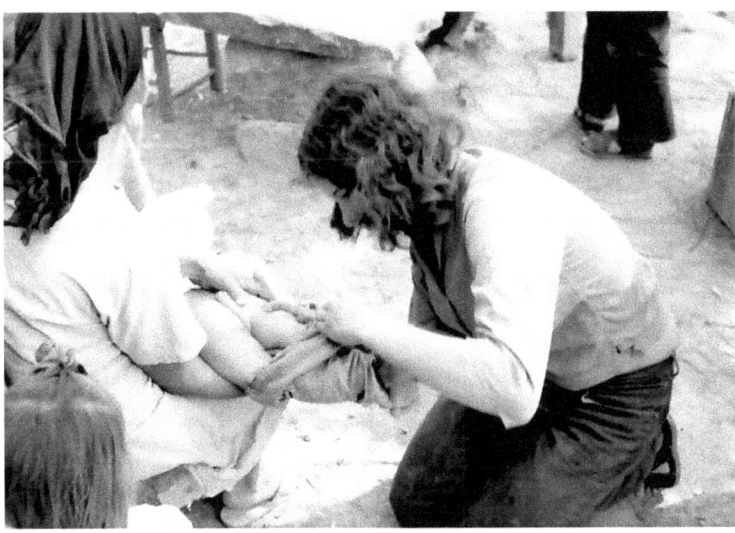

Mexico Special Project with Kerry and Mike Travers

Mexico Special Project with Kerry and Mike Travers

Mexico Special Project with Kerry and Mike Travers

Mexico Special Project with Kerry and Mike Travers

Mexico Special Project with Kerry and Mike Travers

Mexico Special Project with Kerry and Mike Travers

Mexico Special Project with Kerry and Mike Travers

Mexico Special Project
with Kerry and Mike Travers

"Jimi Jett and the Rockin' Bombers" formed a band in the barn for a Special Project, 1960s

"Jimi Jett and the Rockin' Bombers," 1960s

A special thank you for the majority of photos!

Dave Worley,
Chipps (Newsom) Barsky,
Kerry and Mike Travers,
and the John Woolman School archives

SECTION TWO:

THE MEMOIRS: WOMBATS IN THE REAL WORLD

WOMBATS
IN THE REAL WORLD

For nearly 60 years, those who attended and worked at John Woolman School have carried special memories of what it was like to be there. For many, the experience was so deeply embedded that their entire life was influenced by it. Due to Quaker-based classes that taught peace, justice, nonviolent communication and behavior, dispute resolution, and activism, some students even became conscientious objectors and social/civic activists later in life. Woolman taught students how to be advocates for diverse communities, people of less privilege, those wrongly incarcerated or persecuted, those experiencing social and political injustices, and people whose lives are challenged by physical or educational disabilities. The school and its Quaker principles set students up for life to pay attention to supporting the needs of others. As one former Woolman student says, "I will bear witness to and call out both injustice and beauty in the world and use what I learned to make lasting change." Numerous students have.

The John Woolman School mascot was a wombat, a peaceable, habitat-tolerant, vegetarian marsupial found in the forests and mountains of Australia, Tasmania, and parts of New Zealand. Today, that wombat spirit carries forward. A thread of social justice and sustainability runs from the past to present, linked together by justice, nonconformity, active nonviolence, environmental responsibility, and peace. Woolman students, faculty, and alumni still refer to themselves as "Wombats" or "Woolmanites."

In addition to telling the history of John Woolman School, this book also shares how the school affected students and staff from both the school and the Woolman Semester. Alumni said that the unique quality of education at Woolman surpassed anything they would have experienced in a mainstream high school because it encouraged them to follow who they were—and for those who didn't know yet who they were, it gave them the freedom to find out what that was. The school gave them a sense of belonging and became an opportunity to explore what excited them most academically and personally. They also said they had felt disenfranchised in public high schools, that they were getting into trouble; some even reported that John Woolman School likely saved their lives. Others came to Woolman after the sudden loss of a family member, filled with grief. Alongside their education, their healing came from the relationships they made with the land, staff, and other students. Moreover, it was an emotionally safe place for them to develop their personalities and make lasting friendships. They said they "arrived lost but left found." Staff, many of whom also had profound life changes at Woolman, noted that numerous former students became their lifelong friends.

During the 60 years that the school was open, many people called Woolman home. Though there are countless untold stories about how the school and its community affected student and staff lives, this book shares some of the told ones. In interviews with former staff and students, a strong thread of commonality ran through their comments. From those who founded the school right up to staff and students involved in the Semester Program before the school closed, people say they felt a lasting, pervasive sense of place, community, and connection at Woolman. Even today, former students and staff still feel this powerful link to the school, the land, and to each other. The freedoms that students had at Woolman might be unheard of in this day and age, but they happened then and there. It was in every sense a holistic education grounded in Quaker sensibilities and rooted in community. With only a few exceptions, each person interviewed felt that the years they were at Woolman were the best ones for them to have been there. They have all likely been right. As many former students aptly said, "John Woolman School was magical."

| MUSIC |

11

....

INFLUENCE AND LEGACY

"Each of us has our own Woolman."

– N. K. Hoffman

For many students, the unique experience they had at John Woolman School paved their way to success, both personally and professionally. Moreover, numerous students mentioned that the school was powerfully influential in shaping their internal sense of self, confidence, and personal direction. Overwhelmingly, students said they had felt out of step with the rest of the world and arrived at Woolman feeling tremendous self-doubt, traumatized by struggles they'd had in mainstream schools. In contrast, at Woolman, students were encouraged to develop their natural abilities and interests, which often fostered entrepreneurship and fulfilling careers in their later lives. As Rob Sanville (1971-1973) points out, "The Woolman experience was extremely important in my development as a human being. The opportunities to live in a real-world relationship-based life started there."

Jennifer Gershen, (1989-1992), a clinical psychologist specializing in Behavioral Health Therapy, has been working with children, teens, and families for over 20 years. She says, "In my first quarter of high school, I flunked out of all my classes. I was headed down a wrong path, and so miserable and unhappy. My dad lived in Danville, California and my mom lived in Orinda, California, so I grew up in very white-privileged 'people driving their kids to school in Mercedes-Benz automobiles' and 'wearing only designer clothes' neighborhoods. Students were also highly competitive and prided themselves for having high academic achievement. I never felt that I could measure up. Learning was not easy for me. I needed an alternative direction to get out of what was happening to me, which could have led to massive trouble. My dad sent me to a psychologist, who reported that I had no mental health issues or learning disabilities, but that my barrier to success was my home environment. He told my dad he knew of a 'hippie boarding school' out in the woods run by a bunch of Quakers that he thought could put me on the right path, John Woolman School. Thankfully, that happened. Due to the difference in learning style at Woolman, I had the capacity to learn and actually enjoyed it. Initially, it was an incredible shocker adjustment, though. The entire concept of Woolman was different for me. I remember driving into the school for the first time. It was winter, and snow covered the campus. Three students, who looked like they were straight out of Woodstock, walked past us. Two of them were walking in the snow with no shoes on. I thought, 'Oh wow, what have I gotten myself into?' I felt as if I had landed in a foreign nation and didn't know the language. I didn't know if they used drugs, but I could see that these kids had 'rebel' written all over them. Since I tend to be rebellious, had I been sent to a more conservative school, the trajectory could have been just as bad as public high school. Woolman had a lot of misunderstood, rebellious teenagers who were struggling with their sexuality or identity, a whole broad spectrum of humanity. There was a reason we could not survive in public school. We did not fit in that box. My parents realized that leaving me in a place that was going to support me but not dictate to me was the way I was going to find the path to myself. John Woolman School was the right safety raft.

"In the middle of my Woolman life, I had cancer and had to return home for treatment. For a short time, I went back to public high school. Comparing it to Woolman, I remember thinking, 'Nobody cares here. Students and teachers are both playing a game. Wow, this isn't going to work for me.' Woolman gave me permission to shape my life one way and someone else, in tandem, to shape their life another way. The teachers there cared. My experience at John Woolman School helps me in my work with teenagers. Knowing that a teenager needs a voice, and holding space for that voice, hearing it, and hoping that they voice that to their parents is fundamental to what I learned at Woolman. The work I do now with parents helps them understand that opposition can mean there is a fire in their kid, and if they can listen to it, they can harness it. If not for John Woolman, I absolutely would never have become a psychologist, and would have never believed that I would be capable of getting my doctorate. John Woolman School saved my life."

Sylvia "Chipps" Newsom Barsky (1967-1970), massage therapist, also recalls, "I was going to the local high school and didn't fit with the greasers, hippies, or geeks, and was desperately trying to fit in somehow. I was getting average grades, Cs, Ds, and failed a couple of classes. Once at Woolman, I felt completely comfortable with the other students, flocking together from all over. We found each other and created a wonderful community. After Woolman, when I went to community college, I was a straight-A student. I used many of the tools I learned at Woolman and was able to go on in my life. Had more schools been like Woolman and taken students beyond just sitting in class, memorizing the book, and answering questions at the end of the chapter, I think we would be living in a far better, more interesting society. If other high schools had followed the trends John Woolman School set forward, I think so much of what we're facing today—racism, climate change, financial disparity, and more—would have been tempered, looked at and exposed, and therefore worked on. I believe climate change would have been solved 50 years ago. Woolman gave us a broader view of life and the world. Of course, it was the 1970s when I was there. It was a time of a lot of change in our history—language changed, political viewpoints changed, architecture, fashion, food, travel, politics, and economics changed. The stock market went through the roof. We all went through that not realizing how important it was at the time. We look back on it now and say, 'Wow, we were in the middle of something widely historic.' John Woolman School opened those gates to ride that wave. We were not left behind. Many of us are still riding that wave to this day. Numerous fellow students have gone on to do amazing things with their lives, when the parents and teachers from the old schools they'd come from were not so sure they were going to do very well. Now you look at them and it is mind-blowing what they're doing in their lives and succeeding, which has everything to do with John Woolman School. Of this I am certain due to my experience there."

Neal Schneider (1969-1971), who founded a successful interconnect company in San Diego and spent eight years circumnavigating the globe with his wife, Ruthie, on their sailboat Rutea also observes, "Going through public high school would have likely ended my life. I was involved in a lot of dangerous behaviors and was continuously pushing limits that my parents realized they had little control over. That was in the late 1960s, and such a tumultuous time in history and for me. I was the kind of child who if someone said, 'breathe,' I would hold my breath, so Woolman was a fortuitous change. Students and staff became such valuable mentors. Both Ted Menmuir, who went on to be principal, and Hoyt McCurley, who taught sciences, became such close friends with me that we went backpacking independently during summer breaks. As a teenager, to have that kind of experience with highly articulate, well-read, educated adults was fantastic. I had such remarkable experiences at Woolman that I could not have had anywhere else, absolutely phenomenal. I may not have known how valuable they were at the time but as I matured and eventually got married, had a family, and my own business, I realized how much the time I spent with such brilliant people really influenced me."

Jennifer Dickey (1977-1978), computer technology professional, clerk of the Woolman Programs Committee and formerly Executive Director for the suicide prevention program Idaho Lives Project, also notes how Woolman changed her life.

"My dad was in the military, and he had been raised in a very strict, conservative, authoritative family. Mine was that way, too. I was a rebel — if they said right, I went left. At home, I had always been the bad kid, the black sheep. I flamed out in public school, cutting classes, sneaking out at night, taking the family car for joyrides, smoking pot all the time. Woolman totally transformed my outlook and approach to myself and to the rest of the world. I didn't feel micromanaged there, hovered over, or told what to do. There were still expectations, but I got to decide if I would follow them, knowing there would be consequences if I didn't. Courses were scheduled in the same way they would be in college with time off during the day, which made me feel very grown-up. If I skipped a class, staff didn't report me to my parents, and I was not marked truant. I just had to make up the classwork. I was being treated as an adult and any choices I made were my own responsibility. It was like being in a cocoon, where I was safe and supported but doing my own thing in the insulation. I thrived on being my own person and making my own choices. I made breakfast twice a week on my own for 70 people because I was seen as being very responsible. That's where I learned to cook. I was also chosen to serve on the Ministry and Oversight (M&O) Board. Students who got into trouble went before a group of peers who were seen as fair and mature. They picked me! At Woolman, I developed belief and respect in myself, as well as how to trust people. The best part is that I realized I wanted to succeed and not self-destruct. I graduated with straight As, the highest GPA in my graduating class."

Initially, Doug Tweed (1968-1970) viewed Woolman as a way to leave home and be on his own, but once there, he found it was a lot more. "Raised Quaker in La Jolla, California, I was unhappy with the public school system. I discovered John Woolman School through a Friends Meeting newsletter. As for most of us, John Woolman School was a seminal experience. That's why people have such a deep emotional attachment to the place. Populated with like-minded youth, students there were treated as adults. Staff member Dick Miller, who managed the farm, became my mentor, and changed my life path. He trusted me to take the school's flatbed truck into Yuba City to buy feeder pigs at auction. Raised on dining-hall food slops, the pigs were then slaughtered for meat to feed the school. Dick introduced me to labor: cutting firewood, building things, and feeding livestock. Since I was drawn to getting my brain out of my head and into my hands, making pottery in the art studio was also joyous. I work as a carpenter now. Everything I've done since has come down to process, transferred from clay to wood."

After graduation, Doug started a one-month pottery workshop at Woolman that ran for four to five years, and he majored in art at UC Davis. He also developed a summer back-country wilderness experience at Woolman that included snow-and ice-climbing and backpacking. Additionally, in the 1980s, he initiated fundraising and worked for reduced wages alongside volunteers and two crew carpenters to build the larger cabins on the Woolman campus.

Martha Kahane (1973-1974), a psychologist in private practice, also says that Woolman had a big educational impact on her. She notes, "The biggest influence in my life that I got from Woolman was from my teachers. One of them was Susie Van Tine, my French teacher, who had done her junior year abroad in France. Susie taught a tiny class of three to four students who were advanced in French. Since I had already studied French before, I was in it. We met every week and delved deeply into the minutiae and nuts and bolts of French. In fact, the class was so thorough that I scored 799 on my French SAT. Susie also encouraged me to attend a summer six-week immersion program in Quebec, and I did. After that, I was dreaming in French. I went on to study French, German, and Spanish in college. Then I married a man who is an ardent linguist."

Jennifer Shannon (1976-1978) a licensed psychotherapist and a Certified Diplomat in Cognitive-Behavioral Therapy, specializing in anxiety adds, "Five years before going to Woolman, I really hadn't had any formal education other than a short time at Berkeley High, which was so big and overwhelming. I had a lot of catching up to do because I'd been in a free school for four years. I did not do well in biology, or test well. I struggled with algebra and geometry. For other students coming from a public school, Woolman may have felt very different. But for me coming from an alternative school education, Woolman felt just right. I did well there. Woolman was like having a tutor. Plus, since I was such an eager learner, teachers loved me. I was super-interested in learning. I fact, I got annoyed at other students who weren't taking the academic processes seriously and said, 'Oh, we're free – we don't have our parents anymore.' I was at Woolman to study.

"Early on, I knew I wanted to be a therapist and knew I would need a master's degree to do that, but I didn't have a lot of confidence in my academic ability. Woolman gave me the emotional confidence and academic foundation to know I could do it. Math instructor Amanda

Wilcox taught me algebra and geometry with love and support, and ultimately, I could do math. She also fostered a love of German in me and inspired me to go to the four-year Quaker college, Earlham, in Richmond, Indiana. I used tutors there but felt fine about asking for help because Woolman had taught me that it was okay to get extra support to be successful. Had I not had that one-on-one experience with my instructors at Woolman, this would not have been the case. After college, I got accepted into the master's program at UC Berkeley."

Olivia Gay (student 1965-1968, staff in the early 1970s) also feels that Woolman saved her life. "My mother was going to school at Cal Berkeley in the early 1960s and having a fantastic time living in San Francisco. She really didn't want me with her. She had a friend in Berkeley whose son had gone to a summer work camp at Woolman. Since there weren't that many other options for boarding schools in California, I ended up at Woolman, which became a blessing. I think a lot of kids ended up at Woolman because their parents didn't want them to be in Berkeley during that time.

"In some ways, more than changing my life, Woolman saved my life by providing me with a surrogate family and community. I had come from a very small, close-knit community in Vermont and found that again at John Woolman. In that sense, the school allowed me to continue the rural experience I'd had growing up in Vermont. Being in a small community in the countryside felt familiar. Like many other people, I had a very strong social community experience there. I've had other experiences like that but not for that long with that much intensity. Though I don't have a family of my own, I do have that experience of being enmeshed in a community and involved."

Jane Uptegrove (1970-1971) also mentions, "Woolman caught me in my life at a time of crisis. I'd had it with the school I was in and thought they were hypocrites. You could get some support but mostly the teachers said, 'You're on your own.' I kept feeling that I wanted my school to be more of a community, but it kept coming up short. Su Herbert urged me to come out to Woolman, which seemed like barely a school, but maybe that was okay. My first feeling there was if you wanted something to happen, you would have to want to do it and take the initiative. You weren't going to be force-fed anything. The faculty was accessible, backed you up on it, and did not judge you. Compared to where I had been, the fact that it was a Quaker school and staff lived there made them more connected to students. The freedom there was also good because it was such a hard time because of the war in Vietnam and what we were looking at into the future. I had a connection with Michael and Susan Brown. Michael taught a course on African American history. It was an eye-opener and stuck with me. At Woolman, I got the idea of a California-ethos approach to life that stayed with me. After Woolman, I went to China, invited by Putney School in Vermont to join a youth group. The trip was organized by author Bill Hinton, who was researching material in China for a book he was writing. My experience at Woolman left me open to the idea of joining the group. A year later I came back to Woolman to teach a seminar class."

Chris Edgell (1970) says, "My mother wasn't Quaker, but after my parents divorced, we started going to the College Park Friends Meeting in San Jose, the oldest meeting in California. She took us to protest marches that the Quakers were involved with, like Hiroshima Day on the Golden Gate Bridge and Peace and Freedom marches. When I was a kid, I thought Quakers were really weird because they sat around in silence, but what I got out of that experience much later in life was that unlike a lot of religions, Quakers truly live what they believe, not just on Sunday. When I was young, I didn't have a lot of appreciation of Quakers, but they completely formed how I have tried to live my whole life, which is ironic because at that time, I didn't take it to heart. My first wife, Heidi Jett Edgell (1968-1971) was a Quaker. My second wife was also a Quaker. Plus, it was the generosity of Quakers that enabled me to go to Woolman. College Park Friends Meeting and Berkeley Friends Meeting were the two Quaker meetings that founded John Woolman School. There was an elderly gentleman from College Park who had refused to pay his taxes due to the use of tax money being used for the war in Vietnam. He paid my way to Woolman. I don't know where he got the money, but I was basically at Woolman on a scholarship from College Park. Woolman made a huge impact on my life. My daughter, a public health nurse, works with the Santa Cruz County homeless population. She has really strong social societal beliefs about how people should be treated equally and with respect. Though she is not Quaker, some of those things that were important to her mother, Heidi, and me, rubbed off."

Ed McCarroll (1963-1964) attended John Woolman School in its first year. He recollects, "My mom couldn't handle my rebellious nature, so she pawned me off on the good Quakers in Grass Valley. Thirty-six students were there that year. Del Reynolds was principal. I had a blast! Toward the end of my second year, both Del and Bob left, and Harold Blickenstaff took over. Some compared Woolman to Summerhill but from what I could see, the only similarity between the two schools was that staff at Woolman walked around with the Summerhill book in their back pocket. Any behavior was acceptable at Summerhill, which wasn't true of Woolman. Misbehaving had consequences. I was almost kicked out once, and then begged the Spanish teacher to raise my grade from an F to a D minus, which saved me from getting kicked out. I was failing everything but geometry. Woolman's science and math teacher, Bob Creighton, took me on as a personal challenge. He was the teacher who made a difference for me. At Woolman, I learned how to apply logic to geometry. I got a college degree in mathematics. The math department at UCLA had a computer science option, so I got my degree in mathematics without ever taking differential equations. I started teaching sixth grade. I also taught bilingual math, where 80% of the students were mostly undocumented Mexican immigrants. After five years of teaching, in the late 1970s I went back to computer work, which I did until retirement."

Sean Farrell (1981), now an electrician in San Francisco, was so unhappy at the public high school in Nevada City that he financed his own schooling at Woolman. Famous for having been the subject of a 1969 documentary short called *Sean*, which featured his four-year-old thoughts on marijuana, police presence, and the freewheeling lifestyle of his home in the Haight Ashbury district, he was also the subject of a follow-up film in 2005, *Following Sean*. The first documentary received acclaim in the U.S. and in Europe at Cannes Film Festival for its open portrayal of 1960s counterculture. French filmmaker François Truffaut was a fan. *Following Sean* received similar praise. Sean says, "When I watch my four-year-old self in *Sean*, I realize how much my attitude has changed. I no longer have animosity toward the police. I was clearly repeating stuff I had heard, but it was also a fairly rough place to be back then. Regarding Woolman, my dad didn't want to pay to send me there. I was fully invested in going but could not afford to pay full-time tuition. So, I sold my pickup truck and went there as a day student. With only 12 students in my graduating class, it was a small school. I lived in a small camp trailer on my family's property in North San Juan, about a 20-minute drive north of Grass Valley. Now I own property in the same area. During Special Projects, I helped with maintenance on the farm. Even though I wasn't supposed to, because of the way the school was structured with student-built structures and A-frame cabins set out in the meadow, I often stayed overnight. Senior students who had been at the school in prior years assured me that staff never checked cabins after check-in at 10:00 PM. One night, though, we were having a big, raucous party with a keg and a bonfire. Former older students from town supplied the keg. We were making so much noise that we woke instructor Al Chase up. He arrived at the party and told us to put the fire out. Then he walked over, picked up that nearly full keg and put it on his shoulder. We were impressed by how easily he could just pick up that keg and walk away with it. We didn't do hard drugs. We were just teenagers having fun. For the most part, we were actually very responsible. I did my schoolwork and always worked and made money as a teenager. I was wired with a 'get up and go' attitude. In some ways, I feel that we were moderators for some of the kids who were really messed up there. We helped them."

Steven Greenleaf (1979-1981), founder of Greenleaf Education Costa Rica, which provides accelerated classes in environmental leadership, communications, problem-solving, and sustainability, also says he was a troubled teenager. "I didn't go to Woolman by choice and had no initial desire to be there. I went there because it was Woolman or the California Youth Authority. Though I was high-functioning, I had major drug and alcohol problems. If not for Woolman, I would not be here. Woolman literally saved my life. I was interested in science and took physics and advanced biology from Geri (Alcomo) Stout. She definitely added to my interest. Greg Smith also had a big effect on me. He was an extremely kind, clear, intelligent man, and brilliant teacher. He designed an advanced poetry and prose workshop, in which I was his only student. Open to creativity and experimentation, he introduced me to the work of Gary Snyder and Peter Matthiessen. He was a great role model because it came effortlessly to him. I also took fiber arts because I could sit at the Art Barn, knit, and hang out with all the girls. Other Woolmanites were kind to me in spite of what I did or said, which was new to me, since my family situation was not great. Now, even 40 years later, I am in communication with people from Woolman. We are like extended family."

Additionally, students who came from good family situations who liked school express how John Woolman School paved a positive path for them. Paul Jorgensen (1966-1969), son of Mary and Russ Jorgensen (founders of the school), attended John Woolman School for three years. He says, "We were Quakers growing up but the element of nonviolence and working in service projects at the school definitely impacted my life. Just the story of the farm at John Woolman is amazing. Going to Woolman for three years affected me, particularly the work ethic and community spirit there. We carried that on in our family. A large part of what I remember about being at Woolman were activities outside of the classroom. They made a difference. Principal Harold Blickenstaff loved sports. We had amazing sports teams. We were a force in the foothills and built strong relationships. I'll always remember getting into his low-riding limousine and driving all over the place to play games. Also, in the summer of 1969, my brother, Mark Jorgensen (1963-1964), sat down on the piano in the art barn at Woolman. Indirectly, as a result of listening to him play that piano, when I went to college, I took up music at Sonoma State. When Woolman started, my mom was a dedicated fundraiser for the school. Day in and day out in her home office, she was on the phone raising money for Woolman and building relationships. To their dying breath, my parents gave thousands of dollars to the school. They held the belief that the school would survive. Up until she passed away at age 98, my mom was still completely locked into how to save the school. She lived and breathed John Woolman and would do anything she could to save it. What's happening now is the resurrection of John Woolman School. When you see how everything is woven together, then you have no doubts that Divine Will is happening. To me, that's exciting. I also think this book is an honor to Russ and Mary. It gives a historic element to the school, which means a lot to many people."

A Quaker associated with Woolman for many years, Lisa Hubbell (1976-1978), attended Quaker Quarterly Meetings in the campus meeting hall, was active in family work camps (1990s-2000s), and was on the Board from 1989 to 1995 and again in 2018. She also started the John Woolman School Alumni Association. (JWSAA). After college, Lisa lived in Italy for two years. Her daughter, Hannah McKenny (now Thistle Hofvendahl), also went to Woolman in the fall of 2014. Thistle is married to Ben Hofvendahl, who was also a Woolman Semester student in the fall of 2014. His older brothers Trevor and Russell are also Woolman alumni. Lisa earned a master's in museum studies and worked in museums for 20 years. When her museum jobs dried up, she went to library school and has been a librarian since 2013. She says, "Each person in the Woolman community was valued for what they cared about. I was never judged for being smart. People could appreciate that academics were just as much fun for me as whatever they liked doing. I led a madrigal quartet at Woolman and grew up going to the Southern California Renaissance Faire. As a result, I got interested in the Italian Renaissance. Though a class in the Renaissance was not offered at Woolman, I took a phenomenal class from Richard Sanders in how to write a research paper and chose a topic from the Renaissance. This led to getting a BA in European Studies, with a concentration in the Italian Renaissance."

Ann (Croninger) Zedah (1967-1984), who has been active in city government and community organization, was raised at Woolman and also remembers Richard Sanders favorably. Her parents, Chuck and Virginia Croninger, were instructors there. She says, "Academically, our education was like being in college. My teacher, Richard Sanders, left a big impression on me. He was hard on me and the subjects he taught were not my easiest ones, but he taught Research Skills, which served me so well in college. Deward and Louise Drollinger also influenced me. The summer after I graduated, I lived with Deward's family in the Cedar House while I cooked with Marguerite Blickenstaff for the owner-builders. Greg Smith, my English teacher, was also fantastic."

Gordon Smith, biologist, (1975-1977) was also profoundly influenced by his time at John Woolman School. He says, "There is no question that my academic and social education at Woolman influenced my career path. I work as a fish and wildlife biologist with a federal agency, and on conservation of aquatic habitats. My experience at Woolman of reflecting on the importance of the individual in a community gave me the sensitivity to work with native Hawaiian-island communities and care about what drives their small community groups. My exposure to these issues at Woolman has had a lasting influence on how I approach my late-career work and life path to this day."

Susan Miller (1968-1969), who went to Woolman alongside her sisters, Jennifer, and DeBora, relates, "My life was informed by Woolman for at least 20 years following graduation. It was so unlike the schools from where most people had been. I think the way the Quakers made their decisions through unanimity, and the way social interaction was introduced at the school, were unique. We met all the students at the beginning of the school year by spending two days together sleeping and eating in the dining hall. We went there because our parents, Dottie, and Dick Miller, got jobs at the school. My dad was hired to manage the school farm. I was born when mom and dad were 16, so my parents were in their early 30s when we arrived there. The largest education I got at Woolman was social and political. We did a lot of marching for Caesar Chavez and against the war. My dad was also a big mentor to the boys because at the time, there were a lot of boys there from the Bay Area who were struggling socially and educationally. He had a particular influence on Chris Thollaug, Doug Tweed, and John Klingelhofer. While there, our parents swapped partners with two other teachers on campus. Our mom, Margarite, got involved with Harold Blickenstaff and later married him, and our dad, Dick, married Harold's former wife, Dottie. They were all young, and still sorting out their own lives."

Nick Bratt, photographer, and President of 4D Optical LLC (1975), whose father helped build the dorm and desks for cabins at John Woolman, also says that Woolman had a positive impact on his life. "I was an eccentric kid, and a high-school dropout. Woolman changed my life. The school gave kids adult responsibilities. It was my freshman year, I was only 14 years old, and I drove a tractor. I tell people and my kids how unique it was, and they don't believe me."

Sue Opitz (1969-1972) says, "Growing up in a small town and going to Woolman influenced me to live in rural areas. I got my BA degree in nursing virtually. I think Woolman prepared me for that because I functioned well independently. Instructor Jim Corbett said I graduated from Woolman with more credits than anyone."

Paul Schneider (1979) adds, "Because of the way Woolman was set up, it was possible to mold the school operation to meet the needs of the individual. This meant that if a student had a problem or needed help in a particular area, the school could usually fill that need."

For still others, the Quaker teachings of nonviolence, social justice, and community action at John Woolman School left a deep impression.

Josie Chase (1970-1971), potter, says, "I remember a wonderful history class taught by Michael Brown in which we read *Malcolm X* and *Bury my Heart at Wounded Knee*. It was very topical at that time. These important social justice subjects woke me up. As a result, I became very politically active after Woolman. I got very much into the left-wing Marxist world, and was very invested in anti-war work, and civil-and labor-rights movements. I was very much involved in organizing attempts in factories and exposing when unions were complicit with employers."

Suchi Branfman (1969-1971), dance instructor and choreographer, also carried the principles of Woolman and Quaker tenets into her later life. She says, "Social justice has always been the context for my work. I did not grow up in a Quaker family, but I came from a progressive, social-justice-based one. We were secular Jews, and my parents were Communist Party members. John Woolman School was attractive because it was a place that was founded on social justice and on people being engaged with society through our classes. The ways they structured our work—and our time and their approach to our engagement with everything—was very democratic. Yes, it was a "top-down" school with a Head of School, but it was a real community very much informed by social justice. I remained committed to social justice but also opened myself to exploration of an inner, spiritual life. At Woolman, those things melded together; the spiritual, the societal, and the embodied practice. It was a big place: a combination of the real world and ethereal space of the 1970s. Woolman was also a place where I could go that felt like a good match for who I was and the things I valued. It also allowed us to be who we were and be free with who we were becoming and find out who we were in all of that."

Blair Gardner (1974-1976) says that she become a health and childbirth education, public health, and EEG (brain wave study) professional due to the influence of her biology instructor at John Woolman School, Kerry Travers. She says, "Kerry inspired my love of human anatomy. My second year at Woolman, Kerry was pregnant with her first child. I had always been enamored of pregnant women and babies. Even though I was only 16, I had read the book *Spiritual Midwifery* and I wanted to be a midwife. In my teenage brain, because I'd read so many books about it, I thought that I could give her good information to support her pregnancy. The fact that she honored my interest was huge to me. During her pregnancy, she had a lot of early contractions and was put on bed rest for three to four months. I had drawn an elaborate, colorful mandala for her to focus on during her labor. Lo and behold, she put it up on her bedroom wall. I was very touched. During the time I spent talking with her while she was on bed rest, we formed what I interpreted as a bond. I was interested in science only in terms of what I would need to become a midwife. Kerry let me do a special project on the study of female anatomy, which was unusual. Then she told me, 'You know, you're really good at this – you'd be great as a nurse, midwife, or doctor. I think you should go on the Mexico Spanish immersion trip and work in the lab at the medical clinic. You can learn about a lot of parasitic diseases. I want you to see those rare things under the microscope.' I was terrified because I didn't know Spanish and was shy, but I did it. When I got there, Darrell, who spoke English and was supposed to be my staff member in Mexico, had a terrible case of dysentery, was stuck up in the mountains, and could not get down to the clinic. I ended up working with someone who did not speak English, and I spoke no Spanish. I also got extremely sick, and while I was ill, my belongings were stolen. I got in touch with Mike and said it was not working and went up to stay with a friend in San Clemente, California. Even though the trip did not work out, I still appreciated that Kerry thought I could do it."

Priscilla Hockett (1969-1971), who also became a nurse and helps Habitat for Humanity build houses in underserved communities in emerging countries, sums up what many former students feel about the time they spent at Woolman: "So many things we were exposed to at that school were magic. I think about kids now in high school—it was bad enough back then, but their lives now are wrapped up in focusing on computers and cell phones when, in contrast, we were out in the middle of the field dancing with goats. What a miraculous way to spend high school! The bond that we created there was also something very special. I think that school planted something in all of us that enabled us to blossom."

Matthew Bronson (1973-1974), a massage therapist and linguist who taught for 30 years at UC Davis, also recalls, "An invaluable thing I learned from being at Woolman was the capacity to amuse myself. We didn't have the Internet, TV, videos, or computers. A phone call home was a big deal. Back then, an operator would come on the line and ask for your phone number because they couldn't figure out where you were calling from, so you'd have to punch it in. We had to schedule a specific time for placing our phone calls. We felt like we were isolated in the wilderness, but we were never bored. We always found something to do. Kids these days are overstimulated but bored all the time. We had resilient ingenuity. I had a posse of friends, three girls. One night, I got the idea to play-act that I was a mad scientist, and they were my monkeys, escaping from the laboratory. They immediately got into it. I would chase them around the campus, talking in a funny German professor voice as they made monkey noises. We did that for weeks. I do comedy improvisation now, and realize we were doing that all the time. We did not know it was a "thing,' but we would just make-believe some scenario. We had the room, the imagination, and the space to do it."

Amelia Neighbors, (1994-1996) also says that Woolman had a big influence on her life. "Before going to Woolman, I was a sophomore in my second year at Nevada Union High School, where I just felt like I was in a concrete jungle. I was surrounded by people who were not very kind, peers that I did not feel were appreciating the individual differences and uniqueness of each one of us. In fact, I was getting along with my teachers there much more than my peers. I just needed a different place to get decent grades. So, my parents looked around for options. I was living with my mom in Nevada City, and she found John Woolman School. Then we had to figure out how I could apply to be a day student and how to get a ride out to Woolman and back every day, which was a little bit of a trick for my mom, who was a single mom at that time. At that time, John Woolman School was a four-year high school. I think there were maybe 40 students total. I started school there in the second quarter of my sophomore year.

"Every year, the school did a week-long service project somewhere, usually in California. The projects were chosen by seniority. I remember my friend, Rachel, did not like me, or get along well with many others. She was upset with the project she got because of her age and the fact her seniority wasn't good enough to go to the top-tier programs. We ended up on a service trip together for a week. She got stuck with me and a bunch of other new kids she didn't want to hang out with, so she told me, 'We're going be friends.' On that project, we went to the beach and cleaned it up. An invasive succulent, ice plant (*carpobrotus edulis*), that was not native to California, was taking over the beaches. So, we helped clear it. I also worked at a small newspaper on the south coast of Southern California near San Jose, I think, for a week writing articles and doing everything for them.

"Woolman was definitely different than Nevada Union High School. There were no lockers or as many kids. I went from a school of 2,000 students to 40 students total, with a graduating class of 20. There were kids who attended during the day like I did, and there were students that lived on campus. The kids that lived there would get in trouble at night. Even though there was a lot of drama and stuff going on, I actually got to write a science-fiction book for my English class. I never finished it, but they did let me do my own program for English. Woolman was just a completely different environment and experience. For example, we read Howard Zinn's *A People's History of the United States*, which was about U.S. history from the viewpoint of marginalized, disenfranchised, and oppressed people, covering protests and activism. Woolman had smaller classes that you didn't find in other places. For me as a teenager, art class was important and special. I loved my ceramics class with the huge, spinning pottery wheels. In the art studio at Woolman, I was allowed to do projects my own way. Nobody was there to tell me how to do it. When I had an art class at Nevada Union, the teacher would write critical things right on my art, which made me feel violated. Teachers at Woolman may have given helpful critiques, but it was a completely different, more supportive environment.

"Woolman allowed me to enhance the values that I had already had and reinforce them. I could choose to make a stand, and care about what I chose. Immediately after graduation, I went to Evergreen State College, which is like Woolman, a liberal arts college in the woods with a similar kind of hippie atmosphere. Now I work at REI, which means I am still caring about the environment. I love gardening, being outside, and hiking. I work at a place where our whole vision is getting people outside and being anti-racist. I don't know if 100% of that came out of my experience at Woolman, but I definitely feel that Woolman allowed me to align who I was with where I was. It gave me an option to actually be myself, which I still value. When I worked at other companies, none of them felt like I was allowed to be a human being. At REI, employees are allowed to have a religion, thoughts, feelings, and to disagree with things. They allow me to have my humanity and work.

"My son also just recently started public high school and was having a hard time. His first semester, he got bullied by other students who threatened him physically. As a result, he was having a hard time learning. His grades were okay, but you can imagine having to think about other kids trying to beat you up after school. It made learning hard for him. So, I literally did for him what my parents had done for me when we found Woolman. I said, 'You have options – this is not the only school you can go to. There are other programs.' I went down to the Washington School District, and said, 'Okay, what are our options?' That's when we discovered The Learning Center, which is an alternative school in Carnation, Washington. My son is now a part of the Choice Program there, where 15 kids and their individualized learning happens on site. There's no homework. It is the same kids all day with the same teachers for the entire program. It was only because I got to go to Woolman and choose a different route that I thought to offer my son another option."

Former instructor Greg Smith (1978-1984) sums it up best when he says, "I think what impressed me most about Woolman was the degree to which kids who had not even thought it was possible to experience community in the late 20th century found that at Woolman, in fact, it was."

Art/Sketching in the tall grass, learning outdoors,
photo on back cover

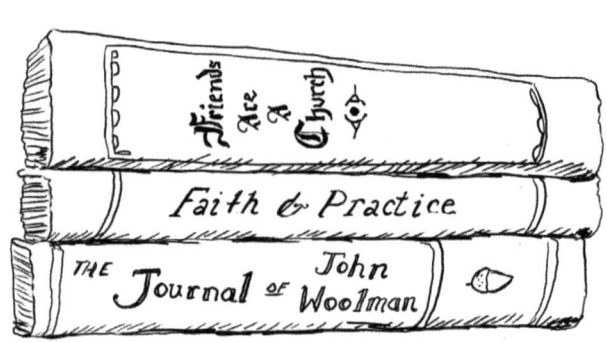

| LANGUAGE ARTS |

12

....

EXPERIENTIAL LEARNING

"We were invited into a deeply interwoven world of possibilities."

– S. Branfman

At John Woolman School, education was exploratory and self-selective. Those drawn to the arts threw pots fired in a Japanese-style multichambered step kiln, fabricated jewelry in an art barn, wove on Swedish floor looms, played music, studied writing, performed plays, or learned to dance in the dining hall. Others drawn to the sciences and natural world raised goats, planted trees and gardens, learned astronomy at night in the campus meadow, or studied chemistry, physics, geology, mathematics, and biology through hands-on applications. Students built a sustainable social community together. They worked on farm projects, grew and prepared food, and were a part of developing consensus for school-related issues during community meetings. Some social learning was even peer-based.

Biology and Chemistry

Lisa Klein Kirsis (1981-1984) observes, "Everything I learned at John Woolman School got me thinking. I consider myself a scientist and I do believe the seeds for doing good science were laid there because it was so experiential. We learned about biology by draining the lake and pulling everything out of it. We learned about field botany by transecting fields or through harvesting 500 mushrooms or anything you could find, anywhere, and dragging it all back to the chemistry lab. We learned about chemistry by having an active, live chemistry lab which was a

little under supervised so we could explore outside the bounds. We had excellent teachers. I was very fortunate. The education I received there was tremendous. I ended up doing a lot of field botany."

Astronomy

Co-author of this book, Catherine (Cathy) Lenox (1969-1971), recalls, "I felt confined in public high school. Woolman opened my eyes to a wonderful unique, hands-on way of learning. I thrived on it. In one memory, I'm tucked into a sleeping bag at midnight in the campus meadow surrounded by classmates, chilled to the bone. The sweet, dusty smell of unpaved roads, farm animals, and hay drifts down from the barn. As I lie there staring up at a wintry, star-filled sky, my astronomy teacher points out Cassiopeia and Orion. Sipping chamomile tea brewed from the meadow's tiny yellow flowers to stay warm, though shivering, I marvel at this exciting, real-world experience. No other school has ever given me anything close to this. Even as young as I am, I know this is education at its best. All my senses are learning. Astronomy comes alive for me that night."

Farm Life

Suchi Branfman (1969-1971) adds, "What was profound about Woolman is that I was able to live there, see the stars every night, grow food in a garden, and raise goats. I didn't know anything about goats or gardening when I got there. We were invited into a deeply interwoven world of possibilities that were expansive, and not separate from the pleasure I took from dancing. It was all deeply connected."

Purpose in the Arts

Shana Maziarz (student 1980-1991, Peace Studies & Global Studies teacher 2004 - 2005, Head of School 2005-2008) has a long family history with John Woolman School. More of her story is in the Woolman Semester chapter. Her aunts, Jan (early 1960s) and Joan (1983) also attended Woolman. Jan remembers, "I was disenchanted with being in a traditional school. Joan was in an innovative program school (IPS) at University High School in Los Angeles, an alternative high school within the public school, chosen by lottery. I was not chosen from my grade. This stimulated my interest in going to Woolman. I liked being outdoors and went to a summer camp. I loved the garden and how we were being taught; however, I decided I did not want to go to high school there because I was interested in riding horses and dancing. At the time, they did not have horses or a dance program. However, Woolman did prompt me to go to a private, alternative high school in Los Angeles."

In the long run, it was her sister, Joan, who decided to go to Woolman for high school. Joan remembers, "I was very troubled in public school. The IPS program was unstructured, and I was lost. School was also not my thing. I was unhappy in a school setting, self-medicating, drinking, and doing drugs; however, because Woolman offered weaving and I was interested in crocheting, I went there. At Woolman, I found a purpose in weaving. It was my first step toward happiness. It saved me. I did a lot of weaving, spinning, and dyeing. After graduation, I ended up with an 8-harness and a 16-harness dobby loom. For a very long time, I was into weaving."

Sex Education

The following story is also so evocative of being a teenage girl at Woolman, especially one in that place in the early 1970s, that it belongs in this book. Written by psychologist Martha (Philips) Kahane, a John Woolman School student in 1974, it speaks to how private and safe the environment felt there, to the bold education of a campus cook, and to the depth of the trusting relationships that students had with each other.

"It is winter, and a group of female teenagers are lying on their backs, peering into the little pink caverns of their vaginas with awkwardness and awe using a mirror, a speculum, and a flashlight. They are students at John Woolman School who, under the tutelage of a campus cook intent on teaching them self-empowerment, are lying supine on the floor of an enclosed kitchen storage room. Outside, the snow is piled high. Someone's cabin is where they all hope to be at night – hope to be invited, that is. Something of the moment's exclusivity and extreme coziness invite both magic and danger, especially in the winter at night.

"The hair on their legs and under their armpits is sprouting freely, proudly unshaven. They are reading *The Second Sex, Our Bodies, Ourselves, and Rubyfruit Jungle.* They are women, not girls, and shame and misery to anyone who refers to them as 'chicks.' They are taking a self-defense class, and no one dreams that the groin kick might actually have to be used on a real-life would-be rapist. They are excited and full of desire in that mind-thrilling way peculiar to this stage of life. One of them wants to be a writer, is sure she will be a writer even if she is fifty before her first book is published. One has chopped off her waist-length blonde ringlets and is trying mightily to be a lesbian. One wears kickass hiking boots and ripped jeans and reminds them of Wonder Woman in the cartoons they only recently stopped reading. She is confident and sexy and powerful without seeming to try at all. All of them are taking AP classes and applying to college in the spring. All of them scorn what is ordinary and predictable, like wanting a boyfriend or applying mascara and lip liner in the mirror. All of them believe their power as women will not be challenged much, knowing all they know about feminism. One of these teenagers is me. I have chosen this school since my mother has moved to Manhattan to live with her soon-to-be new husband and I am not moving to New York!

"Back in my cabin after the brief journey into the inner landscape of my own vagina, I look into the open wood stove to see glimmering jewel embers of apricot and orange. The fire warms my face, and the mingling scents of wood smoke and sandalwood incense intensify my longing for something I am nowhere close to being able to name at this point in my life. My face gets too hot, and I move away as the zipping sound of a match being struck elicits another smell, one that evokes all of this danger and excitement and longing more than any other. Someone has lit a joint.

"When one of the other women (we call ourselves womyn) suggests we take a night walk to the road outside the school and then hitchhike to the all-night diner down the road, I don't really want to go but no one has taught me yet, as I teach my patients to do now, to listen to my own inner voice. To listen to the voice that says no, don't drop acid with your 18-year-old boyfriend in a public garden. No, don't get into the front of a truck cab with two old men while your boyfriend sits in the back in the open-air truck bed. No, don't sleep with that guy you just met on the street in Oregon. None of that has happened yet.

"I tell my children edited versions of these stories now. I don't want my daughter to emulate my promiscuity or my risk-taking. Listen to your Inner Voice, I tell her, teaching her the term as soon as she is old enough to understand. It will lead you to new doors opening. When you ignore that voice the first time, ivy starts to grow around the door. The second time you ignore it, the door gets covered over and you almost can't see it. The third time, the door grows over with thorns and there is no way to open it anymore. What I don't tell her until she is older because I don't want to scare her is that it works the other way too. If your Inner Voice says do not open that door and to walk the other way, the price of not listening could be near fatal."

John Woolman School farm project

| CAMP |

13

....

LIVING TOGETHER

"There is nothing like living in a community in real time."

– D. Drollinger

From those who founded the school right up to staff and students involved with the Woolman semester before the school closed, the sense of true community in every respect at John Woolman School left people who lived there with a deep and lasting impression. Community, in fact, is the word repeated most often in their recollections.

Lisa Klein Kirsis (1981-1984) observes, "John Woolman was a wonderful matrix of hard work, hard play, poetry, life, love, and being a decent human being. It was an experiment with living in kindness and trying to develop an environment where people are listened to and heard, and the individual is experienced, developed, and built without massive over-structure, power, control, and dominance. There are different theories about how to run societies and we saw one that was, in fact, built on Quaker values: kindness, caring, consideration. It was not some 'that will never work' idealistic utopia. It did work. I took every one of those lessons and applied it to my life."

Kristin Applegate (1986-1987) says that she was drawn to attend John Woolman School because of the farm project. "I was working part-time in a veterinarian office. When I found out that Woolman was a working farm and that it would be part of my responsibility to care for animals, I was totally into it. Being of service has always been important to me. I'm a nurse now, so the emphasis that was placed on service at Woolman did have something to do with what I did down the road. Before becoming a

nurse, I was a clay artist. I also did photography and writing at Woolman. I was so excited about learning. Ted and Michelle Beatty had a big impact on me. Ted taught history and Michelle, his wife, was my counselor. Michelle taught me to organize research papers on index cards in a specific way that worked for me. Discovering how you learn best is an essential component of learning in any kind of school setting. This is something I would have never been given at Berkeley High School with 3,000 other students around. Additionally, living in rustic cabins with a lack of urban noise enabled me to spend a lot of quiet time thinking about my place in the community. To be given the opportunity to have silent meetings for worship also put me so much more in tune. The setting lends itself to that automatically. I absolutely would not have had this same opportunity to discover myself in a mainstream school."

Sean Feder (1977-1978), now a business manager for the largest organic food certification company in the country, Farmers CCCOF, says, "I ended up at Woolman because my mom was part of the Peace Movement in the late 1970s. She connected with the Friends community in Palo Alto, who had a nice presence and worship house there, and heard about Woolman. I grew up an atheist, so I had to find other ways to make life meaningful than religion. For many generations, my family did not go to church on either side. My dad was Jewish, but they were secular and not religious. Sitting down together and being quiet and speaking your mind seemed reasonable. It made me aware of the social and community benefits of religion."

Jennifer Gershen (1989-1993) also says that living in the John Woolman School community changed her life. "Though I'm not a Quaker and never knew about Quakerism, the most fundamental, essential, philosophical point of view that changed my life at Woolman was being in a Quaker community. The Woolman experience of showing up for your community, being prepared and working toward a community goal, being as fundamental as your own personal preparedness, and working for yourself – I had never had a system like that. Students bonded with and relied on each other. In the learning community at Woolman, I had to be prepared to contribute to classes because my classmates were depending on me. The same was true of work jobs. We didn't have parents to clean our bathrooms. We participated in cooking meals. I had no idea what it took to take care of myself, but I liked being independent and I wanted to learn it. I hadn't had that level of responsibility in my family life. We learned to resolve conflict and live with and adapt to each other peaceably because we lived so closely together. The framework of collective behavior and the value system that was fundamentally laid out at Woolman was positive. It was a culture that kids were invited into and community where they could contribute. Learning how to be with other people in equal space is so helpful in the real world. As a teenager, that social engagement and responsibility was life-changing. This is the same value system I teach now to my own children."

Lori Bellilove (1970) notes, "As a religion for a young, struggling person trying to figure their way out, the Quaker faith and practice at Woolman was perfect. I loved the silent meetings. I'll never forget when something was stolen – we all fasted and sat on a hill together as a community in protest. At some point, there was a bathroom break, and somebody said something, and it got through to the culprit. I was really moved by that. It has affected me my whole life. I'll never forget that way of dealing with conflict. Human nature tends to not be like that. Look at our wars, how we enslave people, how we steal from others and how we think that they don't feel things. When the girl who stole the money was caught, rather than gang up on her, students responded to her pain with understanding. We came to understand that people steal when they have pain. That was one of my strong moments at Woolman."

Halina Janusz (1981-1982) agrees. "Woolman gave me tools regarding consensus, how a community works, and how everyone needs to lift each other up, from caring for sick people to being responsible for work jobs. We were a bunch of wild hippies in the woods, and some intense, painful things also happened, but I felt very challenged and fulfilled academically and socially there. Sitting in silent meetings was also powerful, and now a part of who I am. Had I not had those experiences at Woolman, I'd be a completely different person. I'm very grateful."

D'Arcy Drollinger (1984-1987) adds, "There is nothing like living in a community in real time. When you're responsible for cleaning, cooking, and milking the goat, and being part of a true community where everyone has jobs and participates to make everything work, it is a real opportunity to witness that in real time as a reality and really does foster community. I also believe that being thrust together and having to live, work, and study with people so closely from all different walks of life has given me the ability to collaborate and be patient with other people. I see that now. I interact with so many people in so many different capacities that I think the strength of what I have, who I am, and how to get along and work with other people was learned through that experience. Woolman was an amazing, safe place – and so progressive. Being present really changes the way you look at life. We even had a same-sex wedding in the 1980s. The cook and the secretary got married. Some Quakers stepped aside because they could not accept that, but the fact that the school was so ahead of its time in creating that environment for students and youth to grow up in and providing a space that had that level of active equality and justice for everybody was somewhat of a utopia in a lot of ways. When I look back on what an indelible imprint it made on my life, I will say that there were moments as a teenager that I wasn't always happy. I was living on those 360 acres all the time. Other students got to leave campus at Christmas and during the summer. I was very connected to the local community, but there were times during my teenage years when it felt stifling to be there all the time. I was ready to move to San Francisco when I had the opportunity. However, it is all relative. Looking back on it, I'm incredibly grateful when I compare it to other childhoods I hear about. At my nightclub, Oasis, I've worked hard to create a space where a cross-section of communities, gay and straight, young, and old, and all different racial backgrounds can all come together in a safe haven. It's been an amazing, satisfying experience for what I've been trying to do – and I can really trace its roots back to Woolman: the importance of it, how to create it, and how to be open to other people's needs for their experience of it. You can't create a community in a vacuum. You really do have to hold the space and give the space over in a lot of ways. I open the doors and turn on the lights, but it's the people who make the community.

The value of a community is that people are there to rally behind you and support you. It's fundamental to everything I do – and again, I can trace that back to Woolman."

Amelia Neighbors (1994-1996) notes, "I distinctly remember moments that you would never find at another school other than Woolman, like sitting in the library with others in silence or having community meetings. There was the feeling of being in a community and knowing if you were going to be there, you were going to do chores. If you were going to live there, which I did in my last year of high school, you were going to do even more chores. You were responsible for more than just yourself. You learned that you were part of something bigger than yourself, and that it meant having both responsibilities and benefits."

Olivia Gay (student 1965-1968, staff in the early 1970s) also says, "Woolman set me in a life direction that had more to do with Quaker principles and was different from what I might have had otherwise. The silent meetings, volunteerism, activism, and living in an intentional community in that way had an impact on my later life. I loved the feeling of being quiet together. The idea 'of God in everyone' was also very powerful. Consensus Quaker dialogue, anti-war pacifism, service, and volunteerism had a big effect on me. Being my own person at John Woolman, I also felt distinctly that people were relating to me as myself rather than as part of my family. As a staff member, I also loved having my counselees and was very close to them. While on staff, some students had famous parents and I remember feeling an equality with them while their kids were at Woolman. Diane DiPrima's daughter, Mini, and Faye Kicknosway's son, Kevin, were at Woolman when I was on staff. Sterling Hayden's daughter and son, Gretchen and Christian, were also there when I was a student. That gave me confidence about being with all different kinds of people."

Blair Gardner (1974-1976) says that Woolman is the first place she had ever lived where she interacted with adults as people. "Woolman was the first place I learned how to be with adults. Whenever I babysat staff members' kids, they also always invited me to dinner first, and I would sit and eat with them before they left."

Head of School Amy Cooke (2000-2007) also shares that there was a great deal of intention to cradle the school in a community with various ages. "Two of us on staff had elders living with us; my husband's mother and Dorothy's mother and father were also there. To have 80-year-olds present was an incredible gift. A lot of those teens never knew their grandparents or hadn't spent much time with them. I think it really added a lot. We also had very young kids; my daughter was there. I think this was true over and over again throughout Woolman's history, that you had a matrix of people that provided something for each other. I always thought that we were recreating a tribe. I believe we are tribal – deeply, intuitively tribal – and we need that range of ages. It's such an artificial thing to stick a bunch of same-age kids together in a building or room and expect that to turn out well. It's not how humans have evolved. So, I think it was wonderful for those kids to have that group of people with them day after day eating in the dining hall, being in meeting for worship and community meetings. That was truly as educational, if not sometimes more, as what was going on in the actual classroom.

"Our society puts up artificial barriers that a teacher must be an authority figure. Actually, you have better education results when you don't have that, but it caused problems too, and that should not be skipped over. Sometimes relationships got too close and sometimes it was difficult. That's part of it too. It was incredibly powerful that students had that there and could see people being real. We worked a lot with conflict. The nonviolent communication course came in just as I was leaving. That gave students such concrete tools to work with conflict. Honestly, conflict is where we get close, whichever weird ways humans are built, which I don't understand at all – conflict brings us close when we can walk through it."

Nina Kiriki Hoffman (1970-1973) agrees that living in a community of all ages also affected her. "I have a huge takeaway of living in that communal experience with a variety of people. Woolman was definitely formative. One fond memory I have is of babysitting Gloria Menmuir. We were friends and ran around a lot. I took art photos of her in a cemetery, and we did storytelling. She was a wonderful little compatriot."

Students often took this sense of "tribal responsibility" and applied it to work or volunteerism in the larger world.

Kate Connell (1977-1978) directed a nonprofit called Truth in Recruitment for numerous years. Truth in Recruitment is a project of the Santa Barbara Friends (Quaker) Meeting, a 501(c)3 nonprofit. Their goal is to educate students, families, and school districts about alternatives to military careers, inform families of their children's privacy rights, and advocate for policies regulating recruiter presence on campuses. Kate's leading to work for justice for youth and nonviolent solutions to conflict came out of her experience as a Friend and was strengthened by her time with other like-minded peers and teachers at John Woolman School. She says, "Woolman added a power dynamic and conversation between students and teachers: knowing each other on a first-name basis, learning to work out conflict resolution, how to dialogue. Woolman encouraged that critical thinking. I think the sense of community that comes from having more than one voice in a conversation is important. Community decision-making isn't a skill that everyone learns. I remember sitting in a circle in meetings and classes at Woolman to discuss school issues, conflicts, and resolutions to arrive at consensus. There was also a student school board. So, I would say that even if it didn't always work perfectly at Woolman, that was part of the goal. We involve youth a lot in our organization. I think that comes from the Woolman idea."

Jeanie Perry (1969- 1970) has worked with mentally handicapped adults, has been a special education teacher, and currently volunteers with the Corvallis Daytime Drop-in Center (CDDC), a community resource for people experiencing homelessness and poverty. She echoes what others have said when she reflects, "Woolman saved my life. I loved the country and the casual atmosphere. I was not doing well at the time due to a disruptive, confrontational home life. For the longest time, I did not feel valued. At Woolman, the focus was on building positive relationships. Forgiveness was also an underlying philosophy. Peter Donahue, who taught ceramics, and Molly Titcomb, who taught Spanish, both influenced and encouraged me. Molly and I went on a Spring Special Project to Coachella to help support the Cesar Chavez movement. On another project, I helped a nearby community of American Indians. At Woolman, I became more aware of people who did not come from economically advantaged backgrounds, which eventually led me to volunteer at the CDDC. So many people in our population feel very undervalued, as if they are invisible and nobody cares, just as I did. They are drowning in feelings of worthlessness, really struggling, and barely making it. Just reaching out to them in the smallest ways can make a difference. Sometimes I will just hand a dollar or two to someone on the street and their eyes will soften and even tear up, not because of the money, but because someone has acknowledged them as being human. They say, 'God bless you' and really mean it. I am so grateful to be able to play a very small part in reaching out to these precious people in Corvallis."

Suchi Branfman (1969-1971) also extended the Woolman spirit of community into action in her later life. She notes, "Woolman expanded my sense of community in terms of food and lifestyle. I'm interested in storytelling, gathering people, and creating places and spaces where that can happen, whether it is through dance or my community garden. I periodically invite community garden people to bring their salad produce for picnics. It's a place of gathering for people to talk together. It's a random part of the work I do which is linked to social practice and engaged to society. It is about exploring ways to get together as a community, grow food together, pick food together, and offer that to people. Perhaps what we need more is for people to grow up in communities where they are well-educated, have access to physical and mental healthcare, fresh food, wonderful schools, community centers, and access to the arts."

14

....

QUAKER CONTEMPLATION

"Quaker meetings taught me the importance of listening to people and giving each person weight. That's a Quaker tradition that a lot of dominant cultures don't value. We practiced it at Woolman, so it became more deeply ingrained in me."

– L. MacKenzie

R eligious studies and Quakerism were an essential part of John Woolman School, though not a mandatory expectation for students. Quaker meeting for worship was held regularly, during which staff and students could sit quietly for an hour on fold-out chairs in the campus meadow or inside the community meeting house, the barn. In that shared silence, everyone participating focused on the "light of God in all people," their own inner light and the light of others. If moved to speak, anyone could break the silence. Quakers believe in integrity, equality, simplicity, community, stewardship of the Earth, service, active nonviolence, and peace. These principles were foundational at Woolman. Numerous students chose to voluntarily attend meetings for worship. Community meetings, which students were expected to attend, usually started with a brief moment of silence, symbolizing the spirit of the Woolman and larger community.

Martha Kahane (1973-1974) says, "Woolman silent meetings were an exposure to an accessible religious tradition. Spirituality became a big part of my life. A group of us would also go into a cabin where Matthew Bronson taught us chants from different cultures. We'd sing the chants together. I still remember some of them. Also, living in an A-frame cabin

and being responsible for building fires and tending the gardens, the beauty of the land, and the seasons – all of that was wonderful. Most of all, living in a community with all those kids was intense, and sometimes even painful."

Matthew Bronson (1973- 1974) adds, "My mom was a Buddhist, and I'm a very 'Buddhist adjacent.' I'm a Tantric Shaivite now, and meditation is a big part of my life. It's a continuation. There was an emphasis on contemplation at Woolman. We were encouraged to reflect. I blossomed there and found a lot of room in the Quaker meeting to just be with myself and others. I loved our silent meetings every week. It was a touchstone. At reunions, there were these Quaker ladies in their 80s with that beautiful shining light in their eyes welcoming me. I love the Quaker resilience and the fierce love which has never been passive. It is love in action in the world. I am absolutely to my core resonant with the values of the community. It was such an important part of my life. The Quakers really saved my life. For ten years, I was also involved in dialogues with Native American scientists in Albuquerque, New Mexico. One of the things one of the elders said is that white people are missing our 'first instruction.' We weren't handed a manual of instruction of how to make sense of life, but he said that their people largely had the 'first instruction' intact, which is to take care of the land, take care of the people, and then take care of yourself. Part of the hunger in the white condition is this longing for a sense of 'being home,' or reconnecting with that clan structure that would have been our birthright for 40,000 years. We feel we've been dislodged from that, and Native peoples still have it. From my perspective, I believe that Woolman was a place of 'first instruction' where we came back to 'first principles.' There are certain root lessons we learned there of respect and taking care of each other on all levels, and if you messed up, you had to deal with it. We were living in a fishbowl. If you had an issue with someone, you would have to see them the next morning for breakfast. There was nowhere to hide. Our only option was to lift each other up. It was a beautiful opportunity to learn how to be with people. I am grateful for the core of cultural medicine we got there that deals with the gaps of how folks are typically socialized. What a beautiful gift to have an opportunity to go back and learn the first instructions that my society could not or would not give me."

Suchi Branfman (1969-1971) also reminisces, "I had never been in a Quaker meeting before John Woolman School. The Quaker meeting was a beautiful model for gathering with people and for listening to them and for giving them a space to speak. A lot of the work that I do now is around facilitating what the plan is, not deciding what it will be. That consensus and community connectiveness is very Quaker-based."

Outdoor community/event photo

| MEETING HOUSE |

15

THE ECO-CAMPUS

*"Only at John Woolman School do buildings
wander around the campus."*

– A. Zedah

The physical campus at John Woolman School offered its own learning, development, and unique joys. Students lived in a dorm on the left side of the campus or in A-frame cabins on the right. Cabins were heated by wood-burning stoves. Each residential area had a bath house, with sinks, toilets, and showers. Life in the dorm educated students in how to live amicably with others in a shared space; living in the cabins let students to feel as though they had their own homes and offered additional "real-world" education. Located in the Sierra Nevada foothills, the campus had 230 acres of woods, meadows, hiking trails and grasslands, a few main classrooms, a pottery and art barn, and a library. Education included interaction with the surrounding natural world. Houses and apartments were used as faculty residences around the campus. The barn was used as an art center. Today, the campus is much like it was then, with cabins still heated by wood burning stoves and a bath house with sinks, toilets, and showers in each residential area. The barn it is still used as the meeting house for the local Quaker Friends Meeting. Behind the Library/Meeting house is a multichambered step kiln, still used for community pottery firings. Many acres of forest and trails still lead through the campus. In 2020, the Nevada County Board of Supervisors designated the site as a county historic landmark.

Cabins

Jennifer Gershen (1989 -1993) describes moving into an A-frame cabin when she first arrived at Woolman. "I went to my cabin and there was a wood-burning stove in it. I assumed I was supposed to do something with it, but I had no idea what. I stacked a bunch of newspapers into it and laid a log on them, which did not work. It was like Survivor Island. I'd never made a fire before in my life or even considered making one. Thankfully a staff member came in and built a fire for me. At Woolman, there was always someone there to teach you and help you figure it out." In the 1980s, larger cabins were added to the left side of the campus. Whereas the A-frame cabins were numbered, these "condo cabins" had names, such as Skier, Beekeeper, Tree-Climber, Spinner, Musician, and Pig.

Central Campus

Staff housing, including the Stone House, the Redwood House, and the Cedar House, the Fern House, and the Arbor House (formerly the Principal's House), plus the campus office, a large barn, and a few classrooms, were situated in the center of the campus. The campus library, originally housed in a Quonset-style building beside a creek on campus, was moved later to a room behind the office. A pottery studio, also located in a Quonset hut, was later moved to the barn. Dubbed "the Art Barn," this structure was filled with pottery wheels and weaving looms. It would later become the Meeting House, used now for Quaker silent meetings.

Ed McCarroll, who attended Woolman during the early 1960s, remembers, "The building currently called the Meeting House was, in 1963, the Dining Hall. Then they built the existing Dining Hall, and the old one became the Art Barn, and later, the Library. At times, the Dining Hall was also called the Rec Hall, or the Wrecked Hall. We called the Fern House the Art Barn since that is where we had art classes. The Quonset House for us was Pottery, and the building above it was intended to be used as a student center. The original library was actually a room at the southwest corner of what's now the Office (and the office was a small room with a desk next to it); two classrooms occupied the rest of that building.

What's now Fern House was built in 1968. I remember the library was just called the Quonset hut. I helped the art teacher at that time, Arlo Wells, install the ceiling, standing on scaffolding inside. The building now known as Madrone was originally the Dorm, and IIRC was also the Academic Building. Arbor House was originally the Principal's Residence, but before it was built, the original Principal lived in the Dorm."

Having moved to the John Woolman School with her parents, Chuck and Virginia Croninger, when she was merely eight months old, Ann (Croninger) Zedah (1967 – 1984) holds the distinction of having lived on the Woolman campus longer than anyone. She says, "Everything at Woolman informed my entire life. I lived in that community for my entire upbringing and went to high school there. When I was in high school, the library was one room behind the office. As I recall, the old library by the creek was a Quonset-style building—kind of a central foyer that ran through to the creek with wings on either side of it. It was one of my favorite buildings. The library was just "down creek" from the pottery Quonset. My parents got divorced when I was seven years old, and my dad moved to Sacramento. He married a woman who is also like a mother to me, and my mom remarried later, too. When Ted Menmuir was principal, he and his wife, Dorla, liked the Cedar House, so we still lived in the Principal's Residence. After they moved off campus, we moved into the Cedar House. My mom stayed at Woolman until between my sophomore and senior years, when she moved to San Diego. After that, I went to San Diego during the summer. Even though my mom was faculty during my freshman year, I still lived in student housing. However, because I was a 'staff brat' and we didn't pay tuition, and since they always tried to fill the housing with paying students, the next year this didn't happen right away. For a while, Emily Hunter and I slept out on the rolling grass between the office and the dining hall until they told us that we could move into the Stone House wing of student housing. Since my brother went to high school in San Diego, my last two years, I was at Woolman alone. It is sad that our first home at Woolman, the dorm, and our last home, the Cedar House, burned in the Jones Fire."

Karen (Baird) Eaton (1975-1976) also remembers a fire that started in the library in the spring of 1976, burning several books. She says, "The spines were burned off many books. The fire burned between the shelf backs and the walls, so many of the books had spines that had burned but the pages were okay. Harriette Smith (the staff librarian) taught me to repair them with a paper saw, string, and glue—then taping over the repair. I rescued one of those lovingly-cared-for library registers. Of course, the list of books is wonderful, too. I think some of those 'repaired' books survived until the 1990s as I remember seeing something like that in the library and wondering why we just didn't get new ones. I guess their history was important.

The Rope Swing

For many years, a rope swing hung on the branches of a large oak tree near the center of the campus meadow. Until the rope disintegrated in the winter of 1977-1978, students loved to grab onto it and swing across the grassy field.

Lisa Hubbell (1977) recollects the night that rope swing disintegrated, "I lived in Cabin 10 in fall of 1977. There was no Cabin 11, as it had burnt earlier. One night, during a very heavy rainstorm, we heard a loud crash. The rope swing tree fell, rotted out from the inside. Within a day or two, we held a memorial meeting in Virginia's/Arbor House. I think Ken Jones was the one who wrote and played a song to the tree. Later, Alan Fischer heard Kate Wolf sing 'Fly Away,' which Kate had written about the tree, and he told all of us about it. I wrote a song, 'Tumblebug,' with one verse based on the memory of holding Allan Stone on my lap while waiting to jump off the rope swing."

Sophie Wood Brinker (2007) observes that singer/songwriter Kate Wolf, who visited John Woolman School in 1977, caught the essence of the Woolman campus spirit when she wrote "Fly Away." Kate's song of swinging on the rope captures the sense of "freedom riding on the wind" that students felt when they did the same.

(Reprinted with permission from Max Wolf, son of Kate Wolf)

FLY AWAY

By Kate Wolf

Fly away, riding high again,

you got me up a tree, out on a limb,

Just to fly away, listen to the wind,

then you showed me an oak tree, standing there so tall,

You know I have seen a thing or two, it has seen it all,

Seen the seasons come and go that made its branches bend,

Held the rope for those who go riding in the wind.

And yes, I guess I see the freedom waiting in the wind.

I have taken all the rope I have got and jumping off the end,

Riding with the swing 'til I touch down again,

Letting go, to go riding on the wind.

The Octagon

Instructors encouraged innovation, and to that end, students often also built their own lodging. Admired among Woolmanites and built by student Karen Reiner in the early 1970s was the Octagon, which had nine sides (so actually a nonagon). Though instructor Nick Wilcox helped her with the project, Karen built most of it and then lived in it. Don Brewer remembers the Octagon: "After crossing into the meadow past the Quonset hut, you would bear forward and slightly to the right to get to the Octagon. Mel's Pond/Lake would be more of a right turn to the south."

One hot sunny day in 1981 or 1982, a few choice students were high up in a pine tree relaxing in the canopy. From their vantage point above the cabins, they looked out across campus, past the soccer field, Richard's trailer, the Grovers' house, the office, the dining hall, and the Art Barn. With a sudden rush of adrenaline, students noticed an ugly column of dark smoke rising up from somewhere in the meadow behind the Kiln area. Throwing caution to the wind as they scurried back down the tree, they began sprinting toward the office. As they ran, they alerted several other students who ran with them until they reached the office buildings and started grabbing fire extinguishers. At that moment, a few staff members saw the commotion and one of them started calling Cal Fire. They continued on down the drive past the kilns and into the woods. The little path was well worn and easy to travel on as the looming cloud of smoke was well visible through the foliage. As they broke into the south meadow clearing, they could see that the column of smoke was just ahead, and the sound of burning, popping, and crackling wood was audible. They raced on and rounded a corner until they were suddenly being faced with a shocking have of heat. The Octagon had been fully engulfed, its frame glowing red like a skeletal monster, popping and hissing and belching fire and smoke into the air. Most of the area around the front of the structure was short grass and dirt, but behind the building were burning manzanita bushes that were starting to spread fire up the hill. A few students immediately began attacking the spreading fire, blasting the burning areas down low and using short bursts, moving steadily around the perimeter. By the time they got back around to the other side, a Cal Fire truck and crew had arrived along with more students and staff. Cal Fire began to mop up what was left of the smoldering building, and the captain walked over and praised the student "fire brigade" for its swift action. That was the end of the Octagon. Although several students had recently slept there and had partied there, no cause was directly found.

The Treehouse

Mary Lambert, who also attended Woolman in the early 1960s recalls another student-built house. "It was a stick-built treehouse with windows, a deck, and even a wood stove, up a tree. It was past the East Side Meadow behind the A-frames, through the tallest manzanita I have ever seen. It was there in 1975 but gone in 1996."

The Garden

There is a reason the garden was dedicated to Russell and Mary Jorgensen. They ardently believed in John Woolman School and were instrumental in the formation of the original garden, which was sadly lost to the 2020 Jones Fire. Original founders of the school, they held Quaker values and were committed to family, education, peace, and social justice. They supported many groups that work for social justice, including the American Friends Service Committee, Sonoma Peace and Justice Center, and the Peace Center of Nevada County. They leave a lasting legacy at Woolman and would be pleased to know that the garden is recovering.

Students have taken an active role in planting and caretaking the garden and campus orchard. Malaika Bishop (1992-1993) says, "It was sweet to see that the dedication sign to Russ and Mary Jorgensen survived the 2020 Jones Fire at John Woolman. I'm working now to restore the farm site from the fire and years of nonproductivity. It's exciting that we are expanding to two fenced acres, with the intention of making the garden both a locally grown organic produce farm for the Woolman dining hall and for everyone who stays on campus during retreats, workshops, and camps, as well as a production farm for produce throughout the region. This is a way of continuing to teach how we can steward the earth in a good way and produce our own food. That understanding of how to be resilient in changing times is very important."

Mel's Pond

Though not part of the central campus, a short walk away down a scrubby, thatched path is Mel's Pond, also referred to as Mel's Lake. Named after the curmudgeonly neighbor who dug it out, it was a favorite swimming hole, frequented by students and sometimes teachers who held classes there. In fact, memories of swimming at Mel's Pond are so poignant for one former student, that he periodically returns there by the light of the moon to camp by it. In a John Woolman School Alumni Facebook page, David Russell (1973-1975) writes, "I remember the smell of the hot pine needles in the summer mornings. On many long-distance motorcycle rides, probably a half dozen times when coming home, when Reno was too short of a day and getting home too long of a day, I would push on and sneak into the school between 10:00 and 11:00 PM, ride down to Mel's Pond, set up my little tent with the fly off, and smell that aroma...the BMW ticking as it cools, the bullfrogs doing their solos, and that aroma wrapping me in memories. I really loved that."

Biologist David Worley, (1970-1972) also remembers Mel's Pond fondly. He says, "A few spots at Woolman held their own specific birds. I found California thrashers, a very vocal bird, only in the dense growth below Mel's Lake. I could lie on the raft in the lake and listen to their calls, and to the snap of ash-throated flycatchers' beaks as they foraged beside the lake."

Jones Bar at the Yuba River

Another favorite place for students that was relatively near campus was Jones Bar, a tranquil glade located on the South Yuba River about five miles northwest of Nevada City. After jobs and classes were done, students would often pile into an open flatbed truck and ride down the rocky, uneven, dusty spur trail that led to Jones Bar – or, laden with packs of food on their backs, trek down. An area on the Yuba River with three stunning natural pools, Jones Bar was inviting, especially during the hot spring and summer months when temperatures could exceed 100 degrees. A social gathering spot well loved by Woolmanites, it was perfect for swimming or sunning on its smooth, hot rocks. Eddies in the river and the pools were gorgeous, brilliant aqua, and so clear you could see right down to their rocky bottom. Diving into that crystalline water and letting its rivulets pour over you or sunning on its smooth, hot rocks was delightful. Alumni and staff who revisit Woolman nearly always add a swim at Jones Bar to their experience.

Yuba River, photo by Dave Worley

A-frame cabins

Mels Lake, photo by Dave Worley

16

....

WORK JOBS

*"The work program was important because
it showed a person the importance of being responsible
for one's own share of work in a society."*

– P. Schneider

A community is only as strong as its people and their wiliness to be an active part of it. In as much as John Woolman School educated students in nonviolent peace action, justice, environmental sustainability, and encouraged personal and spiritual growth, it also required personal, responsible participation in the Woolman community. Work jobs, which were mandatory, ranged from campus cleanup and farm support to maintenance and food preparation.

David Standish (1979) notes that John Woolman School forced students to grow more quickly because of this required responsibility. In a March 1979 issue of the campus newsletter, Outsider's Insider, he wrote, "The sense of community helps you look at and participate in making the place run. If we don't, the place falls apart. This is a large responsibility, and responsibility helps us grow."

For some, the work jobs they did at John Woolman School influenced their entire life. In a letter written to the John Woolman School Board in the spring of 1992, Dayle Hayes (1968) wrote that baking bread in the JWS kitchen was the beginning of her exciting, successful career as a nutritionist. "My career is an enormously satisfying part of my life," she said. Today, Dayle Hayes is a nutrition coach, author, public speaker, and educator. She has dedicated her life to making school environments

healthy for students and staff.

Laurie MacKenzie (1976-1977) also says that working in the kitchen at Woolman influenced her life path. An instructor in the Culinary Arts and Hospitality Department at City College of San Francisco, she attended the Cordon Bleu Culinary School in Paris (1990), took continuing education classes at the Culinary Institute of America, and did a culinary independent study in Nicaragua for six months. For the past 30 years, she has worked in well-known restaurants and food establishments in the Bay Area. In addition to teaching, she works as a chef at Hands on Gourmet, and has worked as a culinary tour guide. Laurie says, "Woolman was part of a culinary trajectory I was already on. I had been involved in cooking for retreats and meetings when I was in Jr. High and High School in Claremont, California where I grew up, but Woolman definitely had an influence on me. One of my work jobs there was to make bread once a week. One semester, I made breakfast three times a week, so I'd get up at 5:30 AM and make breakfast for 40 people. I was in the kitchen quite a bit."

Gretchen Herried Petersen (1969-1971), who spends summers in Fairbanks, Alaska, and winters in Southern Baja on the Sea of Cortez also credits her career success to John Woolman School's kitchen. For 20 years, she and her sister, Ingrid, owned and operated a seasonal bakery in a 50s-style trailer in Fairbanks, Alaska. "Bun on the Run," which the two ran during the summertime, was the first bakery food truck in Alaska. She also wrote a cookbook, *Recipes from the Bun*. Gretchen says Woolman definitely influenced her decision to start a bakery.

"Baking has always been my passion," she explains. "When I went to Woolman, I always took work jobs that involved making snacks or breakfast. I was always in the kitchen baking. I would make granola or lemon bars for eighty people. Over the three years I was at Woolman, I learned to bake in massive amounts and was comfortable with it. After Woolman, thinking I might want to cook on sailboats, I went to Cordon Bleu in London. As it turned out, I got seasick, so that did not happen. At that time, Ingrid was teaching in the Alaskan bush. A year later, we decided we wanted to start a business. Ingrid suggested that since we both loved to bake, we should start a bakery. Though we sold it after 20 years, 35 years later, it is still going strong."

Matthew Bronson (1973-1974) also remembers working in the kitchen. He says, "Work jobs taught us simple things we may have missed in our socialization prior to Woolman. I had mentors in the kitchen. I was a prep-cook. They taught me some of the first things I learned about cooking. We had to get up to speed. Our lunch cook was a sweet guy, Daniel, who was a violin player with a Ph.D. in Ethnomusicology. Our dinner cook was a woman with a somewhat prickly disposition. They were my master cooks. Like the Buddha said, 'Before enlightenment, chop fire, make wood; after enlightenment, chop fire, make wood.'"

For his work job, Sean Farrell (1981) did just that. He remembers, "I worked on the firewood crew. We cut firewood, sometimes on the Woolman property, and sometimes on Nevada County residents' property. We'd then distribute it to the cabins on campus."

Chris Edgell (1970) says, "Whilst I chaffed at the bit at Woolman, I was assigned to clean the boy's bathroom down by the A-frame cabins. I didn't ask for the job. Normally, students got to ask to work certain work jobs, but I guess because they thought I was malleable, they said 'Chris, you can clean the toilets and showers.' I said 'No, I don't want to do that,' which prompted a school-wide meeting of concern in the dining hall. I didn't actually participate in the meeting. Instead, I went and cleaned the bathroom. I also remember quite vividly having kitchen duty and scraping that grill with a piece of pumice stone, as well as stealing a carton of milk every night from the walk-in refrigerator to drink in my cabin at night. I was one of the reasons they started locking up the walk-in at night."

Olivia Gay (student 1965-1968, staff in the early 1970s) says, "The work project aspect of John Woolman had an influence on me in terms of the value of work and how it knits people together. I directed the work program at Goddard College which has work jobs as part of its curriculum requirement. I think the work program at John Woolman set me in a particular direction. It deepened that interest and commitment for volunteerism and shared work.

| HEALING ARTS |

17

....

A SPACE FOR HEALING

*"Being able to be outside in nature with
animals and plants and watching the seasons made
Woolman a place where my mind could process."*

– L. K. Kirsis

Su Herbert (1970-1972) has been an Ayurveda doula in the U.S., Canada, England, all across Europe, and in Italy since 1987. She holds a PhD in neuroscience and teaches meditation, yoga, and primary-school science, music, and English in Naples, Italy, where she has lived for the past eleven years. Inspired by the book, *The Science of Being* and *Art of Living* by Maharishi Mahesh Yogi, she was also a transcendental meditation teacher for 19 years, and for a few of those years, traveled with Maharishi Mahesh Yogi in Switzerland, France, and Germany as his secretary. She also taught high-school physics, chemistry, and biology in intercity London. Meditation, yoga, and breathing exercises have been her mainstay. She recently published a book, *Ayurveda Baby Massage*. She recounts how Woolman gave her exactly what she needed at a deeply formative time. She says, "My dad was part American Indian and was drawn to Quaker meeting in San Francisco, where he was introduced to sitting in silence and to letting God speak through him. When I was 15, he died of acute leukemia. When he shared his condition with my brother, my mother, and myself, he told us, 'Well, everybody's got to go sometime. They've given me three months to live.' Then he turned to me and said, 'Susan, don't play only minor music, it's not sad.' But when he died, I went into an existential crisis, questioning my life and searching for meaning.

My mother was also completely distraught and unable to care for me and my brother. We were shipped off to school at Putney in Vermont, which was far too regimented for me. I told my mom that I needed time and space to just be. That's how my brother and I came to Woolman. The best part of John Woolman for me was Ted Menmuir. He and I had long philosophical talks together and explored the meaning of life in a deep, profound, meaningful way. He was a father figure to me. The Quaker religion class that he and Chuck Croninger taught was a wonderful, nourishing, life-sustaining class and exactly what I needed."

Sonya (Terry) Tefejian (1970-1971), has worked as a consultant to help people set up and secure permits for tiny houses, guest houses, and Accessory Dwelling Units (ADUs) in Sonoma County, California. She recalls, "The year I was at Woolman was a very important, formative year for me. I hadn't grown up with either of my parents, who got divorced when I was two, and I didn't see my dad. Then my mom died when I was seven, so my sister and I grew up with my aunt and uncle. They already had six kids when we joined their family, so I always felt like an outsider. I hadn't felt safe since my mom died. Woolman was the first time I felt that I was in a safe community and part of something rather than being in a family where I felt like an outsider. At Woolman, no one had their parents. For the first time, I felt like I was on an equal playing field with my peers – and that was a big deal for me."

Halina Janusz (1981-1982), a producer, performer, promoter, and booking agent at "Rising Star Entertainment" in Santa Monica, California, also says, "My dad was a well-known, established folk singer/songwriter during the 1960s and 1970s in Los Angeles, California, so I grew up on the folk scene in a musical family. My dad inspired me to sing. He was also very ill, so I spent a lot of time with my family caring for him. At the time, a friend of mine, Grace Moore, had been with me at another camp that I went to in Santa Barbara, California, which was run by Jane Fonda. Through Grace, I found out about a camp session at the Ben Lomond Quaker Center, near Santa Cruz, California. It was a wonderful, amazing experience. While we were there, we met these cool girls who had come out from New York. They happened to be into the Grateful Dead, Neil

Young, and other great music. Most of what I'm doing now is singing. I also play guitar and banjo. One of my bands, a Jerry Garcia tribute band called Jerry Garcia's Middle Finger, has taken off and is really blowing up. We're doing music from a Jerry Garcia side project, the Jerry Garcia Band, which was apart from the Grateful Dead. I've been meeting some of the artists that I have idolized my entire life and performing with them, like Jerry Garcia's keyboardist, Melvin Seals. We're playing a lot of big festivals. As it turns out, Grace and I heard Jerry Garcia's music for the first time at a Quaker camp. Later, a friend from John Woolman School took me to my first Grateful Dead concert. Grace was already a student at Woolman when my dad died. She said, 'You gotta come to this amazing school. You will love it!' In the 1950s, my mom had been involved with Quaker camps and had met Martin Luther King, Jr. at a camp run by the Friends. Since my dad had passed, my mom said yes to Woolman. She used her student loan to fund my tuition. I took my banjo and guitar with me, and immediately felt like I belonged there. Before Woolman, I was not in a great place. I was sixteen, had just lost my dad, and did not feel as though I fit in public school. Had my dad not died, I might never have gone there. It was an awesome way to live. Woolman saved my life."

During the 1980s, staff and some students even served together on a Ministry and Oversight (M&O) Board. Clara Lanyi (1980-1981), professional potter, who served on the M&O Board, notes, "Woolman had a significant impact on my values. Staff really respected the kids, and their development. To be chosen for the M&O Board made me feel as though my opinion mattered, and that I was being taken seriously. If a kid was in trouble, they would go to this committee, which was composed of faculty and their peers. Rather than punish the kid, we would try to come up with a solution for them. There was a student who was coming in front of the M&O committee a lot. One of my more memorable contributions is I suggested that we include him on the committee, which improved everything."

Lisa Klein Kirsis (1981-1984), now a mental health "biopsychosocial" clinical director of a community health center in Alaska, was also floundering when she arrived at John Woolman. She says, "I do not think

I would have excelled the same way in public school. I wasn't thriving. I was skipping school and headed to flunking out. I'm very grateful John Woolman School happened to me. John Woolman School also dovetailed with my own personal trauma because one of the reasons I went there is my mother was dealing with end-stage cancer. That was very hard for me to deal with, so I think going away to boarding school was a solution in that era. My mom ended up dying in November of my senior year. So that entire year was about death and dying. When you are dealing with trauma, and I was, having that open space and large vista of land and being able to walk for miles, swim, and sit in the sun ended up being something that was very helpful for me personally. Being able to be outside in nature with animals and plants and watching the seasons made Woolman a place where my mind could process. Major themes in my life were formed at John Woolman School. I became a hospital chaplain prior to becoming a psychotherapist."

Matthew Bronson (1973-1974) says, "When I came to Woolman, I didn't know if people were going to like me. I had lived in my brother's shadow. He was a handsome extrovert, and I was more of an introvert. When I was 12 and he was 13, he tragically died. Our family dislocated. My mom became a Quaker because she found them consistent with her social values and her gorilla ecology of making up your own world view and coming together with a full spirit and open heart. She helped refugees and was the first person to welcome them when they came into the airport and assisted them in resettling. She was a true community leader and very spiritual. The Santa Clara Quakers kindheartedly gave me a full scholarship to Woolman. At Woolman, I discovered that I was a funny 'ideas guy.' Other students would say 'Matthew, think of something for us to do,' and I always did. I became a beloved member of the community. I remember how wonderful it felt to have 'my people.' I got to belong again. Woolman was a place where I was welcomed back to the human community. We had a lot of mentoring and personal attention at Woolman, too, for which I am very grateful. I graduated high school after three years and got a full Regents Scholarship to UC Berkeley. They only give out 50 in the world."

Ann Sotelo (1969-1971) also reflects, "When I came to Woolman, there was a lot of upheaval in my family that never stopped happening. During that time, I was a ball of confusion. I didn't know how to make sense of anything. Sometimes I play the videos I have in my head of us at Woolman and think 'check, check, check'— (that was a smart one, that was an amazing one, that was an extraordinary one)— many very special people were there."

Judit S. Torn Allen (1966) notes, "John Woolman School allowed me the time and space to explore my person and to become intimate with others at a time when I needed to not be an outcast but a creative member of my community."

Angela Gower-Johnson (Angela Tyznik) (1987-1988) also expresses a similar sentiment. "Woolman saved my life and gave me the foundation to be a better person. I embraced my faith and connection with nature there. It was a clear turning point for me to step out of the darkness into the light. Today, I work with business professionals to help guide them out of their darkness and/or limiting beliefs, discover their own peace, happiness, and love, and have faith in themselves and the world around them. This would have never been possible if it were not for Woolman."

John Woolman School instructor, Gerow Reece, whose Zen-like presence was calming to students

| SENSE OF PLACE |

18

SENSE OF PLACE

"I will arise and go now, and go to Innisfree,

And a small cabin built there of clay and wattles made.

Nine bean-rows will I have there, a hive for the honeybee,

And live alone in the bee-loud glade.

And I shall have some peace there, for peace comes dropping slow,

Dropping from the veils of the morning to where the cricket sings

There, midnight's all a glimmer, and noon a purple glow,

And evening full of the linnet's wings.

I will arise and go now, for always night and day

I hear lake water lapping with low sounds by the shore

While I stand on the roadway, or on the pavements grey,

I hear it in the deep heart's core."

– The Lake Isle of Innisfree - William Butler Yeats

For many students, Woolman's natural land was (and continues to be) a contemplative place of solace and healing. While a student, when she was overwhelmed Sophie Wood Brinker (2007) often went out into the orchard to "sit with the trees," where she also herded sheep. She reminisces, "Sleeping under a full moon in the orchard while another student pulled out a fiddle and played students to sleep under that glow is one of my favorite memories."

Ann Sotelo (1969-1971) remembers, "We had this huge period of time where we were raised among animals. This force and cycle of life was given to us, and we had a deep sense of that. Not that many people get to live on

a farm with intellectuals, as in, "I just came back from milking a goat and now I'm studying Nietzsche and Wittgenstein. Then I'm going to go and sing Mozart. Over 50 years later, I'm still debriefing myself on what that time was. It was a huge experience."

Kevin Moore (1969-1972) says, "What was important to me about Woolman was the freedom to grow and interact with people, to begin to feel and think about what it would be like to live in a community, and to live with other people in all that freedom. My fellow students, faculty, and staff were the most important part of my experience there. Having the woods to be in was also important. I decided to sleep in a different place on campus every night simply because I thought it would be wonderful to experience all those places overnight. Chuck, the principal, thought I did that to evade him, but I didn't have that in mind at all. It was that kind of freedom, playing music with people, living with goats and milking them, and the nurturing at Woolman that made a difference to me. With Ted Menmuir, I took a class in Ancient Egyptian Religion. Jim Corbett's attitude toward life, his Taoism, the utility of going barefoot, and his virtues of living also influenced me. That feeling of wanting to sleep in a different place every night and my instinct to travel to unknown places on a low budget – Europe, Spain, Morocco, the Canary Islands, Choum in northern Mauritania, Senegal, Kenya, the Gambia, West Africa, Egypt, and the Southern Sedan— are all expressions of the same thing. Traveling with nothing but a jug of water and a sleeping bag was very similar to sleeping in different places outside at Woolman."

As an introvert, Jenny Long (1967-1969) also spent a lot of time in the woods surrounding the campus. She says, "That's where I had the intimacy to come alive into the world from a stricken state. This was 1967, mind you, so I had already taken LSD at 13 and 14 years old. I was only seeing black and white when I got there. There were a lot of refugees at the school. It was a raw time. In public high school, we still had to wear nylons and garters. This was the dark ages, before our culture evolved. We were part of that shift."

Ann (Croninger) Zedah (1967-1984) recollects growing up at Woolman when she says, "Nobody lives in a community like that, on a 310-acre farm, with high school students around them. Then I was also a student. I knew everything about Woolman. I saw the whole thing. It was more than a school to me— it was my hometown, my upbringing. Whenever people talked about the possibility of selling the land at Woolman, it would make me sad to think of not being able to visit there because it felt like I'd have no hometown to go back to. As a city planner, I'm a proponent of development but I would be sad to see the land there become inaccessible. I feel connected to where I was raised."

Amy Cooke, Head of School, (July 2000-2007) also touched on why she feels Woolman has such a deep impact on the students and staff who lived there. She says, "When you walk around in the dark and your feet are feeling the path, and you've got the stars and the forest around you and don't need a flashlight, I also think that goes deep into people—that there's a place where they feel that safe, held, confident, and comfortable. For the students who have been there, there's a sense of pride, too—that campus is theirs—and it's still theirs, forty, fifty years later. Ten years later. There are campers who feel that way after being at Woolman for two weeks. There is something there that is extraordinary. I do think there's a presence on that land that's very old. We had a staff member, Lisa Rose, who really felt the native presence there, and felt a lot of grief on that land. But I also think that big, wide bowl, that big valley was such a held place. The geographical configuration of that land was such that you were in a kind of bowl, sort of held. It was also a balance of human and wild habitation that people could experience both of those things. It was a combination of so many things. When you live in a place like that, the smells and the seasons all go deeply into your psyche. So, there is a certain smell there that I really have never smelled anywhere else that happens right after the first rain. It's that mixture of fresh pine, manzanita, and pungent earth—it's an indescribable smell that I think just goes primal in all of us. And maybe that is a way we can always be at Woolman. There's almost a primal sense of being there, and that's very powerful."

Former Principal Ted Menmuir agrees, "For many alumni, the Woolman campus takes on a sacred quality. They return again and again to feel that connection."

Quanset Hut

The Redwood House, photo by Dave Worley

THE NATURAL WORLD

"As a rural school set on 320 acres of semi-wild land,
Woolman was ideal for culturing interest in the outdoors."

– D. Worley

For some students, merely living on the John Woolman School campus, being exposed to its acres of forest land, wide meadows, streams, swimming holes, and vast star-filled night skies, and tending its farmland, influenced their life direction. Their inspiration came from the land itself.

The Woods

By the time biologist David Worley, (1970-1972) arrived at Woolman, his parents had already instilled in him a reverence for the natural world. By extension, the land at John Woolman helped set his life path on course. During his career, David has worked in wildlife jobs and fisheries, studied bird communities, surveyed environmental impacts, and helped a cinematographer with a nature film called *The Flowing Oasis*, focused on the East Fork of the Walker River in Western Nevada. David says, "As a rural school set on 320 acres of semi-wild land, Woolman was ideal for cultivating my interest in the outdoors. Acorn woodpeckers gave their Woody Woodpecker calls and cached acorns in trees all about the central campus. Cliff swallows nested under the eaves of the Dining Hall. I don't recall the specific origins, but Hoyt McCurley, the math teacher at the time, got me interested in birding specifically, and the woods and ponds on the campus were a perfect spot to grow that interest. For spring Special Projects that year (1970), five of us—Chuck

Croninger, the principal, Cathy Smith, the English/writing teacher, and three students, Laurie Morris, Dave Wilheim, and I—took a bike trip down the California coast (Seaside to Pismo Beach). That trip, with help from Chuck, introduced me to sea birds (frigate birds, brown pelicans that cruised seemingly effortlessly just over the water), and the delight of watching Allen's hummingbirds feeding in coastal shrubs. I started an independent study with instructor Hoyt McCurley, working on bird notes and eventually developing a bird list for the school's property. I continued that project all three years, working with science teacher Nick Wilcox my last year at the school. Woolman's 320 acres, and adjoining unfenced properties, supported a diversity of habitats: meadows, chaparral, a lake, pine, and oak forest, which in turn supported a rapidly growing list of birds a well as deer, gray squirrels, gray foxes, and the occasional coyote. More exotically, the second-growth manzanita harbored wrentits, a bird to limited to dense shrub cover habitat on the west coast. Privately, personally, I do love being out in wild places, being washed by desert sunrises and sunsets, being in big forest or big expanses with vistas that go on over range after mountain range. Being in quiet. I'm awed by those places and appreciate the opportunities to experience them."

Sue Opitz (1969-1972), a retired registered public health nurse in Mendocino County, also retained her relationship with the natural world and birds after Woolman. Her late husband, Frank, taught a bird identification class and was employed in Condor recovery in Three Rivers, the gateway to Sequoia National Park. Sue documented the birds' behavior. She also worked with vagrant blue-throated hummingbirds in Mexico and Arizona, which built nests in her neighbor's yard. Other birds also frequented the yard, so the interspecies mated. She says, "We got a banding permit, banded the baby birds in the nest for a couple of years, and wrote a scientific paper about it."

Lisa Hubbell (1976-1978) was so taken with the out-of-doors after going on a summer camping trip for junior-high-school students with a Friends school in Pasadena, California, that she decided to go to Woolman for high school. She says, "There was a strong push among Quaker kids to go to Woolman. We received financial aid to make that possible. Six of us from that camping trip ended up at Woolman."

Matthew Bronson (1973-1974), a linguist and massage therapist, also found his love for nature at Woolman. He says, "I live near Sebastopol, California on two acres in the wine county of Sonoma County. I have a chosen-family compound. It's a place of sanctuary where we invite people to come and replenish themselves. We want to make it a place where people can enjoy events and get back to the land. I hadn't quite made the connection, but I see now that it is a 'straight shot' from Woolman. I wanted to have that for others, so I am paying it forward. I think that's the beautiful part of the Woolman legacy because Woolman connected me with the land. I was just an alienated kid from the suburbs. Woolman turned my whole life around to where I'm now a nature boy. Contact with nature was foundational and it never went away. It is always a human place for me. I get 'nature deficit disorder' if I don't have my connection with the land and the trees."

Sean Feder (1977-1978), now a business manager for the largest organic food certification company in the country, Farmers CCCOF, says, "I grew up in the city suburbs, so I was moved by being out in the foothills, trees, and forest at Woolman. For me, at that time, it was mind-expanding to be out there and get closer to people my age. In urban areas, it is harder to make friends. I had great interactions with friends at Woolman and played music. My wife and I subsequently bought property on Deer Creek near the Woolman site. Staff member Philip Conkling also used to take us cross-country skiing. He pulled together Army/Navy surplus wool pants and ski equipment to take three of us in his truck."

Sonya (Terry) Tefejian (1970-71) who lives in a tiny house near Petaluma, California, and helps others get legal permission to do the same, says, "I grew up in Sacramento and really hadn't lived out in the country much at all. Living in an A-frame cabin at Woolman showed me that not only could I live in an economical space, but I could also have the confidence to live in a tiny house out in the country alone, and not worry about it. I learned to live independently. The tiny house I live in is really like an A-frame cabin. It's all wood inside. There are horses just outside my window. Because of a volunteer effort that I've been involved in for a number of years, Sonoma County has just opened up the zoning code so that anyone who wants to live in a tiny house or wants to have one on their property can do it. Even if the property owner owns the tiny house, it will still give more opportunities for rental spaces. Sonoma County is in a housing crisis right now, with unaffordable housing and homelessness, so it is good this is happening. Living in a tiny house is an affordable way to live in a very expensive area."

Jenny Long (1967-1969), Nevada City librarian, also says, "I think the fact that I was out in the woods a lot leads to my story about Harold Blickenstaff, who was principal at the time. I knew of this one place by the stream that went to the meadows and there were beautiful mossy rocks there—it was a place of enchantment. I went out there one day in my mooning life slumming around in the woods by myself and, to my wild dismay, it had been destroyed, bulldozed, and completely wiped out. So, I went up to Harold and I gave him my feelings on it. I said, 'This was not all right. You cannot be doing this!' I was a very stubborn, self-righteous, animated young woman, and I got right in his face and really let him have it. I was furious! He said something feeble about making a sports field and I just rolled my eyes. That moment was so interesting because at my graduation in 1969, we were out there in the soccer field. He said about me that I was a 'vociferous conservationist,' which is a wonderful use of the English language. Vociferous means exactly what I did. I was animated, yelling—a right-to-the-heart kind of forceful speech. Twenty-five years later, when Harold and Marguerite were living on Willow Valley Road up toward Highway 20, I got invited to Harold's 80th birthday party. I'm not that connected with other Woolmanites who live in the Grass Valley area, but there are almost 15 of us who came back to live here. I scurried out from the library where I was working and went out to his house. There were quite a few of us there, including his daughter Jennifer Miller and other folks. It was lovely. He was going around talking to people and then he turned to the group, and he said, 'Well, Jenny Long was right. She was right to be angry with me.' I was amazed. That the school tolerated that kind of strong communication from youngsters, was incredible. I had absolutely no compunction about yelling at him. None! I was always totally honest with Harold. There was such a permission to communicate."

Jenny Long still lives in Grass Valley, where she worked for many years in the public library. And, yes, having been "given permission" to rant about it as a teenager, she is still an ardent environmentalist.

The Garden

Malaika Bishop (1992-1993) is still connected to the land at Woolman. She has been creating sustainable food systems for over 20 years and brings that love of growing organic produce to it. In 2001, she co-founded the People's Grocery, an organization devoted to improving the health and economy of low-income inner-city communities of West Oakland through local food systems. When she moved back to Nevada County, she worked on several farms, including managing the John Woolman School farm. She also served on the board of the BriarPatch Co-op. Born into a family long associated with John Woolman School, Mailaika is the granddaughter of Russ and Mary Jorgensen, founders of the school in the 1960s, and daughter of Paul Jorgensen (JWS 1964-1969). In addition to her work as the farm manager, Mailaika serves on the school's board. She says, "When I was young, I participated in work camps and eventually worked at Woolman as a farm educator. I started a garden there in 2011. There had been a garden at Woolman from the beginning, but that first garden was small, only 500 square feet. Then it expanded in 2007, and from 2008 to 2011, we tripled the garden to an acre. That's when we had a lot of interaction with the Semester Program. It was a wonderful educational farm. We did a lot of field trips. When I was there, we had an event for members of the Grass Valley Quaker Meeting but ultimately, most of the produce we grew went to the John Woolman School kitchen. We were growing the food to supply the people who lived on campus—$10,000 dollars of produce came out of the garden at that time. I left for ten years, and now I'm back."

The Farm

Chris Edgell (1970) remembers that tending farm animals at Woolman could be challenging. He says, "We had a black-faced ram in the upper pasture. I saw that ram come out of the blue and nail conscientious objector Mickey Barrett, in the hip, tossing him head over heels, ten feet or so. Mickey bounced right back up. I used to carry a 10-inch pipe that I would put at the base of the stile between Mels Lake and the campus to bat at that ram when he tried to ram me. I'd leave it on each side of the stile, so when I went to Mel's Lake, I could pick it up, and when I left Mel's Lake, I could pick it up again. I also remember the Durrett pigs. They were 500 pounds and enormous! I didn't know that you don't take the feed into the pen with them, so I did. They knocked me ass-over-teakettle to get at it. That was a lesson learned. From then on, I poured their feed into troughs from the outside of the pen. We also had apples stored in a shed. Those pigs got into them. Another time, Pam Smith (daughter of Woolman founder Don Smith) had a sheep that was bloated, so she stuck a knife in its side to let the gas out and didn't kill it, something I never forgot. She knew a lot about animal husbandry."

Robert "Bobbie" Stevenson, viticulturist/vigneron (1968-1970) recalls "I don't think I would have made it through high school if I had not gone to Woolman. Academics overwhelmed me but I excelled in helping out on the farm." Today, Bobbie's gorgeous, sprawling vineyards in California supply grapes to regional wineries there.

Jennifer Dickey (1977-1978) also worked on the farm. She remembers, "There was a pig there. I loved that little pig and helped take care of it. In January, I found out that we were going to slaughter it. I had never realized that at the time! But it was part of the Quaker Way that we all do our part. One of the seniors had grown up on a ranch. She had a shotgun and knew how to slaughter a pig. She shot it in the forehead, slit its throat, gutted it out, and hung it up. I had to help. I was so overwhelmed by it, I was taken off the farm work job and became a vegetarian."

Instructor Lew Sitzer (1974-1979) who still lives on a farm in Nevada City, and was active as a Farm and Garden Manager, and math, PE, and photography instructor, says, "Probably the most popular class I taught was farm and garden because we raised all the meat that we ate at the school. I was slaughtering an animal almost every week. Some of these animals, like pigs, were huge. Students had never been exposed to this real stuff of life and death. It taught them exactly what they were eating. I felt if you could not kill the animal, you should not be eating meat. We learned to butcher, smoke the meat, and to occasionally make bacon. It was a back-to-the-land, primitive experience for a lot of kids, including myself. I grew up in cities, so this was new to me. My family was so put off by it, they became vegetarians, but the students were fascinated by it. Everybody went up to the barn for it. It was a big deal, which, when you think about it, was respectful. There was a sense of awe to it because an animal was losing its life. After two years, though, it became too repugnant to me, so I turned the responsibility of killing animals over to the students. I oversaw the slaughters but became a vegetarian. Nowadays, moving to a plant-based diet is the way to go anyway. That is where we are all headed, if we are not already there."

John Malcomson, (1983-1986) says, "The farm program was also very strong when I was a student, with goats, pigs, cows, chickens, and maybe some sheep too. It provided great learning on many levels, but by no means did the farm or garden make the school self-sustaining. However, we did eat, drink, and weave from all the 'products.'"

Sustainability

Steven Greenleaf (1979-1981) also realizes that there is an important connection between environmental sustainability, technology, and entrepreneurship. To that end, he has founded a nonprofit organization in Costa Rica to help accelerate environmental protection management. He says, "Being in the environment at Woolman, spending a lot of time out in the meadows, and feeling a connection to the land influenced me to become involved in environmental work. After Woolman, I taught English to robotics, industrial, and computer engineers at a University in Costa Rica who were required to do projects and could pick any topic they wanted. I started noticing that some chose projects that were 'green.' As a pied piper of environmental sustainability, by the time I left that teaching job, about 30 percent of the projects were 'green.' The projects were brilliant, like the idea one kid had for an automated greenhouse system for organic agriculture. But once these were done, no one supported them. There was no "and then," which may be the biggest failing of the environmental movement. Frequently when there are great ideas, nothing is done. People can dance around the problem, but solving it is always due to lack of money. The goal of our NGO is to give grassroots support to people who have a passion for saving the planet and need ideas of how to do it. We want people to come here and stay. As I walk around our property, I realize that I am very definitely trying to recreate the extended family dynamic we had at Woolman."

Meadow, photo by Dave Worley

Students out in nature

Student reading a book, 1969

Site of John Woolman School, 1960s

| INSTRUCTOR |

20

TEACHERS

"Teach me and I remember. Involve me and I learn."

– Ben Franklin

Founded in the Quaker tradition of peace, justice, and simplicity, John Woolman School offered students both academic and real-life experiences as part of their education—and for many, paved the way in which they would choose to live after Woolman. However, students were not the only people to credit the school as having played a big part in shaping who they are today. Former instructors also say Woolman profoundly influenced their values and life choices, and that it did as much for them as it did for the students.

On the John Woolman School campus in 1970, Kerry Travers, a perky young biology teacher in her early 20s, strode across campus during a parents' visitation day. Mistaking her for a student, a parent expressed surprise that "married students are allowed on campus." Laughing, she replied, "I teach here."

When she taught at Woolman, Kerry was only a few years older than some of the seniors. In a supervisorial role yet close in age to students, she was often a staff member who students felt understood them. Kerry and her husband, Mike Travers (1967-1976) were among those few teachers who stayed a long time. In 1967, John Sullivan of the Seattle Quakers had sent Mike to the University Friends Meeting, where a member knew someone who worked at John Woolman School. Mike's application reached the hands of John Woolman School founders Russ, and Mary Jorgensen, who noticed that Mike spoke Spanish and was also a mathematician. They asked if Mike and Kerry were interested in teaching at Woolman. They were. Mike taught math and science and Kerry taught biology. They spoke enthusiastically of their time at Woolman.

"We credit John Woolman School as having played a big part in shaping who we are today and our values. We think it did as much for us as it did for any student. Our experience of Woolman is like when people involve themselves in 'do-good' projects in South America or elsewhere to do something or build something and they find that the people who benefit most from the experience are them, rather than the people they are helping. This was certainly true of us at John Woolman School."

Mike adds, "When I was teaching geometry, I asked myself what the purpose was in teaching it and I found that it was to teach people how to reason. It should not necessarily be to just teach them about geometric structures. It is to use a person's reasoning ability to determine how one thing implies something else, so we started that course not talking about geometry at all, but about logic. Then we'd make up formal arguments about what constitutes a formal argument. From there, we'd go into geometry since that was what the course was supposed to teach. Then we'd put all that stuff together. What I was really trying to do was to teach students how to think."

Kerry notes, "Many students at Woolman would later say we were influential in shaping the course of their lives in a variety of ways, from music to activism to love of the sciences. This is very rewarding to know. However, Woolman was also very influential to our life path. Dorla Menmuir, who taught music at Woolman, was also a major influence in my life. I was a biology major and was teaching biology there. I had not played the piano or violin for years, other than sometimes playing with a little group in Grass Valley. Dorla came to me and asked me if I would accompany her chorus. Dorla got anyone who could make a sound to sing, so I practiced the piano well enough to play some of the parts for her chorus. She also had me play in the orchestra in Grass Valley for some of the things she did. One day she said to me 'Have you ever heard of this music method called the Suzuki Method?' I said, 'No, I've never heard of it.' She told me a little bit about it. Now, I've used The Suzuki Method to teach violin to students

for thirty years! It's really Dorla who got me back into doing music."
Alongside her husband Mike, Kerry and her family have performed seven
Travers family concerts where they now live (Chelan, Washington), filling
the church every time. Son Christopher, born at Woolman, sets music to
Robert Barnes' poetry and enjoys playing Irish recorder. Two of their other
children, Maia, and Tarn, are professional violinists and instructors. The
musical seed that was planted at John Woolman School continues to grow.

Ted Menmuir, former Woolman Principal, Ceramics/Drawing/Math/
Philosophy instructor, and Farm Manager, (1969-2012) remembers
teaching at Woolman fondly.   "For me, Woolman was wonderful. My most
valuable, rewarding teaching experience was in drawing and ceramics,
which was a real high point. My undergraduate academic training was in
social psychology and philosophy of religion, with masters' level classes in
sociology at the University of Alberta in Edmonton, Canada. Turnover at
Woolman had left then principal Chuck Croninger in need of teachers. He
tracked me down in Canada. Initially, I was hired to teach social studies, but
then an art teacher left under unmentionable circumstances, and Woolman
needed an art teacher. Though I had no formal art education background,
I asked if I could teach art and Chuck said yes. The first two years, I taught
myself ceramics and drawing while teaching students. I self-educated and
learned a lot about myself, which was a profound experience. You could
say that Woolman rescued me from the academic world. Because John
Woolman was a small school, I taught a lot of different classes: pottery,
philosophy, math, drawing, and ceramics. I also ran the farm when the
sheep and pigs were still there and was the business manager for two years.
For thirteen years, I was also principal of the school. I worked at the school
for nearly 43 years. It wasn't a job; it was a way of life. I was a part of it in
so many different elements."

Instructor Nick Wilcox came to John Woolman School in the fall of
1971. His association with the school stretched from 1971 to 2008. He
served 12 years on the Woolman Board, nine years on the John Woolman
School Board, and three years on the Woolman Friends Center Board. In
1971, Chuck was principal when Nick came to the school. Ted Menmuir
was principal when he left. Nick says, "Ted took over for Chuck because, in

the tradition of Woolman's 'swap at the top,' Chuck ran off with my wife. They are still happy together. It worked out, though. I remarried and am also happy."

Nick taught biochemistry and physics from 1971-1975. Before coming to Woolman, he taught at Germantown Friends School for four years. He says, "I saw Woolman through thick and thin for many years and experienced its ups and downs firsthand. It was very different from where I'd taught before. Germantown Friends School was an urban day school. It had a long history of excellence and high achievement, which wasn't true of John Woolman School. However, I found the change refreshing. I loved the land at Woolman. As a biology teacher, I considered it an enormous asset and a living laboratory. Dave Worley was in my physics and biology classes. He had a love of birds and has since worked as a consulting biologist his entire career. As a Special Project for me, he compiled the definitive list of birds at John Woolman School, which was viewed as the authoritative list for decades to come. He was already a well-informed young naturalist when I had him in school."

Nick also taught four sections of chemistry at Nevada Union High School for a semester while holding down a full-time job teaching physics at Woolman. That was the year he met his current wife, Amanda, in the dining hall, 1977. He says, "Though I was no longer working at Woolman at that time, I had pulled a trailer onto the property above Mel's Lake and was living there while helping out at the school. I have fond memories of Woolman. It was a real growing experience."

Nick's wife, former instructor/office manager Amanda Wilcox, says, "I was a senior in college at Earlham, and a career placement advisor there gave me a test that compared my interests with people and various occupations. I scored high as a high-school history teacher. After that, he had a 'bee in his bonnet' that I should try teaching. I'd never had any education courses or background on it. One day I got a note in my mailbox at Earlham that a school in Northern California wanted someone to help with their work programs and ski program, and to teach math. So, at 21 years old when I graduated from Earlham, I drove my beat-up old car out to John Woolman School to serve as an intern. I had gone to Westtown Quaker School, founded in 1779, in West Chester, Pennsylvania (near Philadelphia) for grades 10, through 12. As I drove out to Woolman, I reflected on my own high-school experience. The grounds at Westtown were beautiful. It also had tradition, academic excellence, and a big endowment. I thought that I was coming out to something like that. When I came to Woolman, expecting it to have huge buildings like Westtown had, I kept thinking 'Where's the campus? Where's the buildings?' Woolman was very different from an established Quaker school. A teacher was fired that April and I replaced him teaching algebra and geometry. I lived in student housing, worked in the work program, taught a student German, and taught remedial math. I wasn't much older than the students. That's when Nick also came in to teach physics. I taught the next year. By then, the school was trending toward having only juniors and seniors. The big difference between Westtown and Woolman was that (at Woolman) classes were throughout the day with big blocks of unstructured time. Students who didn't already have some discipline often floundered there. Other students were self-disciplined but had been disenchanted by public schools--they just blossomed. I think that in later years what affected Woolman's viability and financial stability was the charter school movement, in which you could find alternative education tuition-free. I think that created a challenge for Woolman."

Deward and Louise Drollinger (1981-1992) also taught at John Woolman School. Deward was an art teacher and cabin supervisor, and Louise taught Spanish and geology. Together they taught a gardening class. Deward says, "At first, talk of drug use at Woolman scared us off, so we didn't take the job. Then we reconsidered, but someone else had taken the job. Somehow, they left mid-term, so they hired us. I worked there for the last trimester. Louise and the children moved up over the summer. Our son D'Arcy went to Woolman, and while we thought he was the 'perfect son,' we found out later he was not above pulling pranks like sneaking up to the dining hall during the night, taking all the furniture out of it, and putting it on the lawn. Our daughter, Masina (Samoan for 'moon'), didn't take too well to school but dropped out in favor of home schooling. She took to the student culture but not the adult one. The gardening class was a high point for us. Nobody was gardening at the time. That was a very important part of our time there. The garden was located between the Cedar House and the principal's house. D'Arcy did a lot of cooking–brunches and the like. I also built a gazebo and did a lot of manual work. Another high point is, some students and I built an 18-foot concrete obelisk in the upper meadow above the old apple orchard, paid for by the school. It was a combination of an aeolian harp and an obelisk, with an opening down the middle of the obelisk. I strung a G-string piano wire on it so that when the wind blew, it would hum. Lynsey Cleaver was the farm manager there. The myth is that she had the sheep all sterilized but after the obelisk was put up, some of them got pregnant. I cannot attest to that story being factual, but there is some powerful symbolism in it. Everyone came up and circled around the obelisk. I had a cousin who belonged to the Ring of Bone Zendo come and do a Buddhist dedication. That was another high point, and a lasting thing for me at Woolman. As we look back on it, it's all positive vibes."

Louise Drollinger also taught English as a Second Language (ESL) to two Japanese students. Woolman paid for her to go to an ESL class in San Francisco. Deward notes, "One of the Japanese students was my counselee, Masa Shimakawa. We didn't have anyone at Woolman who spoke Japanese, but we did have an exchange teacher who came over from China who spoke a little Japanese. He and Masa bonded. Immersed in the Woolman family, Masa then picked up more English than we taught him. We were very fortunate, because his parents were quite wealthy and paid for us to stay with them in Osaka for three weeks."

Greg Smith, English and music (choral, piano, chamber music) instructor (1978-1984), took his community-based teaching experience at Woolman and expanded it into a thriving school program in the local community in nearby Grass Valley, California. Editor of the book *Public Schools That Work: Creating Community*, which is about alternative schools focused on inclusion and social justice in public school settings, Greg says, "My experience of community at Woolman is one of the reasons I used the word 'community' in the title of the book. My wife, Becky, and I came to Woolman after envisioning the place we wanted to work, which would be a setting where we could pursue our interests in social justice, environmental concerns, music, and teaching. We happened to connect with a woman at a local grocery store and got talking with her about what we envisioned, and she said, 'I went to a school just like that in Canada.' She had gone to Argenta Friends School in British Columbia. The next spring, we interviewed at Argenta and planned to work there. However, we learned that getting an okay from the Canadian government to teach there was going to be very unlikely because we did not have particular skills that Canadians didn't already possess. Argenta told us about Scattergood, John Woolman School, and Oakwood School.

"We chose Woolman. It turned out that Woolman was exactly what we had described and a remarkably perfect match. It was like calling to the universe and having the universe respond. I'd been teaching at Ashland High School in Oregon and had developed a style of interactive teaching that was much more student-centered and tied into dialogue than lectures. This matched well with teaching at Woolman. The main difference was that Woolman offered a much more comprehensive relationship with students because we were all living in the same place. At Woolman, I also appreciated the real focus on what it means to live responsibly in a community and the Quaker emphasis of seeing God in other people. The Quaker concern about peace and social justice, and the attention to what is best in people was instrumental, and one of the things that attracted Becky and me to the school. Also, it was located on a gorgeous piece of 320 acres with gardens, animals, and access to the Sierras. The environmental focus was central to my own focus as well and influenced much of what I did later in my own work. The emphasis on nonviolence was also in line with my thinking. The American Friends Service Committee would come to the school and do workshops in nonviolence. Another teacher, Brian Fry, and I taught a class on peace studies. Part of the class included going down to the Bay Area at the time to participate in protest marches about getting the U.S. out of El Salvador. I've also been a practicing Buddhist since I was in my early 20s, so Quaker meeting tied into that as well. Having the opportunity to sit in silence with an entire community of kids was extraordinary. The emphasis on consensus decision-making, both at the faculty level and the community as a whole, was also of value and carried over from the activism my wife and I had done in our college days. Additionally, for three years, there were some extraordinary classical string players at Woolman, all of whom have become professional musicians; Carla Fabrizio (cellist, Bay Area, California), Masten Brich (violinist for a symphony orchestra in Spain), and Eric Borgir (cellist in Germany/Austria). I played piano. We performed chamber music and played in town at an old church, or at the school. Richard Sanders, who also taught English, played a mean recorder. I learned enough recorder to play with him because Telemann wrote some beautiful recorder duets. Ted Menmuir had also built a harpsicord, so we could use that for chamber music, too.

"After leaving Woolman, I realized that I wanted to find some way to make the community experience and sense of social responsibility students encountered there accessible to a larger number of young people. So I went to graduate school at the University of Wisconsin-Madison to pursue that question and get a Ph.D in educational policy studies. What grew out of that work has been a movement called place-based education (or place-and-community-based education). While at UW-Madison, I participated in a national study of successful programs for potential dropouts that (surprisingly) brought me back to Grass Valley to do research at the Sierra Mountain High School, one of whose founders was Lou Sitzer, a teacher at Woolman when I first got there in the late 1970s. During that time, I wrote or edited five books about this topic as well as the team-written book about the UW-Madison study of successful schools for students who were struggling in conventional high schools, entitled *Reducing the Risk: Schools as Communities of Support*. One of the 14 schools we included was Sierra Mountain School. After working for two years at the University of Alaska-Fairbanks, I spent 23 years as a professor in the Graduate School of Education and Counseling at Lewis & Clark College in Oregon. I used the same style of student engagement in my teaching there as I had at Woolman. Looking at how conversational dialogue could happen in the classroom has been one of my pedagogical aims, and very much what I tried to do both at Woolman and Lewis & Clark College.

"My experience at Woolman was also transformed into an effort to engage public-school students more fully in their communities. One is about the Environmental Middle School in Portland (now the Sunnyside

Environmental School). I was among its early founders and sat on its site council for six years. Its principal was a woman named Sarah Taylor; she is a Quaker who sent one of her sons to John Woolman School. So, I've encountered all sorts of serendipitous connections to Woolman since leaving."

Lew Sitzer, (1974-1979) elaborates, "My late wife, Eddy, and I were at Woolman for five years. She taught Spanish. We moved to the area and set up the Sunflower School, which primarily catered to the John Woolman School children, and did that for three years before she and I moved over to Woolman to teach school there. The Sunflower School lasted for about twenty-five years. I like to think of it as an acceptable, innovative approach to education that did not exist here in Nevada City before. Eddy was deeply affected by the Quaker experience and became a Quaker about a year into our stay at Woolman. The environment of Woolman was intimate, so she was able to make a lot of great connections with students, primarily with young women. Woolman provided a sense of acceptance, caring, and personal connection that the public schools didn't. We were attracted to the Quaker Way of life before Woolman, and I have continued it ever since. Woolman reinforced my life direction in community service and a sense of respect for not only one another but for quiet in silent, Sunday community meetings. It supported the idea that community is the basis for wholesome, healthy contributions. That being said, living in an adolescent, teenage community was very challenging for everyone—teenagers, staff—it stretched everybody. It had some down moments as well as great ones, the full spectrum. There was a special, idyllic, euphoric quality to life there, but there were students that just couldn't live with the lack of structure— they did fall through the cracks."

Lew took his Woolman experience and applied it to the larger community. He explains, "I introduced senior projects to the public schools in Nevada City to connect students to nonprofit organizations in the community so that they had a sense of community needs, and community service. When I was in high school, I started working with blind children at the Foundation of Junior Blind in Los Angeles, and that led to five years of working with blind kids which set me in a direction for service. So, I wanted high-school students who are sheltered to have a sense of what it is like to be at a food bank or working with the homeless or animals that need shelter, with all sorts of community issues. That continues at the high school where I worked."

Elee Hadly, Head of School (1994-2000), cited the ingenuity in the John Woolman School curriculum and its educational process. She points out that students were highly engaged in the curriculum. "We had kids who need to fulfill their U.S. History or English class requirements to graduate. We offered a class that could cover both, with the Toni Morrison book, Beloved as the theme. I team-taught a class with two other teachers, Nick Messer, and a Woolman staff member. Along with us, kids who were involved, including a Japanese student from Argentina, and an African-American student, brought lively, differing viewpoints to the class. We had twelve kids in the class, which was a big class. That experience was a high point for me."

In the late 1980s, Corrina Lasa had founded the alternative school, Global Friends School, the smallest Quaker school that the Friends Council on Education had recognized as one of their own. It, like Woolman, offered students real world education founded in Quaker principles. When the students at Global Friends School graduated, Corinna reached out to then principal Ted Menmuir at Woolman, who offered her a position as the school's history teacher.

She reflects, "These students were smarter than average and needed to stretch themselves. Kids like these can either get into trouble with drugs, sex, or alcohol, or, if motivated and challenged, can become extraordinary and do worthwhile work in the world. On my first day of teaching at Woolman, I established the 'Mutual Admiration Society' with students in my class. If we came to consensus and agreement about anything, every kid was expected to participate. We applied this non-negotiable action to projects and class attendance. Once in place, we could accomplish miracles together.

"The kids decided that our first project would be an Oxfam Hunger Banquet for Thanksgiving, an event that was designed to teach participants about world hunger and poverty. Everyone invited was randomly given food tickets. Based on the distribution of poverty in the world, out of 100 people, two people sat at a fancy table and ate gourmet food, while the rest sat on the floor and ate beans, rice, or nothing at all. Some got ice cream; others did not. The majority of people sat on the floor eating rice or nothing. The kids only expected to invite only elderly Quakers from the community. Though at first there was pushback from them about including local police, my point was that we should invite the entire community so they would have a chance to look inside Woolman to see that students there were not the enemy. At the time, Woolman students were sometimes seen by law officials in Grass Valley as nothing but 'throw-away renegades.' The Police Chief and his staff did come, with the provision that since we were a Quaker campus, they would have to leave their guns in their cars. All the police ended up with poverty food tickets and had to sit on the floor and eat rice, which immensely pleased my class! On Thanksgiving Day, the Nevada City Union newspaper ran a full cover half- page photo showing long-term Quakers Del and Julia Reynolds serving food to policemen sitting on the floor. That's how we started the year.

"Another time, we were watching the film, Gandhi, in my World History class, and I realized that my students did not understand active nonviolence. Some kids came from harsh backgrounds and were fighters. To illustrate hands-on why the active nonviolence Gandhi and Jesus practiced was so powerful, I said, 'Let's do an experiment on turning the other cheek!' One student volunteered to get slapped and another student volunteered to do the slapping. At the end of the experiment, the student who slapped the other felt terrible; however, the one who had been slapped said that by keeping to the decision to not react violently, they had never felt very powerful. Although my teaching style was 'out of the box,' Principal Ted Menmuir supported it.

"Also, because Principal Ted Menmuir was a clear taskmaster about what students could and could not do, kids thought it ridiculous that anyone could even conceive of having consensus about the rules at Woolman. However, believing in the Quaker process of consensus, I asked the kids, 'how do you think the rules should be enforced?' As a group, we first agreed that no one should be expelled, but that the principal had the final say.

Additionally, it was agreed that community service should be expanded to encompass this situation. We decided that it wasn't just the kids who were actually breaking the rules who were culpable but also the students who knew about it and helped to cover it up. For example, six kids might be standing along a campus trail and pass the word down to others who were smoking that faculty was in the area. In these cases, the ones who knew or participated in the broken rule also had to do community service work on the Woolman campus alongside the smoker. After implementing this edict, we had the cleanest windows, floors, and dishes in the dining room, woodpiles staked, and grounds raked because that is what the students themselves considered a fair consequence. They worked this resolution through Meeting for Worship for Business, exchanging punishment for community involvement. Some faculty had difficulty with this flexibility but were reminded that consensus and objection to majority rule were underlying Quaker principles. The Quakers have always stood by the principle of 'Speak truth to power.' Staff were in a position of power and the kids were speaking their truth, so as teachers in a Quaker School, I felt we all needed to get on board. It took months of student meetings, but the feeling of the school changed. John Woolman School became a place where kids were going home and telling their friends what an exciting place it was, and that people actually listened to them.

"For me, Meeting for Worship and Worship for Business were essential at a Quaker School. At first, kids were reluctant to participate but after some practice, especially outdoors, they would sit quietly and respectfully with each other, as well as participate in Meeting Worship for Business.

"We are all children of the light. Recognizing that light within in the students applied to me as well. In my later travels, I experienced very hierarchical societies in different countries where women were treated as inferior. Teaching at Woolman instilled in me the principle of not giving permission to people to make decisions in my life that they did not have permission to make. Before Woolman, I had solely identified as a Quaker—a Quaker women, a Quaker wife, and a Quaker teacher. I had even been a featured speaker at the New England Yearly Meeting, the largest, oldest Yearly Meeting in the country. After leaving Woolman, I was no longer simply a representative of the Quakers. In some profound ways, I felt I had lost my identity. What I came to realize is that I, too, am a child of light, not specifically in any role or definition. So, as a springboard from my magnificent year with the students and faculty at John Woolman School, I gained my real identity. That's what I would say Woolman gave me, not in a limited way but in a universal one."

Kerry and Mike Travers

ENVIRONMENTAL PROTECTION

21

CONSCIENTIOUS OBJECTION

*"Lobbying our congressman and knowing that
I could do this and that it was part of the Quaker tradition
has always kept me politically active."*

– C. Lanyi

Historically, Quakers have objected to military service and have been persecuted for their conscientious objection. They also support people whose conscience calls them to reject military activity. During the Vietnam War era, the natural surroundings of John Woolman School and its adherence to Quaker principles of peace offered a harmonious sanctuary to conscientious objectors who opposed the Vietnam war. Quakers were significantly involved in the anti-war movement in the U.S., so Woolman was a natural and appealing place for conscientious objectors to fulfill their requisite alternative service. They became instructors at Woolman and/or helped with maintenance of the campus. Based on their religious, moral, and/or ethical beliefs against the war, the number of conscientious objectors during this era numbered in the thousands. One of these was former staff member, Peter Nutting, who (with the help of Woolman students) planted the apple orchard in 1971 that is still standing at Woolman. He said he was pleased to learn that the orchard acted as a firewall and helped protect the main structures on campus during the 2020 Jones Bar fire. Peter also taught German and German literature.

Peter says, "Woolman was a life-changing experience for me, as I'm sure it was for a lot of people and sharing those life stories is really important. I was at John Woolman for two years as a conscientious objector. It took

a while to find a place that would accept me, but Harold Blickenstaff, who was the principal at the time, did. I was living in Berkeley going to graduate school. It was 1968-1969, the year of the revolution in Berkeley. Ronald Reagan was the governor of the state of California. Each quarter there was a disturbance, so I was ready to get out of Berkeley. I am not sure if it was through the American Friends Service Committee, but Woolman was on the approved list for alternative service. I knew that if it was on the approved list, I could get it past my draft board back in suburban Philadelphia. So, I went up to visit the school. It was a beautiful day in spring, and I just fell in love with the place, particularly because it meant getting away from Berkeley, which was not fun at all, especially in the spring because of the National Guard and police presence there. Woolman was such a contrast. Harold asked, 'What can you do?' The need was for a maintenance person. I really did not have much in the way of maintenance skills, but I had teaching skills and an academic background. So, I was somewhat hired somewhat as a handy person, but what they actually did need was someone to be in charge of the boy's cabin area. I wasn't supposed to be a full-time teacher, but I also did do a little teaching. I was hired for $50 a month plus room and board. Then I got into gardening. I knew there was a garden at Woolman, and that someone had some garden space but there hadn't been any active gardening in it. That's what made me really feel like I had a role to play at Woolman. I started reviving the gardens, which went along with the teaching. Then, in my second year, the orchard project came along. Just the fact that the trees are still there after all these years—and the fire skirted the orchard, which I find miraculous—is my legacy.

"Even after my two-year stint, I would come back to Woolman from Berkeley to take care of the trees until I got my doctorate seven years later. It became my home away from home. I really learned to love the school in a different way. Somehow, I got my hands on *Living the Good Life*, by Helen and Scott Nearing. Either I found it in the Quonset hut library, or somebody gave it to me, but I read it and was immediately taken with it. I would do intellectual work for half a day and manual work for half a day – and I remembering thinking, 'This is the life.' It's still the life I live today which is probably why my academic career did not go anywhere because I have such a love of gardening and trees. I live on 30 acres and am a steward of them, which I believe is really a part of who I am."

Philip Conkling, who holds a B.A. from Harvard University (1970), an M.F.S. from the Yale School of Forestry and Environmental Studies (1976), and an honorary doctorate from Bowdoin College, also did alternate service at John Woolman School. In 1972, he taught a Beat Generation class. Students read Ginsberg, Kerouac, and other Beat Generation authors. He had a dog named Bear. Shana Maziarz's aunt, Jan, remembers Philip fondly. "He made it possible for Yoshi, my dog, to live with me on campus. Yoshi had been sickly and nervous, but once she was at Woolman, she became free-spirited and confident. I loved having her there." Philip's love of the natural world and environmental sustainability prompted him to launch the Island Institute in 1983 in Camden, Maine, where he served as its leader for 30 years. He was also the founding publisher of *Island Journal*, the author of *Islands in Time*, and the founding publisher and editor for *The Working Waterfront*. His book *The Fate of Greenland— Lessons from Abrupt Climate Change* won the Phi Beta Kappa best science book of the year award in 2011. Additionally, he is a contributing editor to *Maine* magazine. Philip currently serves on the board of Fox Island Wind, a community wind-power company that has brought energy independence to communities off the coast of Maine.

In 1971, Doug Feeney also came to John Woolman School to do his alternative service. An accomplished painter, Doug worked in maintenance. His wife, Mary, taught English, math, guitar, and recorder. Ben Elkington and Dana Meyer also fulfilled their CO service working in maintenance in the late 1960s and early 1970s.

Though instructor Mike Travers was not technically doing his conscientious objection service at John Woolman school, an emotional epiphany working in a small village in the high mountains of Mexico convinced him to abandon his then military career and follow his conscience to an opportunity through the Berkeley Quakers to teach mathematics at John Woolman School. In essence, his motive for teaching at Woolman was an outgrowth of conscientious objection. He explains, "I was arrested at the school on the third day of school in fall 1969 and in detention with the Army for five months. John Woolman School was having a workday at school, and I had been pulling cattails out of the oxidation basin, which was a holding place for liquid sewage. The basin's oxidation broke the liquid down as compost. It was a dirty job. My wife, Kerry, and I were dorm parents at that time and living in the dorm. A student, Kathy Cass, came up to our apartment in the dorm and said to Kerry, 'These two men just came to the school, and they handcuffed Mike and took him away.' Kerry told her that wasn't funny because it could happen and Kathy said matter-of-factly, 'Well, they just did. They just came and took Mike away. They are walking across the field now.' So Chuck (the school principal at the time) followed the men because they had apparently come to the office and asked if Woolman employed a Lieutenant Mike Travers. Chuck had said 'No, we employ a Mike Travers but not a Lieutenant Mike Travers,' and they said, 'Take us to him.' Chuck replied that it was a workday and that Woolman was a 365 -acre farm. He said, 'Well, let me see where he is.' They walked toward the oxidation basin, where I was covered in oxidation water, and handcuffed me. I asked, 'Can I change my clothes and tell my wife? My apartment is in that building," as I pointed at the dorm. They said, 'Sure' but handcuffed me anyway and took me up to the office. The entire time Chuck was trying to get their badge numbers, saying 'Look, we don't have to do that. This is a Quaker school. We are not going to be violent toward you, but we are quite willing to use active nonviolence toward you. We will just lie down behind your car. Then what are you going to do?' So, they finally gave Chuck their identification. Ironically, the last name of one of the men was Loveless. Chuck looked at his identification and retorted, 'Hmm, Loveless, that's appropriate.'"

Mike was in the Nevada County Jail for two weeks, after which he was taken to Fort Ord. (Fort Ord has been dismantled now). There, he was charged with desertion. That was the end of his ROTC life. Kerry continued to teach biology, but went down to Fort Ord in Monterey, California every weekend to see Mike. He was let out in February. Later, Kerry would say that when she went to movies about Vietnam, she would have a visceral reaction remembering what that time was like for them.

Student involvement

John Woolman School also taught students Quaker principles and practices of active nonviolence. In keeping with these beliefs, the school supported social action, peace efforts, environmental protection, and social justice. Periodically, the school would even close its campus and take students to peace/social justice vigils and protest marches. In 1968, with support from the school, students protested on behalf of the national boycott of California grapes. They carried placards that read, "Don't Buy Grapes" and distributed 750 leaflets. Though union truck drivers did not honor their picket line, the message of Quaker social responsibility was firm. Former principal and history teacher Chuck Croninger (1967-1971) remembers the importance of engaging students in active nonviolent demonstrations. He says, "We often took students to big anti-war march and demonstration in San Francisco. That kind of social bonding was very valuable for the school."

In the summer of 1971, John Woolman School students and staff also organized a draft counseling center in Nevada City, California. Paul Gallioni, a graduate of Woolman, served as its draft counselor until Michael Brown, Social Studies/English Literature teacher at the school, took over. The Center was financed by the Grass Valley and Berkeley Friends Meeting.

Olivia Gay (student 1965-1968, staff in the early 1970s) says, "After leaving Woolman, I did community organizing on the local level, organized political campaigns, became involved in aspects of town government, and worked with community action organizations, the State of Vermont Housing and Community Affairs, and a community center in Vermont. Being in a situation where you're connected to people as a student and then being a staff member at Woolman connected to their parents, as I was, gave me a good foundation for that kind of organizing."

Jennifer Miller (Summer Work Camp, 1967), daughter of former staff members Dottie and Dick Miller, says, "We were raised by young parents who were right in the middle of civil-rights demonstrations, peace marches, and civil disobedience, so we were exposed to that at an early age. We came to Woolman having already had that experience. The biggest education I got was social and political. We did a lot of marching for Caesar Chavez and against the war."

Laurie MacKenzie (1976-1977) says that Woolman also influenced her activism. "It was my idea to go to Woolman. Learning about the tradition of Quaker schools appealed to me. For one Spring Special Project, I went with other students to a base across the water from Seattle to protest nuclear weapons. We camped out there. We went to the gates of the base to do a vigil every day to protest nuclear weapons. We also visited a peace center in Vancouver, Washington as part of that trip to learn more about peace and nuclear activism. My mom still talks about how I was arrested later at Livermore in a big anti-nuclear protest. I felt moved to sit down in protest with thousands of people doing the same. We were arrested and there were so many of us, we spent the night in a gym. They told us to give fake names, so I gave my name as Nancy Reagan and the White House as my address. I had also taken Spanish classes at Woolman for the first time. As a result, I studied Spanish at the University of California at Santa Cruz and ended up speaking Spanish fluently. In the 1980s, I got very involved with Central American Solidarity work in El Salvador."

In the fall of 1970, Molly Titcomb, who taught French and Spanish, also offered a class about the history of nonviolence. Only one student Catherine (Cathy) Lenox, co-author of this book, took Molly's class. For Special Projects that fall, Catherine spent three weeks with Molly studying active nonviolence and peace action at Joan Baez's ranch in the Los Altos Hills. She says, "What I learned there further substantiated everything I learned at Woolman about the importance of political and social action."

Sue Optiz (1969-1972) was active in the Women's Liberation Movement of the 1970s. In 1973, she was interviewed on a radio show about her protest actions by the National Organization for Women (NOW), the grassroots arm of the women's movement. She says, "Way before she became famous, Whoopi Goldberg came and talked with us." Before developing multiple sclerosis, Sue also attended Quaker meetings regularly.

Steven Greenleaf (1979-1981) adds that while activism was always in his DNA from his family, "Woolman added to my activism and reinforced it. When I was at UC Berkeley, I got involved with anti-apartheid divestment rallies and Tahoe Forest planning activism."

Kristin Applegate (1986-1987) remembers a special project of peace-march training in San Francisco. She says, "We went through a safety training for active nonviolence and learned how to stay seated if someone tries to drag you away. The next day, we went as safety monitors to an apartheid march. That was great for me, because while my mom would write letters to the editor, she was afraid of going to marches. As a Quaker, I think it's important to do this—I've been a Quaker since Woolman and that has really made me realize that writing letters to the editor is not enough if you want to be part of the change. Recently, I went to Portland and went out a couple of nights to a Black Lives Matter march and stood there in that line of women and got gassed. Woolman taught me how to do it safely, how to reach out to the community members, and how it is very important to ask what will be of service to them. Quakers have taught me that you don't just go in with your own agenda as a white person. Woolman was very crucial in teaching me how to live a Quaker-centered life."

On October 20, 1979, a nonviolence training was also held at the John Woolman School, led by David Hartsough of the American Friends Service Committee in San Francisco. The next day, three students opposed to the death penalty put this training into action by attending an ecumenical service, candlelight march, and silent vigil outside the maximum-security prison in Carson City, Nevada. Also in June 1979, six students (Zack Salem, Peter Koerber, Phyllis Markley, Scottie Lansill, Caitilin Rabbitt, and Greg Smith) worked with the University of California Nuclear Weapons Conversion Project to help organize a rally at Lawrence Livermore Laboratory. The rally was in protest to the university's support of the lab and its design of all U.S. atomic warheads, including those dropped on Nagasaki and Hiroshima.

In 1980, Woolman participated in a March for Survival in San Francisco, organized by the American Friends Service Committee. Seventy organizations concerned with foreign policy issues, nuclear energy, and the military draft, plus politicians, a Hiroshima survivor, Vietnam vets, and many entertainers, including Taj Mahal, carried the message forward: "No Nukes is Good Nukes. Down with the draft."

Ann (Croninger) Zedah (1967-1984) says, "When we were little kids, before I was even a student at Woolman, we would go to No Nukes rallies with the Quaker Yearly Meeting. We had silent vigils around Nagasaki and Hiroshima. So, I was raised in an activist environment. Living in a community, the way Quakers make decisions, informed every community I lived in after that. It made me a person who is always active in the communities in which I live. Learning about consensus was beneficial in all the communities I've lived in, be it college, a neighborhood, or when I went on to serve on the City Council in Fort Worth, Texas."

In 1981, a Peace Studies class, taught by Brian Fry and Greg Smith, organized a trip for more than 50 people from the area to attend and support a peace march in San Francisco to protest the U.S. involvement in El Salvador. Also, that same year the school held a peace vigil to make a public stand against the draft. A silent vigil was held at two post offices in Grass Valley and Nevada City.

Malaika Bishop (1992-1993) has worked with and run non-profits that support social and environmental causes, and with her dad, Paul Jorgensen (1964-1969), has tried to help get supervisors elected who are in favor of protecting the rural quality of the Nevada City/Grass Valley area and fighting development as it is coming in. She says, "My parents, grandparents (Mary and Russ Jorgensen), and the school's influence really help spur a lot of my activism. Mary always had a petition or two or three for you to sign. They were always fighting for something and writing letters to people about it. Russ ardently believed that there was no circumstance that justified a violent response and that anything can be responded to nonviolently. That was quite an education for me. It's hard to separate the peace activism and Quaker experience I had at Woolman from my grandparents, but I definitely got a chance to embody it more as a student there. On Spring Break, we went and protested at the Nevada test site, and I got arrested for the first time. Woolman definitely pulled me into that world of activism."

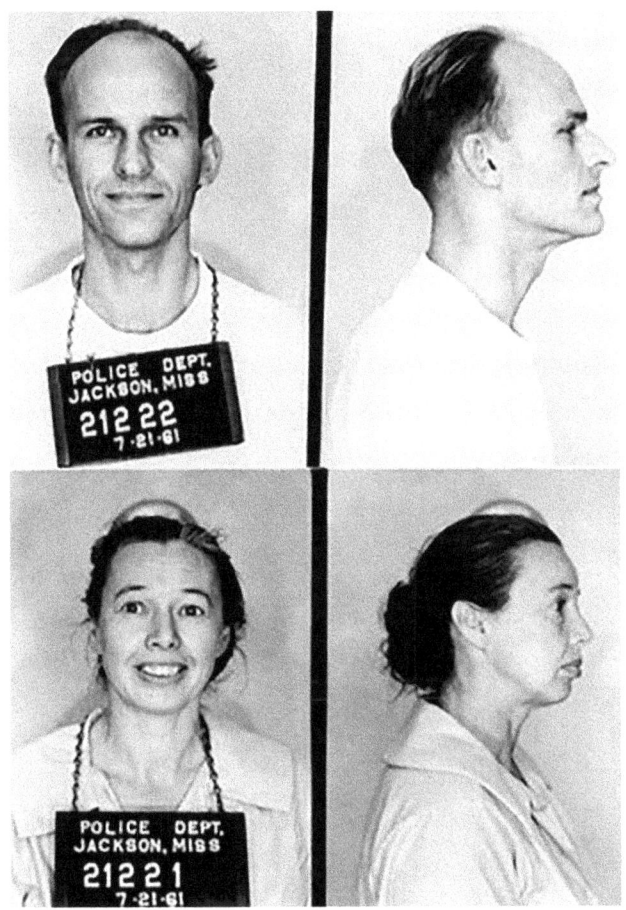

Russ and Mary Jorgensen, arrested at the Freedom Riders'
Martin Luther King March, 1961

| POTTERY DELIGHT |

22

CRAFTING CLAY

"Either I was going to make it as a potter, or I didn't want to live."

– C. Williams

I n the summer of 1971, a group of young Northern California artists hosted a week-long workshop to build a six-chambered, wood-fired climbing kiln at John Woolman School. The leaders of the project included Richard (Dik) Hotchkiss, who currently teaches ceramics at Sierra College; Rimas VisGirda; Ted Menmuir; and Doug Tweed. Ted Menmuir, who still lives locally on former school property, was the school principal, farm manager, and instructor of ceramics/drawing/math and philosophy (1969 – 2012) at the school. Son of former Woolman English Instructor Shirley Tweed, Doug Tweed graduated from Woolman in 1969. Both Ted and Doug were actively engaged in the kiln's early construction and operation, among other school-associated participants.

Ted says, "The original kiln-building workshop attracted more than 40 students of all ages and levels of experience. The kiln is still being used for community firings in the spring and fall of each year. We started building the "Noborigama" six-chambered "climbing kiln" in 1970 and finished it in 1971. It was built as part of the Earth Air Fire Water program. Woolman provided the location for the kiln but did not provide money or support for the project. It was developed by a group of local potters, headed up by potter Dik Hodgkiss who was inspired by the work of Japanese potters living in the mountains of North Central Kyushu, Japan. The Noborigama, which uses the heat of each chamber below it before it is fully fired, dates to 17th century Japan. Doug Tweed, a 1969 Woolman school graduate,

joined me in the project. We secured a site for the project on the Woolman property, located downhill from the dining hall.

"In the summer of 1971, Dik offered a kiln-building workshop to students from art schools across the U.S., Canada, and Mexico, and to interested Woolman students. For $250, students could have access to unlimited clay and as much food as they wanted. Sixty people responded. They lived in A-frame cabins and tents on campus. Woolman's ceramic studio was open 24 hours a day. Firing the kiln required the support of 50 to 60 potters, so the students did not fire it. However, they did join the workshops, but not as part of a formal Woolman ceramics program. It was a memorable event. Even Gary Snyder and Allen Ginsberg came to the school to read poetry while the kiln was being built. The school gave the first participants a lifetime membership to use the kiln. Dik Hotchkiss continues to send out the invitations."

Doug Tweed (1968-1969) befriended Dik and became involved in promoting the program, extending invitations to college and university art programs throughout the U.S. He also later taught pottery at Woolman.

A continuing group of community artists and students gather at the climbing kiln for maybe 180+ total wood firings once or twice a year. Students and friends of Hotchkiss still meet at Woolman to fire the "dragon kiln," which is an intense process of building a fire in each chamber and waiting for it to reach the optimal temperature before building the fire in the next chamber. Workshop participants work in two-hour shifts around the clock to stoke the fires for the three days of the workshop. Students shape clay into pots on and off the pottery wheel. As recently as December 2021, John Woolman School alumni Nancy Garcia (1972-1973) helped with a firing. The legacy of the climbing kiln at Woolman continues to this day.

Su Herbert (1970-1972) reminisces, "I remember going out to a lake to gather the clay and bring it back. Lori Bellilove (1970), Chas Marrow (1970), and I would stoke the fire through night and make raku pottery. I loved it."

Kevin Moore (1969-1972) also remembers long nights by the climbing kiln. "I sat playing the drum all night for people who were throwing wood into the kiln."

Jane Uptegrove (1970-71) observes, "At Woolman, I got a huge dose of good teaching about ceramics. With Ted, the kilns, and the gear we had, it was really original ceramics work. I had so much fun doing that. At Putney School, a small, progressive co-ed boarding farm school in Vermont where I'd been before, it seemed to me that students were tracked. I was a musician, so I had orchestra, madrigals, and chamber music, etc., with no time for anything else because I was doing music. When I got to Woolman and took double ceramics as my curriculum, it was fantastic. Ted really welcomed us to be a part of the entire process."

Professional potter Clara Lanyi (1980-1981) notes, "Going to Woolman informed my world outlook and values in a way that still informs my work, which is really about including misfits and celebrating what is odd and wonderful, including the history of ceramics. It is also nature-based. I started out in sculpture but now I am a potter. Part of the reason that I like pottery is its connection to the humbleness of daily use items, which I feel comes from Woolman."

Darby Huffman (1970-1972) continued to pursue what he learned about pottery at John Woolman School. Today, he owns Laughin'Gnome Pottery in Port Townsend, Washington, where he and his wife, Francie Loveall, have been producing high-fired unglazed pottery since 2005. He says, "I still work about 60 hours a week and love just about every minute of it. I began my throwing career when I attended John Woolman School. I helped build the climbing kiln. We mined the clay and glaze materials and made our own bricks to build the kiln. At the end of the 30-day workshop, we spent three days firing our new friend. As I've grown older, I've realized that this interaction of clay and humans brought me into a closer harmony with Mother Earth and how we are inherently connected to clay throughout our lives. I believe our souls are tied to clay, which is why I do what I do today with passion, a loving attention to detail and joy."

For some students, the profundity of what they experienced in the arts at Woolman stayed deep in their hearts until it surfaced later in life.

Josie Chase (1970-1971) discovered that she loved doing pottery when she was in the seventh grade at Putney School. She went there until the end of her junior year. In her senior year when she arrived at Woolman, she spent most of her time in the art barn doing ceramics, painting, and drawing. She notes, "Later in my life, I wanted to get back to artwork which is all I'd done through high school. That was really my heart's desire. I had dropped it completely and was really starved for it. So, I started back into the Chicago Art Institute when my kids were little and ended up moving east to finish my education. Then I became a potter and high-school pottery teacher."

Susie Schreiber (1970-1972) also returned to pottery after a career in geology, "While I was at Woolman, doing pottery was wonderful. My dad had a Ph.D in ceramics, so I always felt connected to pottery. As a tiny kid, I was running around the pottery studio all the time. That was a fun experience at Woolman. It was my first opportunity to try pottery firsthand. Then, decades later, I came back to it again in Seattle."

Noted potter and painter Cheryl Williams (1976) also says, "I was headed into trouble and Woolman saved me. Quaker Friends teaching was very different from public school education. I got to experience an entirely different world there and do clay in the art barn. Kids with interests outside of the mainstream could excel there." Today, Cheryl is an internationally known ceramic artist and painter famous for her unique prosperity bowls and abstract paintings. She works in a variety of media, including acrylic paint, metal, and clay. Her artwork is prized by major collectors worldwide and has appeared in numerous galleries and art publications. In a White House Ceremony on October 5, 1995, she received the National Medal of Arts from the National Endowment of the Humanities and the Charles Frankel Prize Award for her ceramics and painting. In the Quaker spirit, she says, "The light that is within all of us is reflected in my work."

....

23

STAGING CREATIVITY

"Creativity is intelligence having fun."

– Albert Einstein

Creative expression and the arts were supported and encouraged at John Woolman School. Some staff even took van loads of students to San Francisco to see world-class dance and theater performances. Students also created their own Special Projects, focusing on their natural abilities, talent, and interests.

Dance

Suchi Branfman, (1969-1971) studied dance at Woolman. Today, she is a choreographer, curator, performer, and abolition activist, and she is part of the faculty at Scripps College in Claremont, California. Currently, she is engaged in a five-year choreographic residency at California Rehabilitation Center, a medium-security men's prison in Norco, California. Her project, *Dancing Through Prison Walls*, which began in 2016, examines mass incarceration, the prison industrial complex, and systemic racism through embodied dance practice. Suchi has worked both nationally and internationally as a soloist and member of numerous dance and performance companies including Wallflower Order and Crowsfeet Dance Collectives, which focused on anti-war, feminism, socialism, and anti-imperialism themes. She is also co-director of Catalpa Residency Desert Hot Springs, a space for women and BIQTPOC (Black, Indigenous, Queer, Trans People of Color) activists/artists to create, rejuvenate, work, and reflect. Additionally, she is a community gardener.

When asked if Woolman influenced her dancing, Suchi says, "I was always involved in dance. I grew up dancing. I went to Woolman because I needed to get out of Los Angeles. That was a hard choice for me because I had to leave my dance world, but I was pleasantly surprised. While it wasn't a turning point, I was able to continue dancing at Woolman, in the middle of nowhere, and that was so wonderful. As I recall, we had so much fun—and we performed modern dance with Susan Brown in the dining hall. We had wonderful big dance parties there, too. Dance embodied practices that I started at Woolman that transformed me. One was getting involved in meditation, yoga, Gary Snyder, and this whole other metaphysical approach to the world. A lot of us were doing that. That led to my practicing yoga many decades before it was a big thing to do. That has informed all my dance work—it is part of the embodied work that I developed at Woolman."

Lori Belilove (1970), who also danced at Woolman, is internationally known for her interpretation of Isadora Duncan dance and is the Founder and Artistic Director of the Isadora Duncan Dance Foundation & Company in New York City. As a master teacher she has held residencies at Harvard University, The Juilliard School, Northwestern University, Smith College, University of Alabama, Ohio State and Drexel University. In 2015, she was appointed Artistic Director of the newly established Duncan Dance Academy in Shenzhen, China, with affiliate branches in 15 countries. She is also the leading dancer in the PBS documentary *Isadora Duncan: Movement from the Soul*, narrated by actress Julie Harris. She says, "When I came to Woolman, I had already been introduced to Isadora Duncan because when I was twelve, my family had traveled from London through Amsterdam to Athens, Greece. There, we looked up Mr. Vassos Kanellos. founder of the Kanellos Dance Company. He started talking about Isadora Duncan. My brother recalls that we all asked Mr. Kanellos a lot of questions about Isadora. Mr. Kanellos said that he had studied with her when he was younger. I did not know enough about who this phenomenal woman was to even be surprised. I was very precocious, and in the conversation, he said, 'I think you're the next Isadora. I think you have to come study with me.'

"When I was at Woolman, I wrote to Mr. Kanellos and felt the Isadora Duncan style of dance was a good match for me. In the lower floor of the women's dorm at John Woolman School, we did grand contractions and floor work with our dance instructor, Susan Brown. She was one of my first dance teachers, and I kept thinking that I really didn't like dance but that I was interested. However, I didn't have a choice with Isadora Duncan. She got ahold of me. I loved her thinking, her philosophy, her free-spiritedness, her bravery, and her courage when that was what we needed. She was a feminine feminist. She wasn't a radical 'lead in your face' woman and that appealed to me—that is my nature. John Woolman opened me up to that experience."

A former modern ballet soloist, Anne Sotelo (1969-1971) also remembers how dance at Woolman influenced her life. She says, "For one Special Project, a handful of students and I studied dance with Susan Brown and put on an interpretative dance performance in a chapel at Mills College in Oakland, California. Susan treated us very much like young modern dancers and showed us the studio we would be working in. Our group was made up of some of the students who liked to dance in the dining hall during our wild Friday and Saturday night dances with the records playing. Over a number of days, our group had rehearsals and learned choreography. It was very special. I felt honored to have that opportunity." Ann went on to perform and choreograph for dance companies in the United States and Europe from 1975 to 1989, until injuries prompted her to study dance medicine rehabilitation. She now owns Soma Syntax Studio in Los Angeles, California, where she does Rolfing, visceral manipulation, integrative manual therapy, craniosacral therapy, and the Melt method, which uses small balls and a soft roller to ease pain. In 1998, *Los Angeles Magazine* selected her as one of the best Pilates teachers in Southern California.

Theater

A paragraph from an article written by Kerry O'Regan on April 1, 2019, "Finding Lightness in the Light" for *Friends Journal* could easily be describing the work of John Woolman School alumni D'Arcy Drollinger

(1984-1987). (This article originally appeared in the April 2019, issue of *Friends Journal*. Reprinted with permission. Subscribe at www.friendsjournal.org/subscribe/) It reads:

> "There is value in the particular quality of humor that welcomes the unexpected and unpredictable. This can be freeing, allowing us to cast aside those constrictions and rigidities that can be both limiting and divisive. It can help nurture a climate where we are open to those Aha! moments where we arrive at the unexpected and unpredicted outcome that is as right as it is surprising. Open, if you like, to the promptings of the Spirit which may seek to take us to places our more cautious tight-laced selves could not have imagined. And, besides, what fun we could have along the way..."

D'Arcy is an actor, writer, director, producer, and choreographer known for his playfully irreverent-campy/vaudeville-style stage productions and films that combine slapstick, farce, and drag. They are edgy, experimental, riotous fun. Recently chosen as the first inaugural drag laureate of San Francisco, and the first in the U.S., D'Arcy plans to open a fully functional film production studio in the city. In a May 2023 statement, San Francisco Mayor London Breed said, "While drag culture is under attack in other parts of the country, in San Francisco we embrace and elevate the amazing drag performers who through their art and advocacy have contributed to our city's history around civil rights and equality. I am proud to invest in programs that create a platform for individuals who, like D'Arcy, are sending a message to the nation and the world that our great city is a beacon for acceptance and opportunities for all." Acceptance, advocacy, civil rights, and equality—D'Arcy lives these Quaker values to the core.

A founding member of the post-punk art band Enrique, which in the late 1980s to mid-1990s had a loyal following and toured nationally, D'Arcy has also directed for stage and screen. With twelve plays & musicals, eight parodies, and one film to his credit, whether he is performing on stage as his flamboyant, charming alter-personality, Champagne, or as the loveable Golden Girl, Rose Nyland, his/her productions and performances are delightful.

Deward and Louise Drollinger, D'Arcy's parents, were teachers at John Woolman School. Deward was an art teacher and Louise taught Spanish and geology. D'Arcy's father taught a semester at the end of the school year in 1980, after which the family joined him in 1981. D'Arcy was a "staff kid" at Woolman before being a student. D'Arcy's uncle, as well as family friends, lived on the North San Juan Ridge, so the family had spent summers there and were already quite connected to Nevada City and Grass Valley. Noted poet Gary Snyder's family lived on the same road as D'Arcy's aunt and uncle. The family knew Gary Snyder well, and Gen Snyder, Gary's son, was D'Arcy's roommate for a while at Woolman. D'Arcy remembers going to a little schoolhouse at North San Juan to hear equally well-known poet Allen Ginsberg read poetry, and lights up in a huge smile, saying, "Growing up at Woolman changed the way I related with other people in the world in a lot of ways. I was much more politically minded and had a stronger, clearer idea of what was going on in the world. I feel like I had a big head start going to college because I had a larger view. It was a pretty magical place." D'Arcy also fondly remembers creating theater works at John Woolman School. "Woolman was a college prep school, but we were also able to explore fun classes. You could take anything from stick-making and massage to psychic healing and musical theater appreciation during two weeks in December, and fiber arts and pottery classes were part of the curriculum. There was no theater department, and since drama was really my love, I was allowed to create plays. At Woolman, you could pretty much do whatever you wanted to do. I was very driven, so being able to forge my own way and develop confidence to be creative in it was great for me. It was powerful to have that base of support. I took a lot of the angst I was feeling (a combination of my eyes being opened to world politics and teenage hormones) and produced a play for a "peace fair" we had at Woolman every year during the four years I was there. I would write, produce, and make the costumes for a musical relevant to whatever I was on fire about. I think the peace fair and peace plays gave me a foundation of courage. I wrote and produced my first play in San Francisco in 1993. I had the courage to do that because of what I'd been able to accomplish at Woolman. A lot of times in life, we do what we think we can. That experience gave me the ability to feel that I could. To do that at such an early age was great. I would absolutely not have had that opportunity in a mainstream school. I'm very active in theater and film now."

After Woolman, D'Arcy revealed the true spirit of an entrepreneurial, enterprising Wombat by opening the famous cabaret-style theater and club, Oasis, in San Francisco. That's when the farcical hilarity began that has left audiences laughing ever since.

Melodrama, The Suspenders, 1966

24

VISUAL INTERPRETATION

"The image educates emotion where reason never reaches.
The significant image held, recalled,
has the power to transform."

– Dorthea Blom, Author - *The Life Journey of a Quaker Artist*

Mixed Media

Laura Cooper (1978) works in multiple media, including painting, collage, photography, and fiber. She has exhibited at major galleries in New York, Palm Beach, and Oahu, and at Vassar College, Block Museum of Art, Norton Museum, and Northwestern University. She is on the fine art faculty of ArtCenter College of Design in Pasadena, California.

Textiles

Laurie MacKenzie (1976-1977) had already dabbled with fabric arts in public high school, but Woolman is where she delved into it. She says, "My roommate, Kerry Hamilton, had a spinning wheel. We also had looms in the art barn. At Woolman, I got interested in natural dyes. I did a Special Project harvesting wool from sheep. I carded the wool, gathered plants, learned about natural dyes, did some spinning, and made yarn. Then I went to the Mendocino Art Center and took a workshop on natural dyes. Mary Lou Girtzen was one of my classmates. Her mother was an amazing stitchery and watercolor artist. I gave her some yarn for stitchery. I still have the beautiful work she did with it."

Influenced by the artistic environment at John Woolman School, Sylvia "Chipps" Newsom (1968-1970) studied fashion design at Rhode

Island School of Design and became a model manager in New York City. Also, due to the gentle influence of weaving instructor Gayle McCurley, Catherine (Cathy) Lenox (1969-1971) became a lifelong hobbyist weaver. In the late 1980s, she wove fabric for a design studio that supplied fashion houses in New York with high-end garments. As a part of the curriculum at John Woolman School, in 1978, nine students, directed by Susanna Calderon, also learned how to make hooked rugs.

Photography

Former principal and history teacher Chuck Croninger (1967-1971) is now an avid photographer. He remembers buying his first camera while he was at John Woolman School. "At that time, Woolman had a darkroom in the laundry room underneath the dining hall. Biology instructor Paul Patterson was into photography and had something to do with putting the room together. It had an enlarger and chemicals. I've retained that interest all my life."

Kate Connell (1977-1978) has a BFA from the Art Center College of Design in Pasadena, California, and has worked as a commercial photographer in New York and nature photographer in Austin, Texas. After 2 ½ years in Kyoto, Japan, she moved to Santa Barbara, California where she currently lives and works. She has participated in numerous solo and group exhibitions in Texas, Japan, and California, recently at the Santa Barbara Museum of Art, the Atkinson Gallery, and Channing Peake Gallery.

Camille (Jenny) Ross (1980-1981) of Native Light Photography, also posts on the John Woolman Alumni page that she is a professional photographer in a variety of media. She says, "I remembered Clara Lanyi's brother, Sean, taking pictures of a napkin holder. I really liked them and knew then that I would become a photographer. So, right after JWS I went off to an amazing college as cool as JWS, Goddard! I absolutely loved it and thrived. Then I went to Cranbrook Academy of Art for my MFA. None of this would have happened if I had never attended our magical loving and healing school, Woolman."

Stained Glass

In 1978, five students traveled to local artist Donna Whittaker's farm each day to study in her studio and, in exchange, to help her with work on the farm. They cut glass, learned to make leaded bindings, and soldered the pieces. That same year, the American Friends Service Committee invited two students to their printing shop in San Francisco. Working with Margaret Jolly, press operator, they learned to make plates for offset printing, and how to operate and clean the press.

Photography in action

Wood block print poster, 1973

25

....

MEANING, MYTH, AND MAGIC

"Into the forest I go, to lose my mind and find my soul."

– John Muir

John Woolman School literature and writing instructors were forward-thinking, inventive, topical, and experimental. They also introduced students to college-level thinking and creative writing.

Martha Kahane (1973-1974) remembers that writing instructor Shirley Tweed had a big influence on her interest in writing. "Shirley had us write our memories of childhood in a sensory way – what did we see, how did we feel. I remember how alive I felt in that class and how much I learned about writing."

In Peter Nutting's German class, Su Herbert (1970-1972) loved reading the existential poetry of Rainer Maria Rilke. Kate Lacy (1978) and Jenny Ross, Elizabeth Johnson, and Terry Miller (1980-1981) also remember renowned poet Gary Snyder coming to the school to read poetry on campus in the Stone House.

Additionally, the school spawned many writers, among them Nina Kiriki Hoffman (1970-1973), who started publishing short stories in 1975 shortly after graduation from Woolman. Her first novel, *The Thread That Binds the Bones*, won the Bram Stoker Award. Other novels include *The Silent Strength of Stones* (a sequel to *Thread*), *A Fistful of Sky*, and *A Stir of Bones*. She has been recognized for her fantasy novels, adult literature, young adult books, and children's literature. Her short story "Trophy Wives" won a 2008 Nebula award. As of 2020, she teaches small classes in science fiction, fantasy, and horror writing via Zoom for the Fairfield

County Writers' Studio. Nina says, "Michael Brown was my first writing teacher. I wrote a lot of little pieces in his class, for which I received positive feedback that encouraged me to keep writing. Recently, I wrote a story that will be published soon in an anthology. It was supposed to be about schoolbooks and sorcery. It was about three students at a pseudo Woolman School, but it's in a school of magic. I have this idea that someday I'm going to send one of my characters to a Woolman-like boarding school. It would have to be a period piece because we didn't have cell phones or ways to stay in contact with the outside world then. We had each other. That's a lot different than today, so if I was writing a young adult novel, which is what I envision this being, it would be interesting. Young adults have to navigate all kinds of social strata now."

Rob Sulllivan (1970) also worked as a reporter for the LA Weekly (1987-1993), *LA Times, SF Chronicle*, and *Village Voice*. He has also been a stage actor and has had small parts in movies. He has published five academic books about urban theory, as well as poetry books, with a book of fiction to be published soon. Rob says, "I read like crazy and enjoy writing a lot. I have had fifteen plays produced in Los Angeles. When I was 13, I went to see Bob Dylan sing. That changed my life. I started writing in earnest then. From the time I was 14, I was always writing, but my study with Jim Corbett at John Woolman School changed me a lot just in terms of his knowledge. Before I went to Woolman, I just tried to get by with Cs and Ds. I hated public school. A few teachers read a couple of my short stories and put them down. That really upset me. (Fifteen years later, I read the stories and they were actually pretty good.) It took all year to open me up to the idea of education and then I really got excited by it. Jim and I would go out and herd the goats and talk, mostly about theoretical things, political theory and philosophy. I loved Dr. Seuss' wordplay and rhythm. The most important thing about Woolman is that I fell in love with attaining knowledge and learning. Other than reading poetry and Bob Dylan, I did not have that before. When I was young, 18-30, there were times I wasn't writing, and got very involved in acting. Around 34, I stopped acting and concentrated on writing. I did three one-man shows: 'Flower Ladies and Pistol Kids,' an autobiographical piece; 'The Long White Dress of Love,' about romantic obsession; and 'Thinner than Water, Thicker than Ice,' a fictionalized version of my relationship with my first wife. When the Bethlehem Steel plant in Vernon closed, I worked with steelworkers at the mill to write and produce a political artistic docudrama, 'Lady Beth: The Steelworkers Play,' about steelworkers who'd been laid off during the 1980s. Millions of workers were being sent overseas and steelworkers were being laid off in the U.S. It got attention. Bruce Springsteen loved it and financed our tour of the Midwest. It became a Springsteen event and made the Northeast tour possible. We were dedicated to this issue. At age 53, I went back to school and got my PhD in geography at UCLA. I taught there as a lecturer for two or three years."

Author David Mellon (1971) is an accomplished storyboard artist working in film and television in Los Angeles. After Woolman, he went to San Francisco Art Institute and California Institute for the Arts and graduated from the Art Center College of Design in Pasadena with a degree in illustration. After years of painting pictures and drawing storyboards for film and TV commercials, he attended the UCLA Extension Writers' Program, where he was nominated for the 2016 Allegra Johnson Prize. His novel, *Silent*, tells the story of a young woman who poses as a soldier to rescue her twin brothers during WW1. He says, "My grandfather was the director of the Del Gato in New Orleans (the New Orleans Museum of Art), and my grandmother was a painter, so I was already set for work in the arts. Woolman was that moment for me to kind of take a breath from being at a traditional Louisiana high school to being out in the world; it was a lot of experimenting with being a young teenager. I got a hugely wonderful shot from Woolman to carry on from there."

Niles Dolbeare (1976-1978) has written scripts for actress Lily Tomlin's one-act shows and penned entertaining newspaper columns. He mentioned being particularly influenced by author Faye Kicknosway, who had studied writing at SF State University. Niles says, "Faye was hired as a Poet in Residence at John Woolman School. She was definitely my strongest influence as a teacher. I'm still in touch with her. What attracted me so much to Faye is she knew exactly what you should do in life, what you should write, and what you should not do and not write. Everything was black and white with her. She was not wishy-washy—and not that I don't think consensus is a good thing, but when you're trying to get something out on the page, it's good to have a direction. I went on to get my BA in English & Creative Writing from San Francisco State University."

Co-author of this book, Catherine (Cathy) Lenox (1969-1971) also has a BA in English & Creative Writing from SFSU. She has worked as a journalist, magazine editor, and nonfiction ghostwriter. She remembers taking an influential one-on-one writing class from instructor Gerow Reece, who arrived at Woolman in 1971 after studying calligraphy in Kyoto, Japan with Morita Shiryū in the mid-1960s. The class was held up a tree in a student-built treehouse, where Gerow lived. She reminisces, "The class, 'Reflections,' was Zen-like. Gerow would light a fire in a wood-burning stove. As we sat cross-legged next to it discussing my journal entries, he taught me how to listen to life and to use all my senses to observe it. Through Gerow, I learned how to write about sense of place and emotion; the sound of leaves crunching under my feet as I hiked to his treehouse hermitage for classes, the pungent taste and smell of the green tea he served me, the warmth of the stove fire, and my feelings as I sensed them all. He taught me to notice and appreciate every one of these in detail. This sensory approach to writing has influenced everything I've written since. It was foundational."

Kevin Moore (1969-1972) is a linguistics lecturer at San Jose State University in San Jose, California, with a Ph.D. in Linguistics from U.C. Berkeley. He also works on Wolof, spoken in Senegal and Gambia, West Africa; has published a technical book based on his dissertation, *The Spatial Language of Time*; and has written poetry. Shortly after Woolman, he went to Africa with fellow Woolman student, Erik Silverman, to learn drumming. He says, "It was life-changing to be in rural West Africa in a culture that was very different from my own. Before that, I was a real rebel. In West Africa, I realized that tradition could be a good thing and that I didn't need to rebel. I learned about community. I was also always interested in linguistics. When I was four or five years old, I remember cutting my finger and saying 'ouch.' I remember wondering if everyone in every language says 'ouch' the same way and uses the same intonation when saying it. My parents were good at languages and encouraged me to pursue this interest. At Woolman, I was influenced by my German language teacher, Peter Nutting, who challenged me to think about language origins. In terms of language, I remember he asked me to guess what "der Fürst" might mean. I didn't know but, in the broad sense, it meant Prince, the first in line to the King. Language and the concept of time are also connected. In language, there is an entire system of movement. For example, in English, an event in the future can be described in two different ways, "The middle of the semester is coming, which means it is approaching us, or 'We are approaching the middle of the semester' which means we are approaching it.' Sentences are also governed by rules and structure. I wrote a poem for linguists, 'I wish I had a language with fifty-million words for star, where adverbs compliment their adjectives at night, touching each other's hearts and speech, and copulas* copulate freely, causing little baby verbs to pop out unlicensed." (* a copula is a verb that joins the subject of a verb with a complement, as in "the stew smells nice.")

Author Jennifer Shannon (1976-1978) says that if not for the influence of Woolman English instructor, Richard Sanders, she might never have had the confidence to write. Today, Jennifer is a licensed psychotherapist and a Certified Diplomat in Cognitive-Behavioral Therapy specializing in anxiety, and author of *Don't Feed the Monkey Mind, The Anxiety Survival Guide for Teens* and *The Shyness and Social Anxiety Workbook for Teens*. She says, "I like reading and love writing. But I was always nervous about writing. Writing was an area where I had a lot of problems because I hadn't had any formal teaching in grammar and wasn't a good speller. English instructor Richard Sanders was so supportive and also gave me tremendous guidance. It was a wonderful balance between helping me catch up in writing and being extra supportive of who I was and wanted to say. He had complete faith that I could say it; I just needed to figure out how to do that in a more educationally formal way. So, he was very influential to me. I had no intention of growing up and becoming a writer, but then one of my kids developed severe social anxiety in middle school. I was already a psychotherapist specializing in anxiety, so I wanted to get her a book on cognitive behavioral therapy (the kind of therapy I do for social anxiety disorder). But for the onset of adolescence, there were no books about it, so I had to write one. (You need books to give to teens so that they realize they are not alone.) When that book did well, I wrote more. I've now written six books. One just came out last year. It is about perfectionism—and I used John Woolman English instructor Richard Sanders in one of the stories."

Outsider's Insider

A student-driven publication that was published for many years at Woolman was the *Outsider's Insider*, now a time capsule of the years that Woolman was active as a school. Another publication, *Torp*, was published by the students in 1963, but the *Outsider's Insider* continued to be published for many years. Mary Lambert remembers its first publication. "We had a contest to name the new newsletter. David Sherman won with his submission: *Outsider's Insider*. It must have been 1966-1967."

Meant to acquaint students and Friends with the life and thoughts of Woolman, the newsletter featured student articles, poetry, school news, and photography. During his long career with John Woolman School which started in 1962, Don Smith edited the *Outsider's Insider*.

In the fall of 1968, early in the school's history, in the *Outsider's Insider*, then Principal Harold Blickenstaff wrote, "It may well be that the most practical learning that takes place here is the sensitivity and flexibility that develops from trying to reconcile our differences and live together in harmony. Living here is truly a lab course in human relations." He was right.

Collage in newsletter

Research at John Woolman School in the library, 1960s

| HARMONY |

26

....

PLUCK YOUR MAGIC TWANGER

*"Music is probably the only real magic I have encountered in my life.
There's not some trick involved with it. It's pure and it's real.
It moves, it heals, it communicates and does all these incredible things."*

– Tom Petty

John Woolman School encouraged a well-rounded education based on students' interests, abilities, self-expression, and innovation. In 1970, inspired by fellow student Doug Tweed, students at John Woolman School dubbed the annual parents' visitation day, "Pluck Your Magic Twanger Day." Meant to pay homage to stringed instruments, the name bemused staff and some Nevada County residents but gave students giggles over what seemed to be a double entendre. One student conga player even decided to "pluck his magic" by riding bareback on a horse across campus without a stitch on, much to the dismay of administration. Yet, it was the music program at John Woolman School that spawned numerous professional music teachers and musicians. Of the students who went on to make a career of playing or teaching music professionally, many agreed they were given the trust and freedom to explore music at Woolman. Whether they came to the school already inspired by it or they discovered it there, they said staff supported their interest and helped them learn.

Folk Rock - Jimmy Jett and the Rocking Bombers

In a rustic recreation room during the 1969 Spring Special Projects break, a group of long-haired, wildly creative teens crowded together to form a band. Uninterested in participating in service projects off-campus, with staff approving their plan, they spend their break forming a band and

writing songs for it. Legendary in the history of John Woolman School, just their collective name, "Jimi Jett and the Rocking Bombers" brings a smile to anyone who knows the band. The group went on to delight students at John Woolman School during dances in the dining hall and for years after graduation at the school and at venues in town. At the school, band members Jimi Jett, Rob Holland, Bob Mora, Rhone Scoggins, Erik Silverman, Sandy Smith, Brett Gollin, Doug Tweed, Dan Koppick, and Robert Kaplan created a legacy. Susie Schreiber also joined the band on saxophone a few times.

When he was 14 years old, before coming to John Woolman School, Rhone Scoggins (1967-1969) was in folk-rock bands, playing guitar in Los Angeles, California. Rhone and his sister were also troubadours at the Southern California Renaissance Pleasure Faire, coincidentally a festival started by Rob Holland's mother. Six months after arriving at John Woolman, Rhone connected with other band members to start the band. Rob would become a part of Rhone's band. Rhone notes, ""There weren't many kids, so we formed little tribe groups. To this day, Jimi Jett is my best friend. We started singing do-wop songs in the bathroom under the dining hall because the acoustics were good there. When staff said we could do anything we wanted to for Special Projects, I suggested we start a band. Rob Holland, Doug Tweed, and Bob Kaplan were in that first group. Rob's brother loaned me a guitar, and Rob brought a bass and a bass amp to campus. We started rehearsing in the barn."

In 1969, when Jimi Jett and the Rockin' Bombers band first started, they were playing James Brown's music. They were also writing their own soul songs at a time when they could have been lynched for doing that, given the culture in Nevada City in the late 1960s. Despite pushback from town folk, John Woolman School supported their creative endeavor. Rob notes, "When we were in town, with our long hair all we saw from pickup trucks was people giving us the finger, threatening us, and yelling 'are you a boy or a girl?'"

Stan Koppick wrote lyrics that Rob Holland would describe later as the "voice of Burl Ives" and the "writing of E.E. Cummings." In fact, John Woolman School provided the musical culture that was anything but acid rock and country music in Nevada County in 1975. Singer/songwriter music, reggae, Latin, funk—they played the alternatives. Brett Gollin also started taking drum lessons the following year. After Woolman, he founded Bongo Logic, a Cuban dance music group that produced five albums.

Says Rhone, "We had cool songs. We had character, and we weren't trying to get the groupies. We would have done artistic, esoteric albums because we weren't trying to be great musicians. We were writers who just wanted to make the songs sound good with the skills we had. I didn't even know that that you could play guitar and make money at it if you were especially good. I just thought, 'let's start a band!'"

"Doug Tweed did not continue with the band after graduation, but Sandy Smith bought his drum set and became the drummer. Then it was like we'd get a weird itch to start the band again. It was kind of like a comedy movie; we'd say, 'Hey, let's start the band again,' and we'd drop everything. After graduation, I was working at the post office making decent money as a high school graduate. But Rob would say 'Hey Rhone, come up to Nevada City and start the band again.' Or, I'd say, 'Hey, Rob, let's go start the band again' and we'd talk to Jimi and, he'd say, 'okay.' It was just crazy. We'd drop everything and go start the band again and suffer."

After graduation in 1969, the band nearly advanced to stardom. Moving to London, they started Jimmy Jett and the Rockin' Bombers there. Playing acoustic guitar with Bob on harmonica, they performed Americana-style music. Connecting with a producer in London and working from midnight until 6:00 AM, they recorded an album, mastered at Apple Studios. The producer took the tape to BNG in Hamburg. When he came back, they were all on pins and needles.

Rhone says laughing, "The guy said, 'Sorry, boys. Another American got the gig.' Then he pulled out a picture of James Taylor. We said, 'Let's hear him.' So, he played 'Fire and Rain' and we said, 'Oh, that'll never go anywhere!'"

Rob adds, "A funny thing is, my dad might have been playing percussion on that album. He played on a bunch of James Taylor albums."

Over the next ten years that Rob Holland was in Nevada City, he continued to lead semi-pro bands that were interested in Cuban music;

a 14-piece band, a mixed-up smaller band; and a Charanga band with strings, flutes, and a Cuban rhythm section; and a band with trumpets. In 1979, he also played with the first African dance troupe in Nevada County with former John Woolman School student, Paul Jorgensen. Additionally, in 1978, Rob and another former student, Kevin Moore, led nine students through a study of percussion, focused on Latin and African rhythms. The group was shown how to make a guiro, a simple rhythm instrument. The ensemble performed at Woolman.

Bob Mora also still plays music. His band, Bob Mora and the Third Degree is a hometown favorite in Nevada City, Grass Valley, and Northern California. He brings deep country blues harmonica and vocals to the band. He says, "Parenthetically, I married Lily, who is from a longtime ranching family in the Grass Valley area whose great-grandparents homesteaded not far from John Woolman. Her cousin married Jack Stillins, whose family used to own John Woolman. Jack Stillin's father carved the mantlepiece that was over the fireplace in their house that was later turned into the infirmary at John Woolman. I think the mantelpiece is still there."

Today, Rhone Scoggins is a professional musician, and Bob Mora and Jimi Jett are semi-professional. Though some band members are more professionally involved than others, the music they started at John Woolman School has remained a theme in all their lives.

Sean Feder, (1977-1978) adds, "I was 'spaced out' as a teenager and not very focused. I was distracted by girls. I play a lot of string music now. My wife, Rita, is also a singer/songwriter. But I did get influenced at Woolman to do something I've done a lot: hand percussion and congas. I don't know the history of it, but someone brought the tradition of Cuban and African drumming to Woolman. There was a nice set of congas in the Art/Music Barn. There were people around who knew what they were doing, so someone taught me congas. That became part of my career for 20 years. I was a teacher of congas and played in a lot of bands in Northern California as a semi-professional."

Most likely Brett Gollin and/or Rob Holland had something to do with the congas left at John Woolman School, and perhaps even taught Sean to play. Their legacy lives on.

Classical

The year was 1970. Dancing barefoot across the wide campus meadow in a long, pale blue muslin skirt, dark hair spilling down her back, Kei Salz played a flute. Strapped across her body with twine, the flute went with her to classes, to the dining hall, and even to the barn where she tended goats. Like Euterpe, the Greek muse of music and lyric poetry, the 15-year-old was never without it. She borrowed a flute from another student, put it together, and never took it apart. She trilled tunes on it wherever she went. Noting her intrigue for the instrument, that summer her parents gave her flute lessons and bought her a flute. Kei discovered her lifelong passion at Woolman.

Kei Sundt (Salz) says Woolman shaped the entire course of her life. She explains, "I was basically self-taught at Woolman. I started playing duets with another student, Su Herbert. We went down to Arizona and played duets there. When I got back, that's when I started doing duets with music teacher Kerry Travers. She played violin and piano. Kerry was who helped me but if you were interested in anything at Woolman, there was always someone who could help you learn. Choral teacher Dorla Menmuir also influenced my singing. Though I spent a lot of time with goats, music has been the most important thing I got from Woolman that I've done my entire life and continue to do."

Now retired, Kei has had a long career of teaching music. After herding goats in Arivaca, Arizona after Woolman, she graduated from the School of Music at the University of Arizona, where she has been the woodwind teacher for 30 years. She also taught high school band for nine years. "My relatives thought I was this total free spirit and there I was teaching a quasi-military band yelling at kids to march around," she says laughing. "However, I absolutely loved working with kids in marching band. I no longer teach band, but I still play music in the orchestra, a jazz band, and a soft-rock country group. I play alto flute, saxophone, light percussion, and sing back-up vocals."

Su Herbert (1970 – 1972) also remembers playing music at Woolman. "Kei Salz played her flute, and I played my oboe. We played music all the time. It was wonderful. I've always played in an orchestra or a small ensemble. I played professionally in an orchestra that toured Europe, and in those days went behind the iron curtain in Romania. I also sang in an a cappella choir in a Catholic church and received a scholarship to study at the Institute des Haute Études Musicales in Montreux, Switzerland. I still play classical oboe, jazz saxophone, and sing. Music is still very much a part of my life."

Josie Chase (1970-1971) also played music with both students and staff at John Woolman School. She says, "Woolman was a playground for me in ways because I could completely invest myself in music. Jane Uptegrove played violin, I played cello, Peter Nutting (staff) played viola, and Kerry Travers (staff) played violin. We had a blast playing on campus."

Additionally, Emil Borgir (1973) is a professional musician with "Acoustic Soul." His first album, *You Flow Through Me*, started as a remembrance for his daughter, grew into a 12-track devotional tribute to African American music.

Choral

Jane Uptegrove (1970-1971) says, "Since I was introduced to music as a child and already doing it, at Woolman, I connected with Dorla Menmuir right away. She aligned students with a Seventh Day Adventist Church in Nevada City that was performing the oratorio, "Elijah" by Felix Mendelssohn. We sang with them. Another time, I went with Dorla to San Francisco to find music for the madrigals group. She took me to the music store so I could help her pick out music, and it was wonderful."

Sean Farrell (1981) also observed, "My mom, who is a music teacher, piano player, and singer, was surprised at how good the chorus was at John Woolman School and how we were corralled into singing decently."

Lisa Hubbell (1976-1978) agrees. "Choral singing was supported well at Woolman. Dorla Menmuir had a choir, and she also directed the choir at Nevada Union High School. One of the years I was there, she organized a mass choir to do Vivaldi's Gloria with people from town and both high schools."

In addition to taking writing classes that would lay the foundation for her future work as a professional science fiction/fantasy writer, Nina Kiriki

Hoffman (1970-1973) also enjoyed Dorla Menmuir's choir and madrigals group. She says, "My love of singing choral music started at Woolman. That experience was so exciting that I continued to be in various choirs for years after Woolman. I'm still musical, and in a four-part a cappella group, Sacred Harp. I think Dorla and her madrigal class had a lot to do with that long-term effect."

In 1973, Nina was also part of a student-inspired musical event. Nina, along with Mary Jane Chastain (drums), Walter Thomas (song), and Peter Bradt (guitar) put on a production of "Tommy" (by the Who) on the John Woolman School dining hall deck. She remembers, "We even invited people from town to come see it. I made a poster for the show, and we posted it in town. Dorla gave us permission to do this project and provided staff oversight. Peter taught me to love The Who. It was really fun."

Nina also took her first fiddle lessons from the cooks who worked at Woolman, and for one of her Spring Special Projects stayed on campus and learned to play the banjo out of a five-string banjo book by Pete Seeger. She says, "Now I mostly play mandolin on my back patio with a bunch of Oregon old-time fiddle, upright bass, and guitar players."

Martha Kahane (1973-1974) says that the music program at Woolman also influenced her life. "Dorla Menmuir had a big impact on me. I took her class in choral music. She had an incredible voice and was a really great musician. She even had me conduct a piece for graduation. We did some big choral pieces with a pickup orchestra in town and had these glorious choral musical experiences. Choral music is still a major part of my life. In fact, I'm currently writing a piece about choral music. There were also other people in my class who were incredibly gifted. We were in a small chamber music acapella group. Music has been a huge part of my life. I ended up majoring in music at U.C. Berkeley. If I hadn't gone to a high school where music was such a big part of the curriculum, this might not have happened. I also ended up marrying a really great musician who is quite well known."

| SPECIAL PROJECTS |

27

SPECIAL PROJECTS

"Getting outside of yourself and seeing the world and multiple ways you could contribute, as well as the education we got outside of the classroom and the options we had for choosing it was a unique route to learning."

— J. Gershen

Twice a year, once in the Fall and once in the Spring, as part of the John Woolman School curriculum, students participated in a rare educational experience called Special Projects. Fall Special Projects focused on service to the community, from hammering nails at a Quaker Retreat Center to trail restoration in Pt. Reyes, to helping farmworkers build homes. Students also worked with Chilean refugees, developmentally disabled children, people living at a dump in Tijuana, or foreign children in the San Francisco as English Language tutors. Spring Special Projects focused on real world activities meant to expand students' horizons and give them exposure to other cultures and alternative ways of life. From visiting a Buddhist intentional community at Green Gulch Farm in Marin County to living in a small Mexican village, learning how to survive in the desert and domesticate wild goats, rafting, hiking, or building enclosures for wolves on the east side of the Sierra Nevada Mountain range, Spring Special Projects stretched students' understanding of the world. Additional Spring Special Projects included visiting Pueblo and Hopi locations, living in a Quaker community in Canada, studying peace action at Joan Baez's ranch, and participating with other organizations against the war. Some students also chose to do

independent projects, mainly in the arts. Both Fall and Spring Special Projects taught students to become involved in their communities in a more substantive, meaningful way.

Service Projects

Former Principal, Farm Manager, and Instructor of Ceramics/ Drawing/Math and Philosophy Ted Menmuir (1969 – 2012) remembers taking student crews to Visalia, California to help farmworkers build and paint their homes. He says, "The program required families to take part in building their homes in exchange for ownership of them, once they were completed. We worked with the American Friends Service Committee (AFSC). Students assisted families in framing houses, roofing them, and overall construction. I also took a crew to the Quaker Community Center located in Ben Lomond, California to assist with maintenance and building of the center. Plus, I took a crew to the intentional Quaker community in Sonoma, California, at Monan's Rill to assist the people living there."

Jennifer Shannon (1976-1978) also recalls the AFSC experience, as well as a Special Project she designed herself. "Visalia was a great opportunity to be around Latino farmworkers in central California and get exposed to another culture. They cooked a pig for us by burying it in the ground and then ate everything on the pig, including its brain. I remember how exotic and different that was. For another Special Project, I wanted to go to Southern California to a family systems workshop. I was very interested in psychology. Woolman staff said that I could not go alone, so I went to a Special Project at the War Resisters League in San Francisco and left after two days to go to Southern California to the Family Systems workshop. I guess I was a rebel. Obviously, I got in trouble for leaving my assigned special project and doing my own thing."

Nina Kirki Hoffman (1970-1973) was also impressed by the AFSC housing projects and participated in two of them. She reminisces, "We were on the roof nailing down shingles. It was exciting to learn how to work on building houses. An African American family also invited me to their home, so I got to see a way of life I had not seen before."

Sue Optiz (1969-1972) also visited an Indian Rancheria on the California coast with English instructor Michael Brown, and student Kim Dryden. She says, "Initially, we planned to help clean up junk there, but what the people really wanted us to do was clear brush from the land so they could plant crops. While we were there, the Native people allowed us to watch their ceremonies. Through sharing their dance and music, I think they accepted us. What I learned from this experience is when you want to help someone, ask them what they need. Don't assume you know what is best for them."

Jennifer Dickey (1977-1978) also recalls going to San Luis Obispo, California to build outhouses for an Indian village. "The terrain was granite, so our small group had pickaxes and dug all day. It was January, cold, and the showers were outside. After digging outhouses in granite all day, I wanted to get clean. The water was so icy, it felt like needles were piercing my head. The first night we got there, I was also wicked thirsty. Going into a tipi, I saw a juice jar sitting on a table. I thought it was filled with water and took a swig. It was kerosene for the stove. One of the men there also tried to assault me. However, working together as a group, getting to know the Native people, having meals with them, and being included in the community was wonderful. We also went to a pow wow. Overall, it was a great experience."

Jennifer Gershin (1979-1983) adds, "Getting outside of yourself and seeing the world and the multiple ways you could contribute, as well as the education we got outside of the classroom and the options we had for choosing—it was a unique route to learning. The school made education fun and inspirational. It allowed us to celebrate diverse ways of learning. It didn't matter what the subject matter was, the school engaged kids, lit a spark for learning, and related our education to the real world."

Cultural Projects

For Spring Special Projects Fred Harris and Brett Golin (1968-1970) chose to work at the Pacifica, California radio station, KPFA in Berkeley. Kim Drayden and Mickey Barrett (conscientious objector and ardent naturalist) spent a Spring Special Project at Catalina Island in California on a survival hike eating wild goat meat and natural food plants. David Ginden learned to navigate by current and winds on a rafting trip. In 1969, Dennis Kendall visited a local vegetarian farmer, where he learned about organic produce, and in 1973, students backpacked into the high Sierras. Plus, in 1977, David and Mary Levy, Olivia Gay, Kerri Hamilton, Niles Dolbeare, Suzy and Marlee Steelman, Jennifer Selser, Jonica Smith, Emily Allison, and John Storer explored the deserts of Death Valley, Joshua Tree National Park, Anza Borrego, Palm Springs, La Jolla, San Diego, and Tijuana. Staff member Stephen Miller also helped start the student band, Salsa Band, that year.

Teachers Kerry and Mike Travers also recall Spring Special Projects with a smile. "When we were in Mexico with our students in the spring of 1973, we rode on mules 50 miles up the mountain to the place where we were going to work. We had this Mexican foreman, Juan, who was helping us do what we were supposed to be doing. We'd show up in the morning, and if it was later, around 8:00 AM, he would slowly enunciate, 'Good morning." If it was after that, he would say with even more animated enunciation, "Good afternoon.' That is particularly funny if you know Spanish. 'Buenas tardes' is Spanish for 'good afternoon.' But 'tarde' also means 'late.' So, they were never sure if the foreman was saying 'good afternoon' while also insinuating that we were late. We also took Spanish language students several times to Mexico. The kids were all from urban areas, Los Angeles and San Francisco. We took a first-class bus down to Mazatlán, and a second-class bus to Saint Ignacio, and then we took a third-class bus to Ajoya. The third-class bus was basically a flatbed truck with seats in the back of it. Then we got on the mules and rode them for another two days. There weren't enough mules for everybody, so some people walked, and some people rode the mules. It took us two days to get up into the mountain where we were going. At first, students fought about who got to ride the mules. After a few hours of riding on the bony back of a mule, people were fighting about who could walk. We got up there and they had corn, beans, and tortillas for every meal every single meal. After days of the same meal every day, the kids were dreaming about burgers and fries. But with their help, we built a clinic there. We dug with hand tools to make the foundation with rocks and mud, made it as level as possible, and then we'd lay logs on it. Then we'd build a 'Lincoln-log-style' house on top of it. The men would cut the trees in the forest and drag them down on their horses. We'd have to strip the bark off, cut the notches, and then fit the logs together. We completed it all in two weeks."

Matthew Bronson recalls going on a formative Special Projects trip to Mexico with Kerry and Mike. He says, "I had a very life-changing experience of a month in Mexico building clinics and vaccinating kids. It was my first trip abroad, first contact with poverty, and my first chance to speak another language. Post-Woolman, languages became my thing. I speak fluent Spanish and Portuguese, and can get by in French, Russian, German, and Catalan. I think Mike may have also been inspired to become a doctor on one of those trips because we were working with a gentleman, David Werner, who wrote *Donde No Hay Doctor (Where There is No Doctor)*, which has been used around the world as a self-help medical manual for rural people. The service element to Woolman and the idea that it is not 'all about you' was very important."

Annie Fourt also wrote of her trip to Mexico in 1976. "I learned a great deal about Mexican culture from living with my family. They were most patient with me as I tried to make tortillas (without much success), wash clothes in the creek on a flat rock (total failure), or remove corn from the cob to make tortillas (no way). Every morning, we'd get up at about 5:30 before sunrise, start a fire, and make tortillas for breakfast - they are a lot of work! First, you remove the corn from the cob, wash and soak it, then grind it, add water, roll it into dough, pinch off bits and flatten them, and then finally fry them. I burned my fingers many times. After breakfast, we'd clean up, make the beds, etc. The younger children would go off to school for half a day while the women sewed or did other little jobs until noon. After lunch came the big chores, like laundry, which took a good two to three hours. Fixing dinner took another hour or so. At dinnertime, the men would return from working all day or from hunting or fishing. I think it was a very worthwhile trip. It really changed my ideas about life in foreign countries. I had an excellent experience."

Lisa Hubbell (1976-1978) says going to Mexico with Kerry and Mike

Travers was also memorable for her. "As a Special Project one year, I went with a group to El Hoyo, Mexico. It was a great experience. A lot about that trip was intense, as well as the feeling of going back 100 years back into the past. We flew to San Diego and then took two buses to get to our destination. The second bus was filled with chickens and small livestock. It was such a culture shock. The Hesperian Foundation had a medical clinic there. The town had no electricity. They could run generators for light, but that was it. Most of the work was gardening at the clinic. I was sun-sensitive, so I got to help sort through all the medical supplies and throw away anything that was expired. Each of us lived with a family within an hour's walk of the clinic. Along the route, we were dropped off at homes where we'd each be staying. I was let off at a house, but no one was home. I walked into the house and a photo of a Woolman student who had stayed with them before was on the wall. It made me feel at home. While there, I played guitar a lot. The kids loved one song I played, 'Passing Through,' by the Weavers. 'Passing through, passing through, sometimes happy, sometimes blue, glad that I ran into you, tell the people that you saw me passing through.' One time my family hooked up a little record player to play a record the son had picked up in Mexico City. It was "Hey Jude.' It was curious how little bits of culture had made their way down there. The men who ran Hesperian had paid for the family son to study medicine in Mexico City. The daughter in the family had wanted to do the same but was denied the opportunity. She ended up committing suicide."

In 1973, Mike and Kerry Travers and student Migue Dozier also took a small group of students on a Special Project trip to the Southwest. To help underserved communities, both Mike and Migue became doctors after Woolman. Today, Migue is an internal medicine specialist affiliated with Los Alamos Medical Center in Los Alamos, New Mexico. Before retirement, Mike also practiced medicine in Idaho and Washington. Mike says, "The Special Project was only a part of something bigger. Migue and his sister, Anya, had a father who was an anthropologist, and a native member of the Santa Clara Pueblo in New Mexico. He had made his name in anthropology studying the indigenous Kalinga people of Northern Luzon in the Philippines. After that, he had turned his attention to his own people, writing the definitive works on the Pueblo Indians of New Mexico. Migue and I put together a semester anthropology course on the Pueblo Indians, using his dad's books in the course. As a Special Project, we then took a small group of students to New Mexico, with Migue as our student guide. There, we hiked in Bandelier National Monument, camped in Chaco Canyon, spent a few days at Santa Clara Pueblo, (near Espanola, New Mexico), and went to Santo Domingo Pueblo, (also known as Kewa), near Albuquerque. Then we went to Arizona, where we visited the Walpi Pueblo on the Hopi Reservation and Oraibi, the oldest continuously inhabited settlement in America, located in Navajo Country, and founded by the Hopi." Kerry adds, "In the fall of 1969, we also took a group of students to the Northern Cheyenne Reservation, located south of Billings, Montana. We stayed in a house with running water but no plumbing. We had to use an outhouse and it was snowing. The kids found that distasteful. Another shock for them was a domestic violence situation that happened in our cabin when a wife dragged her drunk husband out by his hair. It was a real eye-opener for them to see the depression and mental health issues on the reservation. We did a service project there for a week and went to two tribal celebrations. A guy named Lyman Weasel Bear told us the first one started at 2:00 PM; we waited for three hours, and nothing happened. The next day, we were told it would start at 5:00 PM. Not wanting to wait for hours again, we showed up at 6:00 PM. By that time, most of it was over. We learned that Indian time is based on whenever the Spirit moves."

Kristin Applegate (1986-1987) went to Camp Chaw'se at Indian Grinding Rock State Historic Park, located east of Jackson, California. She says, "I was there with Gen Snyder, beat poet Gary Snyder's son, and one of my dearest friends at Woolman, along with four other students. Being of service in an environmental way, learning about the history of the place, and honoring people who came before was an amazing, magical experience."

Kevin Moore (1969-1972) remembers a different magical experience. "With the school's permission, I took myself on a Special Project to the Morning Star Commune in Taos, New Mexico, in the Sangre de Cristo

Mountains. I went to a Peyote Meeting there, which is a Native American special ceremonial spiritual practice. I got there by hitchhiking and riding freight trains. The meeting was run by Native Americans in a tipi. In the middle of the tipi was a sand altar called 'Arapahoe Road.' There was singing, chanting, drum playing, sage-smudging, food, smoking tobacco in corn husks, and eating little pellets of dried peyote. It went on all night. The peyote effect came on slowly. When it did, I remember a strong spiritual feeling of the unity of life and being impressed to see that this Native American tradition was still being practiced."

Jane Uptegrove (1970-1971) also remembers, "For one Special Projects, we went into the Big Sur wilderness on a backpacking trip for a week with Peter Nutting to collect trash. The terrain was so different from anything I'd hiked in growing up. There were hot springs right next to the Big Sur River that flowed through the valley. The parched hills around us were covered in golden grass with occasional oak trees. We'd hike down into little notched ravines and walk among these enormous redwood trees lodged in the crevasses where they could get water. Since it was a thermal area, we would find hot springs. Somebody created a pool at the base of a redwood tree that was about 5 feet in diameter and 1½ feet deep. The water was flowing from the hot springs to it. About four or five of us could sit in it at the same time. It wasn't commercialized, it was just there in the middle of nowhere. Experiencing Big Sur in that way was spectacular."

Kristin Applegate (1986-1987) learned to enjoy the rugged outdoors at Woolman. "Instructor Ted Beatty and Steven Greenleaf, an alum who was teaching Introduction to Ecology and Plant Biology that fall, took us on a beginning-of-the-year backpacking trip. They taught me about the outdoors, which deeply and profoundly changed me as a person and how I interact with nature. Initially, I was terrified. Yet, at Woolman I learned how to trust others and do things that frightened me. In fact, the first thing I bought myself when I went to college was a tent."

Susie Schreiber (1970-1972) was also initially unfamiliar with backpacking. She says, "I went on a trip to Big Sur to clean up campsites with instructors Gerow Reece and Mike Travers. As an East Coast kid backpacking was something I'd never done. I borrowed a backpack, a sleeping bag that wasn't warm enough, and boots that were too small. I had the worst blisters all over my feet and froze every night, but it was a cool experience."

Equally unexperienced with outdoor adventure, Nina Hoffman (1970-1973) went on a canoe trip on the Sacramento River, Russian River, and Feather River led by staff member Phil Conkling that was a formative experience for her. She says, "I decided to push myself into doing something I would not normally do to challenge myself. Some of it was glorious! We were canoeing down rivers and past pastures. We'd pull off and have lunch. It was idyllic and wonderful. The group wanted to do Class 3 river rapids, but I didn't want to do anything scary. On that trip, I was canoeing and Phil, who was in the canoe with me, said, 'Watch out for that rock!' I replied, 'What rock?' That's when I learned that I needed glasses—and we still had two weeks to go! That was a revelation. Later we were rained out, so we slept under the canoes. The highlight of our day was to load our canoes onto the truck and drive to the laundromat and put our clothes in the dryer. It was a weird setup because we'd park the truck and off-load the canoes – and then go downriver on the canoes for two days. Then we'd pull all the canoes up and somebody would hitchhike back and pick up the truck and drive it down to where we were. One time, we were in Red Bluff camping out in this really cool place, and I walked into a pay phone booth and called my mom. I said, 'I hate this, and I'm really scared!' She was a great parent because she told me, 'If you want to get out of it, we can make that happen.' Just knowing I had an escape route made it possible for me to go back and have a really good time. Another student on that trip, Herreid, was a real comfort to me." Jane Uptegrove (1970-1971), who was also on the canoe adventure, recalls, "After the trip, we dovetailed into an anti-war demonstration in San Francisco."

Su Herbert (1970-1972) also went on rafting trips but remembers them fondly. "We went on a rafting trip led by Ted Menmuir. He loved whitewater canoeing, so he taught us a lot about it. That was fabulous!"

Former principal and history teacher Chuck Croninger (1967-1971) also notes, "Before I came to Woolman, I'd done a lot of hiking in Southern

California, and to Mount Whitney on one occasion, with the Boy Scouts. So I was quite happy to move to an area that was mountainous and rural and be able to do our school opening hike with all the students going backpacking. Desolation Valley was a popular destination. I thought that, along with Special Projects, was a valuable thing to do with students. A middle school down the road from where I live now in Santa Barbara, California did something similar to what we did at John Woolman School. They had their student body carry heavy jugs of water down the road and back up to the school, which was quite an elevation gain. The purpose was to give students an idea of what it is like for people in a great deal of the world who have to carry water to their homes. Some of the students were doing it barefoot. It is a very powerful lesson with a similar intent to what we tried to instill in students at Woolman."

In 1980, five students and two staff members also went snow camping in the Donner Summit/Castle Peak area. They spent one night in a Sierra Club ski hut, and the second night in tents, and then went on to Sugar Bowl Ski Area to Squaw Valley, with a night at a ski hut along the way. A second trip took students to the Desolation Wilderness camping for five days. Al Chase (1980) remembers the trip, "Bellies full and spirits high, we traced our tracks backward for a short time until they disappeared in a windswept clearing. In the ensuing hour, my compass and map and some strategy led us through thick blowing snow and terrain devoid of distinct features to little Lake Margery, beyond which the route-finding was easy. With the sight of the lake came my greatest sense of accomplishment

Ski Trip Special Project with Kerry and Mike Travers

during the trip. Still, the wind, snow, and cold, though part of the nurturing of that piece of earth, at that moment seemed unforgiving. We skied on and finally descended into thick trees beside Tamarack Lake. As our camp took shape and the cooks readied dinner, the weather lifted; we were treated to golden day's-end sunshine on the snowy ridges and scurrying clouds. We went to bed under cold stars."

As a tall, lanky 15-year-old, Rusty Brown (1970) recalls enjoying backpacking and hiking on a Special Project in Big Sur with Mike Travers that influenced his life path. After his year at Woolman, Rusty put a backpack on his back again and traversed the world. He saw firsthand the struggles of other people in emerging countries. He says, "I was very influenced by John Woolman School's emphasis on community service and wanted to make a difference in people's lives and health." Later, while living in Hawaii, the U.S. Department of Energy hired Rusty to develop solar dehydrators with an application for developing countries. With an interest in sustainable food-processing systems and small-scale technologies that respect and protect the earth, Rusty developed a unique fresh drying process that uses tropical foods from around the world. In 1979, he founded Fine Dried Foods International, (FDFI). Today, FDFI specializes in fresh-dried, high-quality tropical fruits. Rusty employs hundreds of workers in agricultural areas of Mexico and Peru, staying true to his initial vision of increasing food supplies, and introducing and developing organic sustainable farming techniques while multiplying market options for farmers and workers in rural areas. The company works with growers to provide education and resources that lead to organic certification of their crops. Rusty adds nostalgically, "I wish I could go back to Woolman and do 100 Special Projects!"

Ski Trip Special Project with Kerry and Mike Travers

28

....

GOAT HERDING IN ARIZONA

"The program should provide ample opportunity for
people to learn, grow, and toughen, but it is not likely to be
a good trip for dedicated hedonists...there seems to be
agreement that the group should plan to practice
radical simplicity."

– J. Corbett

On November 15, 2020, Ann Russell, Ph.D Associate Research Scientist - Earth and Planetary Sciences (JWS 1970-1972), wrote of a Spring Special Project to a ranch outside Tucson, Arizona led by Jim Corbett, an instructor who was mentioned by numerous students as being highly influential. Joining her were Woolman students Neal Schneider, David Feazel, Scott Silver, Kim Dryden, Gretchen Herried (Peterson), Kei Salz (Sundt), and Su Herbert. A year later, Sue Opitz and Nancy Washburn also went to Arizona. Ann documents her experience so well that it is included here in its entirety: "Walking through wild land with a herd of sheep or goats, looking for forage and water, is a kind of wandering experienced by shepherds and goatherds, but few middle-class white folks have the opportunity to try it. In early 1970, I was 16 and a student at John Woolman School when Jim Corbett arrived with his dog Puck and his goats Sancha and the Togg to teach philosophy. Jim was thin and had a goatee, blue eyes behind wire-rimmed glasses, and a direct gaze. He wore a sweat-stained broad-brimmed felt hat, blue jeans, a denim Western shirt with pearl snaps, and sandals to give room to his arthritic toes. He slept with the goats in the scrub oak and manzanita hills behind the

school and was comfortable with long pauses in conversation, perhaps because of his time alone on the range as a cattle rancher and shepherd in Wyoming and Arizona. Jim had a master's degree in philosophy from Harvard and had lost a job as a college librarian for describing himself as a communist—all worthy accomplishments in Quaker eyes.

"One day Jim held a lottery in the dining hall to choose eight students to wander in the Arizona borderlands, to 'stray from the proper course or standards,' to fit into the untamed wilderness as members of the community of plants and animals. The chosen eight were to become goatherds errant. I was wildly excited by this proposition. He pulled a slip of paper out of his hat and read 'Ann...' and Anne Sotelo screamed, and my heart sank. Then he continued on '...Russell' and I felt a little bad for Anne Sotelo but overjoyed for myself.

"In September 1971, the eight of us arrived at the Sopori ranch, on the Arivaca Road halfway between Tucson and the Mexican border. A dirt driveway ran past an adobe house and irrigated fields toward a mesquite grove spread out along the Arivaca Wash. For the next few months, we slept under those mesquite trees at night and became friendly with Orion. Jim and his wife lived in the house. Pat was slender and tall, with crinkly blonde hair in a tight braid pinned up behind her head and covered with a bright bandanna. She loved horses and books, tolerated Jim's odd ways, and liked to feed him but refused to sleep in the mesquite grove.

"Jim bought a herd of white Saanen goats from an ancient woman on a steep hilly ranch just west of Tucson. The White Queen, Nero, Dearly, Beloved, and Magpie Socialite Piddleteat were uncannily adept at robbing the barrel cactus of its fruit while avoiding the long, curved spines, and had small udders with short teats that were less likely to become impaled than those of the buxom dairy goats one sees at 4-H shows. We also had a small Mexican horse, Chapo, and a flock of elderly White Leghorns we bought cheap from an egg factory.

"The course requirements for the Sonoran Desert Study Group were 'Ultra-Reactionary English Composition,' 'Buddhism, Taoism, and Quakerism,' 'Geography of the Sonoran Desert,' and 'Indians of the Southwest.' We read from Buber, Thoreau, Leopold, and Abbey. We met in the mesquite grove and made ourselves comfortable sitting on roots or on the sandy soil, watching ants and occasional scorpions crawl across sand and among plant roots while Jim led discussions in his soft gravelly voice. Our assignments were mostly writing responses to Jim's questions, including:

- What responses to the war in Vietnam would be consistent with Taoism? Buddhism? Quakerism?
- If the ten of us were collectively to live according to the and ethic with the water, earth, and other productive means at our disposal here, what changes would we have to make in our behavior, consumption patterns, and technology?
- What changes would Quaker simplicity make in our everyday patterns of production, consumption, speech, entertainment, political activity, and social behavior?

"To practice errantry, we went on extended walks with our herd. On the first goat walk, we wandered over 70 miles across low hills and dry washes, from the lower Sonoran Desert up into the high maple and pine forests of the Galiuro Mountains. We loaded our herd into the horse trailer and Pat drove us in the old green GMC pickup out a dusty washboard road. When we were nearly out of gas, she let us off in the middle of the trail-less desert, short of our intended drop-off point. We headed off up a wash, hurrying to get out of sight of the road to avoid any potential conflict with the owner of a ranchette a quarter mile away.

"We made a dry camp that first night when we were unable to find a spring for water. We gave the water in our bottles to the goats and drank only a few sips of water and warm goat milk ourselves. None of us had ever been hiking where there were no trails or faced uncertainty about something as basic as water. We were shocked and dismayed that we had to save most of the water for the goats and couldn't drink more ourselves. The next day we found a rancher's dirt tank, a small spring-fed reservoir trapped behind a low earthen dam and surrounded by desert willow and Bermuda grass. We spent that night and another day there filtering and boiling water, washing, and resting, and I spun a ball of wool as Gretchen read aloud from The Lion, the Witch, and the Wardrobe.

"In my backpack, I carried oatmeal, raisins, brown sugar, a bowl and spoon, a change of clothes, a sleeping bag and pad, water, my journal and pencil, and my drop spindle, carders, and wool. The first page of my journal was a list of plants that the Navajo use to dye wool; I hoped to learn these plants and collect some to try back at the Sopori place. We ate oatmeal with raisins for iron and goat milk for protein. For variety, we added Cream of Wheat to our supplies. All of us looked forward eagerly every day to our oatmeal, but everyone dreamt of sumptuous feasts, and told each other about their dreams at breakfast. Eventually we all lost our spoons and made ourselves chopsticks to eat oatmeal with, and then perfected the art of making lumpy oatmeal so our chopsticks would work better. Every night we built a fragrant fire, of mesquite at lower elevation or of juniper as we climbed, and Gretchen read aloud.

"When I first milked Nero (short for Neurotic), I knelt with a foot on her tether to keep her from running away and blocked her kicks with my elbow. I remember the moment she decided I was her adopted kid. Instead of fighting me, she turned to gaze at me with melting maternal eyes, stood patiently chewing her cud as I milked, and searched for me, bleating anxiously, as I stepped out of her sight. In a goat's-eye view, relationships with humans fit into certain flexible categories. When you milk a goat, you become her kid, when you are leading the herd out you are the buck, and when you decide on a place to spend a few minutes browsing or resting, you are the herd queen. The herd queen bosses the buck around and tells him when to move on. When the White Queen wanted to move on to a new foraging patch, she lifted her head and stared with her slitty golden eyes at Jim. He rose to his painful sandaled feet and led the herd out at a slow walk, whistling 'Shenandoah' in a warbly whistle I've never heard from anyone else. He called to them by bleating 'yeah, well, hey girls, ho girls, let's go.' At the ranch when he called Pat, he called 'hey Pat, ho Pat.'

"There was something about the way we traveled, without trails or campsites that were easily returned to, that opened my eyes. The pace of our days was governed by the goats' need to browse, drink, and rest, chewing their cuds, and by our arrangement to meet Pat at a campground in the Galiuros two weeks later. Jim rose with the goats at first light and followed them as they foraged for catclaw, barrel cactus, and other desert delicacies. We roused ourselves, milked, built a fire, and cooked our oatmeal. While the goats browsed and we waited for the White Queen to raise her head, we had ample time for solitude, daydreaming, and browsing for ourselves. We steeped mesquite beans to make sweet minty tea and ate jojoba nuts. I examined a creosote bush and its seed, a furry five-pointed star with a black spine coming out of the center; each section of the star was a seed. I wrote in my journal that I enjoyed being off alone, that I felt like a wild animal, freed of a few of the dictates that lead to dead ends, that I felt like a rock being worn by a river, being worn smoother and freer of sharp corners until I was sand carried away by the current. I felt joined with the desert.

"From that first camp, we continued wandering generally northeast up and down the hills and across washes to Hooker's Hot Springs and into Redfield Canyon. The canyon was overgrown with wild grapes because it was partially blocked by boulders that kept the cattle out but were no match for goats and teenagers. We spent a day and a half at a camp with flowing water and then made our way slowly up through the narrow canyon, camping one night underneath a vast rock overhang. As we climbed in elevation, tall saguaro cactus on the hills gave way to short, twisted juniper trees, and then, higher up, to oak and tall upright juniper.

"One day we broke out of Redfield Canyon to climb up into the mountains. The harsh hills were steep and brushy with catclaw and white thorn. The sharp rufous gravel, unsmoothed by running water, kept us sliding downhill with each step. When we finally topped out onto the ridge, scratched and sweaty, we entered into a silent grove of naked maple trees, as grey as a fog bank. We walked for a long spell on a soft bed of red leaves, our footsteps muffled. Deer hunting season arrived, and we tied bright red bandannas around the goats' necks to distinguish them from game. Eventually, we met up with Pat and the horse trailer at a campground and headed back to the Sopori ranch to resume our regular classes in the mesquite grove.

"It was on this walk that Jim asked me if I had a calling in life. 'I don't know,' I responded, 'I guess not.' 'Think about it,' he said. 'You are smart enough that if you don't figure out for yourself what is important to you in life, someone else will find you useful.' How will I find my calling, I wondered? In his early twenties, Jim wrote an epitaph for himself that friends used when he died at 67: 'I saved a lamb or two from freezing, I cleaned out a desert spring.'

"I had no such important and poetic deeds to recount and had no clear vision for the future, only a love of color and wool and books and music and an instinct to seek adventure. Are these callings? Is it so bad to be useful? Since then, for over fifty years I've wandered the world, submerged to the ocean floor in a research submarine, climbed Mt. Rainier and other volcanoes, learned two languages, become a scientist and a mother. Sometimes I measure my life's value by looking up on Google Scholar the number of times my journal articles have been cited by colleagues. But maybe the value of my life is as ephemeral as water in a dry Arizona wash, found in small acts of kindness, remembered by a few people for a short while and then forgotten."

Su Herbert (1970-1972) also remembers the Special Project with Jim Corbett. "We had a wonderful three months just north of the Mexican border in Nogales on Jim and his wife Pat's Appaloosa ranch. They caught, corralled, and tamed wild horses. We had to help them train them; to take a bridle, a bit, a saddle, and eventually our weight, and ride them. On my first day, I was able to mount a horse and ride around the ring on it. Pat said I was ready to jump, so I raced the horse forward, and right as we got to the jump, the horse balked. I went over the jump and the horse's head, did a somersault, and landed on my feet, still holding the reins, facing the horse on the other side of the jump. Pat laughed, called me an acrobat, and said I should be in the rodeo.

"There were ten of us on that trip. Being just 20 miles north of the Mexican border at night, we would see people coming over the mountains with torches, disappearing into America; illegal immigrants. Jim also had us read *On Walden Pond* by Thoreau, *A Sand County Almanac* by Aldo Leopold, *Silent Spring* by Rachael Carlson, and other wonderful books that talk about the relationship of humans to nature, our place in the world, and what we're doing to the environment. He had us learn firsthand how hunters and gatherers lived. Then we went to a remote place and each of us had to catch two wild goats. We had to tame them, milk them, and take care of them. Then, with Jim leading the way, we went into the desert with our two goats. One time I was leading the way through the cactus with my two goats on tethers. Suddenly this wild javelina (boar) with its huge tusks shot out of nowhere straight at me! I was terrified but thrust my hiking pole in front of me and froze. My part-American Indian father had taught me that when the lead person freezes, everyone does, and no one talks. The javelina came up to my pole, looked right into my eyes, and walked away. My heart was still leaping. We then camped, pegging our animals into the sand. In the morning, all of our goats were gone and there were cougar tracks in the sand. Thus began our learning how to track. We walked through the desert for three days trying to find them, concerned because we knew their udders would get too filled with milk and drag on the ground through the cactus if they were still alive. After three days, Jim went back to get the truck. On the fourth day, we heard Jim's distinct whistle for the goats. Then we saw all the goats coming toward the truck. They had escaped the cougar.

"Finally, we learned how to plant gardens and build our own houses. Under each stone, there were at least three scorpions and occasionally huge, hairy tarantulas climbing up the walls, so I did not want to make an adobe hut. We studied all the types of houses that could be built, and I quite fancied a Mongolian yurt. I figured cloth would be easier to put up and take down—but, then I came up with a completely better idea that would take me off the ground altogether. I found a billboard and hung it between two trees, fashioning a tarp over it. I built a tent in a tree. We learned history by living it. This was perfect."

In a *Friends Journal* article written by Arden Buck in October of 2013, Jim Corbet was noted for being a "brilliant thinker, writer, and fearless activist, who insisted on putting his Quaker principles into action, rather than just talking about them. The article read, "A rancher and goatherder, in 1981, he started a Sanctuary movement to shelter Mexican refugees.

Risking considerable peril through inhospitable routes, Corbett guided them across the desert to safety. He went on to help thousands of Central American refugees during the 1980s. He was also an ardent goatwalker and willingly shared the experience of goat walking with others."

Coincidentally, Suchi Branfman (1969-1971) ended up years after graduation from Woolman at a function honoring Jim Corbett. "We were doing a benefit when I was dancing with my dance troupe, Wallflower Order, for El Salvador to support people who were coming up over the borders from South America. They brought Jim Corbett up on the stage. While at John Woolman, I had learned to raise goats with Jim and there he was doing this beautiful, radical work of being a 'Coyote,' bringing people across the border. He was getting a reward for his help in border crossings, and for giving assistance to people who needed to come through the desert. It was so astonishing. I said to him, 'We were in the desert, and I raised goats with you.' I found out that he had been doing all this social justice work at the same time as he was doing the projects with Woolman. I did not know that at the time. He had all these skills that were being used in beautiful ways to save people's lives, using love and knowledge to guide people through the landscape that he knew so well."

The Arizona Special Project, (left to right) Neal Schneider, Ann Russell, Scott Silverman, Jim Bonacci, Jim Corbett, Gladys Corbett, Ray Corbett, Jim's daughter, David Feazel, and Kim Drayden; seated (left to right), Pat Corbett, Gretchen (Herreid) Petersen, Su Herbert, and Kei (Salz) Sundt

29

THE SHADOW SIDE

"The dark side of Woolman was its inability to sometimes 'hold the line'
and 'rule of law,' but that was also the Zeitgeist of its time."

– A. Sotelo

As idyllic a place as John Woolman School was for many students, staff, and instructors, it was not without its struggles. Not mentioning these difficulties and pathos would be disingenuous and untrue to the true story of Woolman.

Instructors' viewpoints

Former principal Ted Menmuir notes, "When I think of someone trying to write the school's history, I realize how inspiring and contradictory it is. There is a tendency to romanticize it, thinking of it as providing a constructive understanding of alternative education and institutions—and it was a wonderful place of incubation for self-motivated, creative students. The faculty was impressive. Plus, people you speak with are apt to talk with you because they had positive experiences. But if you look back at the records, the extent to which students were expelled or left the school is overwhelming. For those who were not ready for it, it was destructive. John Woolman School was not without its difficulties. A shoestring operation, Woolman was never well-funded, which put the school in a bind financially. Thus, our temptation was to accept students that we probably should not have. In the early years, everyone was accepted. Over the years, soon after I arrived, I realized that we had real problems because of it. In the 1970s, the strongest influence on socialization at Woolman was the youth culture itself. It took on its own

dimension. Students often came from broken, dysfunctional homes or families where they felt disconnected. Woolman became the students' school and their own culture. They protected their private lives. Life at Woolman took on its own dimension. We found that the less desirable aspects of that student culture were so strong that returning students would perpetuate them and pass them along to incoming students. It was very frustrating. Other than a few crazy people, staff did not stay very long—a couple of years led to burnout. I remember interviewing a well-educated couple who bent over backward to become a part of the John Woolman School community. Initially, I'd warned them that the school wasn't just a job, that it was a way of life. They'd assured me they understood and would far exceed expectations. A few months later, they returned to my office looking completely beaten and exhausted. They said, "You didn't warn us that this wasn't just a job, that it was a way of life!" I was amused because they had repeated my words back to me. For the most part, working at Woolman was far more intense and involved than anyone expected, with both painful and rewarding experiences."

Nick Wilcox (biochemistry and physics instructor 1971-1975 and John Woolman School Board member for 12 years) had a similar view. "We had more students than housing the first year I was there, so we housed students out in the woods in treehouses. After my second year, the drug culture became so all-encompassing that by my third year, we really cracked down and did not re-admit a lot of students. That year, we opened the school with 30 wonderful students, but it created a financial hit on the organization, from which I think the school never recovered fiscally. Having been on the Board for so many years, and at one point being the treasurer, I can say that. When they started the Woolman Semester program, the school was basically bankrupt, so they solicited a loan at 11% to finance it, and the loan was crushing. As treasurer, I was expected to fix the problem, but donors were already giving to their max. I was faced with this conundrum. We had a huge loan that was killing us. Luckily, Amanda (Nick's wife) had a college friend she had known at Westtown and Earlham who refinanced that loan, so we liquidated that loan and brought the debt inside among Friends rather than from banks, enabling the school to survive for quite some time. However, the school was really never able to pay down that debt. Lenders were constantly under pressure to forgive their debt. Amy Cooke, Head of School at the time, also held the Quaker belief that a way would open, and God would provide. As a nuts-and-bolts guy, I said, 'If God writes us a check tomorrow for two million dollars, I'll be a believer, too.' In a way, God did provide because private lenders stepped up. But in the end, what allowed Woolman to pay down the debt was the Jones Fire. Ironically, God did provide by burning down a portion of the campus. The school was adequately insured, so they were able to pay off the remaining loans with fire insurance money. Over the years, plenty of loans have also been forgiven. When I was at Woolman, there was talk of forming an intentional community, but what has stood in the way of that is the property itself which is big and landlocked. It only has one access. Any kind of development of the property would have been impossible without the establishment of a second ingress/egress. During the time I was on the Board, we tried for years to get such an easement unsuccessfully. From a planning perspective, those 325 acres of land were suitable for only one residence. John Woolman School operated under a special use permit in Nevada County. They were grandfathered in, and only allowed to operate a school there. Another problem Woolman had was that they avoided this ordinance and allowed others to live on the property, claiming that these people were 'auxiliary staff.' Woolman's programs were not really the programs described in their use permit. As long as Woolman did not get too grandiose in their plans, city planners were willing to look the other way. Having been a Board member through all this, I can say it was not a good situation."

Amanda Wilcox adds, "In the late 1990s, during Nick's third year, there was another rampant drug problem. Staff decided again to clean things up and not invite students back. Essentially, there were no students, and that is when they had to do a resurrection as The Woolman Semester which worked for a while but was not sustainable. It has been hard to find something with enough enrollment, sustainability, and financial viability to make it. Now Woolman has a cushion, so prospects for going forward are different. Realistically, from a financial standpoint, with the high costs of college these days, I think a semester program will be more manageable for families. Meanwhile, they've had summer camp programs and science camp programs that have been very successful."

Instructor Deward Drollinger also recollects an experience that was not favorable. He relates, "There was a principal at the school in the late 1980s, and she did not do well due to some controversy. I can't recall exactly how it happened, but we were fired mid-year. It was our last year there. We were at a Halloween party with some other staff and students and got a call from the Board that we were going to be let go at the end of that winter trimester. There was a period of adjustment for the new principal, and ones who spoke up about certain things were let go. Some people just left. Being let go mid-year in January, we couldn't find teaching jobs elsewhere. We had signed contracts for the year, so we said we wouldn't teach but we also wouldn't leave until our contract was complete. Students were upset at teachers being let go. Everyone had their favorites. School meetings were held about it. Then that principal left mid-year, and Ted Menmuir took over. As a result, we were reinstated and worked to the end of the year but there was still a certain amount of upheaval. This is the only downside we experienced at Woolman."

Students' Recollections

At Woolman, staff had every bit the same unfettered freedom as students, and they were sometimes also irresponsible with it. Every year the school was in operation, students say, they were dismayed at the tendency of some staff, a few who were even married, to become sexually involved with students. This was likely due to the insular environment of Woolman, but it was still not copacetic, nor did it set a good example for students.

Ann Sotelo (1969-1971) has a vivid memory of a personal "shadow event" when two staff members doing their alternative service at Woolman were driving on a winding dirt road coming back from a day trip on the Yuba River. The narrow road, which was not much more than a dry creek bed, was filled with numerous twists and turns. As it pulled up the mountainside, the truck bounced in and out of potholes in the uneven terrain, dust flying. The staff members, only a few years older than students, were laughing, joking frivolously, and frolicking as they drove up the trail. Suddenly, the driver swerved at one of the hairpins, overcorrected, and the flatbed truck, loaded with students in the back bed, spun off the hill. Ann was among them, thrown under the truck and jammed up against a tree. She suffered a concussion. Another student broke a leg. Still another student broke a collarbone. Ann says, "That accident is one memory in which I did not feel safe at Woolman. It profoundly violated and destroyed my sense of having a 'safety bubble' there. I had an out-of-body experience. I was thrown out of the truck, down the ravine, and then the truck followed my vector and came down, tipped over, and landed on me. Luckily, these two little saplings kept the truck from rolling completely down the hill, which would have been horrific because, for one, it would have scraped me along the bottom and who knows what would have happened to me, but also, everyone else had been thrown from the truck. If the truck had kept going, it would have run into them as well. When I got pulled out from underneath the truck, though dazed, I couldn't help but notice that the truck was wedging against these two little saplings that were holding it from continuing down the slope." The two staff members driving that day were lucky that collective Quaker light was on their side, and, though injured, student lives were spared.

Nina Leshan Dreyfus (1969-1970) is a teacher, sociologist, mother, and midwife. She also questions the permissiveness of Woolman during the year she was there. She says, "As someone who attended several alternative schools, and who grew up in Friends meeting with parents who also started a school, I have some understanding of the philosophy of letting children be free to explore. I was raised in La Jolla meeting. My parents were extremely involved in the meeting, and I was the Pacific Yearly Meeting Junior High Clerk. I also went to Walden in Berkeley and Peninsula School in Menlo Park. These schools, in line with Quaker tradition, believed in letting children freely discover their gifts. I could climb trees all day or study math with a Stanford professor. The choice was mine. While it is the role of teachers to help students develop their gifts, I feel we did not get the basics at Woolman. It was 1969, the height of the hippie experiment. I never went to classes. There was a revolutionary effort in line with Quaker ideals to have egalitarian relationships, but providing more leadership and guidance would have also been a good thing for kids. If you are writing an honest account, obfuscation of this, while illuminating the good, would be mendacious. The truth is, Woolman was both good and bad for students. It wasn't the only school where students were not cared for during this period, but I feel that during the year I was there, adults were extremely negligent, and still in the process of growing up themselves. They weren't ready to take on the responsibility of wild kids like us. In the hopes of establishing egalitarian relationships, they let us run free. But we weren't ready to be adults. We were allowed freedoms that we weren't ready to have. It wasn't safe. For example, when I was 15 years old, I went to Twin Pools to camp with my boyfriend from Pacific High School, was gone for five days, and nobody noticed. I understand that my year was particularly bad, and other years might have been better. Dick and Marguerite and Dottie and Harold were partner-switching at that time and likely this detracted from the attention and care they could have been focusing on students. When I was there, one teacher was also having a sexual relationship with a student, and when the student tried to break it off, the teacher threatened to tell lies about her, and to get her sent home. I think it was better when Ted Menmuir became principal. That being said, Quakerism has influenced my life entirely. I was taught to always go to the light, give goodness, to pour love into discord, and to create a fire of love. But I struggled with the darkness. How do we deal with love and light when it doesn't work? My mother was a World War II concentration-camp survivor. I am a first-generation immigrant whose family was uprooted by war and genocide. As a Quaker, I was taught to not feel angry. When I was a child, I thought that meant I was not supposed to be angry at Hitler, but I was. My father was a theoretical nuclear physicist, and some of the knowledge he had about statistical samplings was used in the making of the nuclear bomb. He refused to work after he found that out, became involved with the Palo Alto Friends Meeting, and started a kindergarten class in the La Jolla Meeting.

"Twenty years ago, I had a brain tumor. At that time, my father told me something that helped me reconcile the darkness. He said, 'The world is only a learning place, so don't get caught up in the drama of it. Some people have light inside but are so busy learning that they have no love left over to give to you. It's okay to stay away from those people. You're important too.'"

Despite the uneven experience at Woolman, Quaker beliefs were planted in Nina and continue to flourish. She adds, "Though I cannot go back a generation to hold my own mother's hand, I can use my voice to support the migrant children at this historical moment. I've been volunteering as a translator between Spanish speaking children and their volunteer lawyers for three years. Separation of immigrant children from their families at the border rips my heart and threatened to render me hopeless. Volunteering with Kids in Need of Defense (KIND) folks has ameliorated my personal pain and transformed hopelessness to hope. The artificial but legal boundary between nations will never impose a border between me and others. As a mother and midwife, all children everywhere are my children. Each one of us is a member of the human family. They belong just as every one of us belongs, and we can work together to make the world a kinder place for everyone."

Joan Flax (1983) also had a troubling experience while at Woolman. Though not the school's fault, since John Woolman School was outside of town, hitchhiking was typically how some students got into Grass Valley, or even home on four-day weekends. Joan left the school to hitchhike to Stockton, California to see her cousin. (Students went to school six days a week, so each month included a four-day break.) She says, "I had a bad experience hitchhiking and was so traumatized by it that it tarnished the rest of the year I was at Woolman. Weaving and cooking at Woolman helped a lot, though. I spent a lot of time in the kitchen."

Olivia Gay (student 1965-1968, staff in the early 1970s) also points out that while Special Projects were usually a good, expansive, educational experience for students sometimes the freedom they experienced while doing them was too permissive. She says, "When I was on staff at Woolman, I took kids to Mexico, and we were together more of the time. I also supervised a trip where three or four boys and I went to work on a farm. That was very circumscribed. As a student in the early 1960s, though, I went to Mexico in a van with a group led by two college students from Antioch College. They were not much older than us, so we had a wild time. On another Special Project, I worked with a Quaker Friends Committee on legislation in the San Francisco Bay Area. Friends of mine were working with another organization that was run by a very charismatic black man, so that looked much more fun and appealing than what I was doing. Gradually, I left my job and hung out with them. That was completely unsupervised by anyone from the school. One of the girls started sleeping with the head of the organization, got pregnant, and had an abortion. I had a bad experience too, a violation from a guy in the program. It was not a good situation. That's a little of the shadow side of Woolman. On the one hand, we had a lot of freedom and that is good for kids. On the other hand, kids could get into real trouble with all that unsupervised freedom. I'm sure if I had been in high school in San Francisco, things would have been even rockier. It was a historically wild era—there was a lot of tumult everywhere, but I don't know if it was any worse temptations and pitfalls than teenagers can get themselves into anywhere at any time.

"I wonder if the people who got into worse trouble at Woolman are ones who aren't talking with you. It was a place of privilege, and some kids who didn't come from that struggled. It wasn't as good for some students who came from working-class backgrounds, who had a rough time there. Being in an environment where people notice you can be good or bad. But when I worked at Goddard College, I saw freshmen go through similar challenges from being on their own for the first time. Plenty of kids have these types of experiences when they are young."

Of what Woolman lore would later call "the swap at the top," Jennifer Miller (Woolman Work Camp – 1967) also reiterated, "There's no way to forget the Miller clan. Our family life changed there. Our mother, Marguerite, was originally married to our father, Dick Miller. Dick was hired as the farm manager. At the time, Harold Blickenstaff was Head of School. At Woolman, our mom, Marguerite, got together with Harold Blickenstaff and Dick got together with Harold's wife, Dottie. They were all young, in their 30s, and living isolated together in that close a proximity at Woolman likely prompted the 'exchange.' But ultimately, they all stayed happily married."

Resident cat

| WOOLMAN SEMESTER |

30

THE WOOLMAN SEMESTER

"Everyone who goes there [to Woolman] has
this same sense of connection."

–S. Wood Brinker

I n the fall of 2001, Amy Cooke was Head of School when John Woolman School closed its doors as a full-time school. As she was helping a student pack to leave, heartbroken, he said to her, "Have you ever heard of The Mountain School? It's a semester program affiliated with a well-known boarding school on the east coast. I went there. You know, there are no Quaker Semester programs; why don't you look at doing that?" This comment planted a seed with Amy, who started researching every program she could find. It prompted her to take a trip to The Mountain School and Chewonki (another semester program in Maine) to try to find out everything she could about their structures. At the time, the board at John Woolman had a committee that met intensively every week to discuss the future of the school. After input from Amy about the success of East-Coast semester schools, the group built a program using the Woolman model for transformative education, an intensive sixteen-week program called, "The Woolman Semester."

Ted Menmuir, Principal of John Woolman School at the time, was impressed with The Woolman Semester. He says, "Students did live on campus but since there was a break in student continuity from one semester to the next, I think the Semester Program broke the hold that the youth culture students had on Woolman. I feel that the semester program benefited greatly from the quality of education students received and the work they did. During this time, I continued to work in maintenance and teach art classes, but I did not work in administration."

The Woolman Semester was four to five months long. Students took wilderness trips together, went backpacking, and studied global issues and environmental impacts, as well as movements of non-violence throughout history. They took art classes such as drawing and pottery, and short-term Spanish classes. In content, classes were quite similar to the ones full-time three-and four-year students took, albeit shorter in duration, and there were no core classes like science and math. Similar to full-time students, semester students also shared responsibility for work jobs on campus. Short-term Woolman Semester students agree with long-term students that Woolman had a big impact on shaping their lives.

Shana Maziarz (student 1980-1991), Peace Studies & Global Studies teacher 2004- 2005, Head of School 2005-2008) taught classes during The Woolman Semester. She says, "The Woolman Semester was a very different model from John Woolman School. With a very tiny student body, it was very interdisciplinary. All teachers taught together. We did a lot of road trips. We took kids to Mexico or studied water in California by going to the east side of the Sierras, or by going to Los Angeles to talk with Los Angeles Water and Power. It was very hands-on in a way that is only possible when you only have 12 students in a van. However, when I was at John Woolman School, there were only 35 students. A lot of teachers had left the year before and the number of students went from 85 in attendance to 35. The school nearly closed. The principal at the time had not been a good fit, and the school was in financial crisis. They had to sell 100 acres of land. So, all the students were new, along with most of the teachers. Ted Menmuir came back on as principal. Woolman was a very free space and there wasn't a lot of structure or oversight, so some people, due to that freedom, had some bad experiences. However, it was very liberating and affirming for people like me who were independent. Because Quakerism is so rooted in activism, the idea that you live what you believe was very impactful for me. The kinds of kids we ended up with in The Woolman Semester were very smart and looking for something that was higher level."

Sophie Wood Brinker (2007) was a student in The Woolman Semester. A professional graphic designer whose drawings appear in this book, Sophie now lives in the permaculture garden retreat center, Commonweal, in Bolinas, California, a center for health and healing, art and education, and environment and justice. She is also helping alumni sort through the John Woolman School archives. Just like many students from other years, Sophie says that Woolman changed her life for the better. "It was a very radical education, short but incredible. We were asked to question everything and to look into our water and food systems to see where the money was coming from, who was benefiting from it, who wasn't, and really parse out our own roles in all these systems to see how we could help. We also did food intensive trips, which was one of my favorites. We would drive to farms throughout California, and see different food distribution systems and community gardens, and learn the ways in which people are feeding their communities. All of the teachers were amazing. I remember one time I was writing a paper about the United States war machine and how many generations after war are affected by people who are forced to go into it. I was feeling very emotional about it as I sat outside of the computer lab at 10:00 PM. I was weeping. One of my teachers walked by and gave me a big hug and just sat with me, talked things through with me, and listened. To have a teacher who would just sit with you and be with you while you were crying—at that moment, it felt very powerful. It was meaningful to me to realize that while learning these hard things, you really need this kind of emotional care for each other. That she was there for me had a huge impact on me. When I was an intern, I saw students going through similar feelings. One student was terrified about the loss of topsoil and paralyzed about how to do anything about it. Both staff and students showed up for him and were with him in his grief. That emotional support was so radical at Woolman and very special."

Sophie, like countless students before her, was also influenced by Woolman instructors when choosing where to continue her future education. "I was completely set on going to a different college until Marie Cope Nicholson, who had contacts at Woolman and Earlham, came to talk to Woolman Semester students. Marie's description of Earlham College as being a private liberal-arts Quaker college with values of peace, social justice, and community decision-making sounded a lot like Woolman. It was a beautiful oasis in Richmond, Indiana. If not for the Woolman Semester, I would have ended up at a totally different place. My decision to study illustration was also directly influenced by a charcoal-drawing class I took from Ted Menmuir at Woolman. I felt a grounded peace, confidence, and inner knowing in that class."

After graduation from college, Sophie did a Woolman Intern program for a year, and then stayed on to help run it. The year-long internship program was composed of eight people who were interested in farming, Quaker education, or working with teens, and who wanted more experience. They helped with shared work on the farm, assisted teachers on field trips, worked as teachers' assistants, and sometimes even taught their own elective courses. After working as an intern, Sophie became a Quaker Life coordinator. She helped with community meetings, and with teaching and sharing Quaker history and process. Many students who came to the school did not have Quaker backgrounds, so Sophie helped bridge that gap. She says, "I feel that some of my most special gathered meetings were at Woolman. In so many different programs, everyone who goes there has this same sense of connection and, when there, feels some kind of magic. There is so much wisdom and energy in the land that always feels very magical. I have no name for it, but it is really special. Who I am is deeply connected to Woolman. What is interesting to me about this book project is the fact that issues discussed, and the importance of adhering to community values, are the same now as they were at the beginning of the school. In a way, it is beautiful how they circulated year after year. I loved feeling how everyone's behavior affected each other in that tiny community."

31

REUNIONS

*"Returning to Woolman after so many years
is a powerful experience. I'm reminded of what an
important time it was for me."*

–D. Covington

For many students who had a positive experience at John Woolman School, regardless of when they attended, its campus continues to be an emotional touchstone and a spiritual place of renewal. Reunions give students a chance to explore their memories, reconnect with the land, and experience a sense of community again that is unlike anything they've found anywhere else in their later lives. They ignite old friendships, too. Whether they were there for all three years or merely weeks, the profound impact Woolman has on its students extends over their entire life.

In a March 1997 issue of the John Woolman School Alumni Association newsletter, *Wombats in the Real World*, a section read, "Those who attended the 1996 JWS Association Gathering came away with renewed enthusiasm for the school and its purpose as well as a deep connection with old friends. Hand in hand in a circle that last day during a moment of silence before saying goodbye, I think all of us felt it: a pervasive sense of belonging to something deep and constant and the luck of having somewhere that will always feel like home to refer back to in our daily lives."

One of those at the 1992 John Woolman School alumni gathering/ reunion, David M.V. Calderon (1976-1980) says, "Walking around this

campus, the hills, the meadows, sitting on a cabin porch, I'm repeatedly caught by strong memories that renew feelings of change, teenage angst, bondings, and partings."

A simple reunion with the sweet smell of hot pine needles in summer on the Woolman campus is also nostalgic for many former students. Blair Gardner (1974-1976) says, "I hadn't been to Woolman for years because I lived out on the East Coast for a long time. In 1993, I flew out to Reno, rented a car, and drove up to the first reunion I'd been to since leaving Woolman. As I stopped at Donner Pass. I got out of the car and that smell of hot sun on the pine needles just hit me. I started crying. It all welled up inside me and brought it all back. Now, every few years, a group of us who went to Woolman in the mid-70s get together in Grass Valley, rent an Airbnb, and stage a small reunion. The friendships that I made at Woolman are the deepest, longest-lasting, most enduring relationships of my life. I think because we were thrown together with little boundaries, it allowed a significant amount of deep bonding, both with the land and with each other. When I tell people I went to the hippie Quaker school in the Sierra Nevada mountains, they have no idea what that means. Woolman was like the family you want. When I talk with former classmates, there is no time lost. I only get that with Woolman people."

In the October 1994 issue of *Wombats in the Real World*, Nina Kiriki Hoffman (1970-1973) also put into words what many students feel when they return to visit the Woolman campus: "I have forgotten so much about this magical place. As I drive toward it, the rosy-red earth in road cuts reminds me—even though the earth is tan at Woolman, seeing iron-reddened earth and long-needled Ponderosa pine hints to me that I am coming closer. I turn a corner and pass Bitney Springs, where cold water still floods from pipes under and open-sided shelter, whether anyone collects it in bottles or not. I arrive as dark is falling. Jones Bar Road looks different: expensive houses with manicured lawns have risen from what used to be a dusty scrub hillside. I remember clearing weeds out of an irrigation ditch that used to run through here, hard heavenly work on a hot day, because at least you could lie down in the ditch to cool off. The driveway is still long and dusty and familiar. I remember digging ditches alongside it when frost ferned the ground. I drive slowly, not stirring up too much dust, and think of all the things I want to see and all the memories I want to tease back to the surface of my mind. Mel's Lake. The Oxidation Basin. The grass ocean on the far side of the creek. The barn. The dorm. The Stone House. The cabins. The dining hall. I have always wanted to set a book here and am greedy for details. I drive my car around to the cabin area, where I unpack into Cabin 2: instruments (guitar and fiddle), computer, food, clothes, bedding, book, towel. I make the bed and lie down. There is graffiti on the wall, but it's philosophical rather than crude. I experiment with remembering what it was like to look up at these sloping walls/ceilings every night when I lived here. I lie on the bed with the light out and leave the cabin door open, thinking, 'this is what amazes me.' This is what I remember, what I've sought all this time and haven't found anywhere else. This is a place where the fantasy fed of innocence returns, strong and beautiful. This is a place that is utterly safe."

The Barn

POSTFACE

By Catherine Lenox

In October 2002, shortly after John Woolman School ceased full-time operation, I wrote a piece for the alumni newsletter, *Wombats in the Real World*. It reflects much of what students and staff say about Woolman, as well as the profound effect the school had on me. It also illustrates what motivated me to write this book with Lisa so many years later. The Woolman story needed to be told. This is the piece:

"As I drove many miles down the coast from Washington last summer to attend the John Woolman School reunion, I had mixed feelings. On the one hand, I was excited to be seeing old friends. On the other, I felt an enormous sense of nostalgia. Something intangible seemed to be passing into history, both my personal history and the school's. The fact that future students would not have the opportunity to experience the same rich educational and community/cultural experience I had, which shaped so many of my internal values and ideals in such positive, deep ways, felt infinitely sad.

"Once at the reunion, I expected that I would have to let go of my memories of John Woolman School, and that something essential was passing away. It seemed the memorial service planned for the reunion was not only a memorial service for classmates who had passed on, but also a reverent tribute to the sad demise of Woolman. With these thoughts in mind, I was pleasantly surprised to discover that I came away from the reunion with a much different feeling. It was a sense of renewal. How did that happen?

"It began with a moment of silence with the John Woolman School Alumni Association (JWSAA). People were asked to say one true thing about John Woolman School. Alumni said that Woolman is the most soulful place on earth, a touchstone for values, and has had a lasting effect on their lives. They said the essence of John Woolman School is relationships and building community. They added that Woolman was a place where people were known deeply. One person noted that

psychologists say that the one thing that makes the biggest difference in a child's growth is if a child was deeply known and loved. This was most certainly true about John Woolman School. It was a place of creativity, self-discovery, and self-expression where we all had the chance to be known deeply. Quite an education! Quite a gift! Alumni envision the Sierra Friends Center as broadening that community.

"In listening to these comments, I began to see a thread through all of them. John Woolman was and is a special place unlike anywhere else in the world. People were touched and moved in a variety of ways during their stay there. The name 'John Woolman School' is still anchored underneath the new sign at the entrance to the school as surely as the human experience of John Woolman School is anchored in all of us who went there. We carry the essence of Woolman and its Wombat community wherever we go. Nothing could have shown this fact more truly than the laughter of old friends, swimming together in the cool waters of the Yuba River, eating and dancing in the dining hall, and hiking through all the familiar meadows. The land remembers. We remember. The future of John Woolman School may well be uncertain. But 'one true thing' is that the seeds that were planted there will grow in all the communities populated by the people who had their roots there. If we all make our communities a better place to live, love each other well, actively speak out against injustices, and live peaceably in the world, we manifest the memory of John Woolman School and keep it alive forever. Those quirky, wonderful, vibrant, often challenging things that happened to us there will filter into our lives and carry on in an active way. If we remember what we learned there, these will never 'pass away.' While it is true the sign at the top of the road has changed, the school's soul is most definitely still there. Regardless of what happens to the grounds, the spirit planted there will always be there, spreading out like a beacon from the hearts and minds of everyone who went there, bringing many 'true things' out into a troubled world. The thread of Woolman may well be a subthread now, but it is still very pervasive and alive."

- Catherine (Cathy) Lenox, (1969-1971)

ACKNOWLEDGEMENTS

It is with our Woolman spirit that we thank and recognize everyone who contributed their thoughts, perceptions, and memories to this book. Without you, this story could not be told, and with you, it will never end.

Special thanks go to the following people who helped fund this project:

Kristin Applegate, Liza (Sieber) Artman, Angela Birkeland, Jesse Bradford, Nick Bratt, Matthew C Bronson, Jonica Brooks, Robert Perry Broz, James Wright Broz, Lisa Hubbell, Aaron Cole, Kate Connell, Angelina Conti, Amy Cooke, Laura Cooper, Amber Davenport, Lenel De Emma, Jennifer Dickey, Louis N. Dolbeare, Kim Drayden, Jessie Dunn-Gilbert, Chris Edgell, David Esposito, Carla Fabrizio, Sean Feder, Peter Fogel, Jonathan Fohrman, Paul Fritts, Brian and Donna Fry, Neil Fullagar, Blair Gardner, Nancy Garcia, George Gastil, Olivia Gay, David Gengoux, Jen Gershen, Annie Goldman, Mark Greider, Jane Harris, John D. Hanavan, Justin Hersh, Christine Heycke, Honolulu Friends Meeting, Elisa James, Elizabeth Johnson, Margarett Jolly, Connie Jolly, Paul Jolly, Kristina Keefe-Perry, Lise Kirsis, Mary Klein, Keya Taylor Kressler, Maura Hogan Leos, Jennifer Long, Melissa Lovett-Adair, Shelley Lowrie, Carol Lustenader, Laurie Mackenzie, Dana Mallozzi, David Matchett, Laura McGee, Nancy McPherson, David Mellon, Sandie and Ted Menmuir, George Millikan, Ann Millikan, Marlee S Mitchell, Ruth B. Montague, Ean Murphy, Tanya Noda, Peter West Nutting, Mary OKane, Gwen Owen, Juliet Loughborough Pierce, Tracy Porter, David Russell, Joyce Samati, Rob Sanville, Neal Schneider, Robert Shaw, George Shea, Tania Simirenko, Lew and Eddy Sitzer, Gordon Smith, Greg and Becky Smith, David Standish, Kory Steelman, Anne Stephenson, John Stirton, Kei Sundt, Sarah A. Tyrrell, John Tecklin, Eric Tomb, Aaron Tomb, Cynthia Evans Trueblood, Jonathan Vogel-Borne, Emily West, Abbie Whitehead, Amanda and Nick Wilcox, David Willheim, Patrick Williams, Susan Winston, Bruce Yarnall, Meg and Eric Yerkes.

ABOUT THE CREATIVES

Sophie Wood Brinker is a Natural Science Illustrator. She is an alumna of the Woolman Semester, has a BA in Peace and Global Studies from Earlham College, a Certificate in Graphic Design from UC Berkeley, and is a graduate of the Science Illustration Graduate program at Monterey State University. She has lived in a Quaker community on and off for much of her life and considers the Sierra Friends Center her heart home. She currently lives in Bolinas, California, on Coast Miwok land, where she works as an illustrator and librarian.

....

Book Designer **Sonja Gerard** is the owner of Oei Graphics in the Greater Seattle Area. She graduated with a Fine Arts Degree from Whittier College, Whittier, California. Sonja was especially interested in designing *The Woolman Way*, which she calls "a collaborative journey," since Whittier College was founded by the Religious Society of Friends in 1887 and named in honor of the Quaker poet and advocate of the abolition of slavery in the U.S., John Greenleaf Whittier. With a spirit akin to Woolmanites, Sonja says her greatest accomplishment has been raising her two boys. She also has a love of family, friends, helping others, and creating.

....

Anita Anderson, our copy editor, is the owner of Anita Anderson Writing and Editing Services in Seattle, Washington. She is skilled in editing documents at all levels, including conceptual/substantive editing, copywriting, and proofreading. A great fit for editing our book, she has edited other memoirs as well as architectural history.

Author **Catherine Lenox** is a John Woolman School alumna (1969-1971) and owner of Write Contact, where she writes website features and ghostwrites memoirs. She lives in Duvall, Washington with her partner, Ray, and dog, Tugger. With a BA in English from San Francisco State University, she has been a managing editor and feature writer for numerous magazines, websites and newsletters, as well as a radio news reporter. Writing *The Woolman Way* has been one of her lifetime dreams come true.

Author **Lisa Frankel** is a public historian. She holds a BFA in Art from The University of Connecticut and an MA in Public History from Arizona State University. Her current work includes oral history projects and focuses on community studies and California Native American community relations. She lives with her husband Eric in Grass Valley, California where the history of the John Woolman School is part of the community history of the region.